FROM POSITIVISM TO ID

From Positivism to Idealism
A Study of the Moral Dimensions of Legality

SEAN COYLE
University College London, UK

Routledge
Taylor & Francis Group

LONDON AND NEW YORK

First published 2007 by Ashgate Publishing

Reissued 2018 by Routledge
2 Park Square, Milton Park, Abingdon, Oxon, OX14 4RN
605 Third Avenue, New York, NY 10017

First issued in paperback 2021

Routledge is an imprint of the Taylor & Francis Group, an informa business

A Library of Congress record exists under LC control number: 2007009760

Notice:
Product or corporate names may be trademarks or registered trademarks, and are used only for identification and explanation without intent to infringe.

Publisher's Note
The publisher has gone to great lengths to ensure the quality of this reprint but points out that some imperfections in the original copies may be apparent.

Disclaimer
The publisher has made every effort to trace copyright holders and welcomes correspondence from those they have been unable to contact.

ISBN 13: 978-0-815-38909-5 (hbk)
ISBN 13: 978-1-351-15796-4 (ebk)
ISBN 13: 978-1-138-35694-8 (pbk)

DOI: 10.4324/9781351157964

Contents

Series Editor's Preface

The objective of the Applied Legal Philosophy series is to publish work which adopts a theoretical approach to the study of particular areas or aspects of law or deals with general theories of law in a way which focused on issues of practical moral and political concern in specific legal contexts.

In recent years there has been an encouraging tendency for legal philosophers to utilize detailed knowledge of the substance and practicalities of law and a noteworthy development in the theoretical sophistication of much legal research. The series seeks to encourage these trends and to make available studies in law which are both genuinely philosophical in approach and at the same time based on appropriate legal knowledge and directed towards issues in the criticism and reform of actual laws and legal systems.

The series will include studies of all the main areas of law, presented in a manner which relates to the concerns of specialist legal academics and practitioners. Each book makes an original contribution to an area of legal study while being comprehensible to those engaged in a wide variety of disciplines. Their legal content is principally Anglo-American, but a wide-ranging comparative approach is encouraged and authors are drawn from a variety of jurisdictions.

Tom D. Campbell
Centre for Applied Philosophy and Public Ethics,
Charles Sturt University, Australia

Preface

This book is intended as a contribution to jurisprudential reflection on the nature of legality. The term 'jurisprudence' in the Anglo-American legal tradition generally refers to the philosophical study of the general features of law, both as a social phenomenon and as an intellectual object of moral significance. As such, jurisprudential theories have as their main goal the elaboration of the general properties of law and legal order, at a level of abstraction that is in some degree removed from the immediate sphere of concern of the practising lawyer. Contemplation of these more abstract theses and concepts is the central aim of jurisprudence; in doing so the legal philosopher may hope to clarify the intellectual basis and presuppositions entailed by the practitioner's activities. The detailed application of such general theoretical insights to the concrete substantive issues arising from practical, legal and doctrinal argument is then the secondary business of 'applied legal theory.'

The present work is an instance of 'applied legal theory' *not* in the sense that it seeks to apply a general theory of legality or ethics to a particular problem (for the central argument of the book is that such a distinction between theory and practice is misleading). Rather, it represents an attempt to show that theoretical insights can be grasped only *within* particular practices, so that theory and application go inevitably together. It is, therefore, an attempt to understand the nature of legality not in general, but within the British polity specifically. In this respect, the book seeks consciously to depart from the predominant forms of jurisprudential inquiry carried on in Anglo-American law schools at the present day, and hopes to reconnect with the traditional jurisprudential investigation of the moral nature of law. Modern jurisprudential arguments increasingly hinge upon a limited number of disagreements as to the correct way in which to refine a series of conceptual distinctions and categories. When not concerned with conceptual boundaries, they tend to concern the proper description of essentially the same theoretical object, a 'liberal theory of justice'. These efforts, I argue, are misguided for they fail to grasp the essentially practical or 'applied' character of jurisprudential thought.

I have endeavoured in writing this book to keep its length as short as possible. In the face of a vast and ever-growing jurisprudential literature, there is (I hope) some virtue to be found in a shorter work seeking to develop its own set of arguments and concerns, rather than engaging with established and well-worn arguments in an exhaustive way. The book's brevity has necessarily entailed a certain ruthlessness in pursuing a particular argumentative course at the expense of many possible lines of development. I hope in time to explore these broader themes in other published books and essays.

Much of the present work represents a deepening engagement with themes that have been developing in my mind for a number of years. Parts of Chapters 5 and 6 appeared in earlier guises in the *Oxford Journal of Legal Studies*, 26 (2006) 257–288 under the title 'Positivism, Idealism and the Rule of Law' and in *Law and Philosophy*, 25 (2006) 417–452, entitled 'Practices and the Rule of Recognition'. An earlier version of a portion of Chapter 8 (and short sections of Chapter 7) appeared as '"Protestant" Political Theory and the Significance of Rights' in the *Northern Ireland Legal Quarterly*, 56 (2005) 551–584. Thanks are due to Oxford University Press, Springer and the Society of Legal Scholars (NI) for permission to republish.

I have benefited enormously from discussions with a large number of colleagues during the writing of this book. In particular, Brian Bix, Neil Duxbury and George Pavlakos read and commented upon early versions of the initial chapters. Emile Perreau-Saussine and Nigel Simmonds provided much-needed encouragement, intellectual inspiration and discussion of some of the book's main themes. I learned much from conversations with Ross Harrison and Amanda Perreau-Saussine, who directed me towards sources that were to have a major influence on the direction of the book, but which I would otherwise have overlooked. Finally, Fiona Smith has provided incisive and valuable commentary on successive drafts of the whole manuscript. It is my great pleasure to thank them all here.

The bulk of research and writing was conducted during a term of leave spent as a visitor to the Law Faculty at the University of Cambridge. I am extremely grateful to the Faculty and Library staff at Cambridge for their cheerful help and assistance, and to my own colleagues at UCL for granting me a period of leave from teaching in which to think and reflect. I would especially like to thank Tom Campbell for his unfailing support and encouragement throughout the period of writing, and for his valuable suggestions about the way in which the argument could be pursued. Lastly, my thanks to Sherman for constant correction of my typing.

Sean Coyle
University College London, 2007.

Chapter 1

Reflection on Law's Nature

This book is intended as a contribution to analytical reflection on the nature of law within the British polity. Jurisprudential theories that describe themselves as 'analytical' are often presented as attempts to clarify the concept of law: by revealing the necessary and sufficient conditions for the use of concepts within legal practice, such theories purport to uncover the form of our practices by exposing their 'conceptual foundations'. Hence, it is supposed, jurisprudential theories enable us to determine the form of our legal practices prior to any substantive engagement with moral and political questions *about* those practices. Theoretical enterprises of this kind leave us with the impression of having gained important insights into the essential nature of our legal understandings, without those impressions depending on contestable political assumptions or moral ideas. The insights we have achieved are, we feel, permanent rather than illusory or transient.

The present work is conceived as a departure from such approaches, in that it represents an attempt to resurrect a tradition of reflection on law's nature in which analysis focuses not on 'abstract' or 'necessary' concepts and categories, but rather upon aspects of law's role within the wider currents of political thought and practice that shape our way of life. This book hence concerns the British, and more particularly, the English experience of political and social life under the rule of law. The focus on conceptual connections in modern jurisprudence has been, in the end, an unfortunate one, in that it has served to reinforce intuitions about the role of philosophical analysis and its relationship to ordinary legal scholarship that are at odds with the traditional concern with law's moral nature.

It is often assumed that jurisprudence consists of the task of clarifying the intellectual commitments of legal practice. The legal practitioner devotes his energies to the exposition and application of legal rules, concepts and doctrines by subjecting them to established patterns of reasoning and argument. A clear understanding of such concepts and doctrines, and of the distinctive modes of reasoning used in their elucidation, might then be thought to depend upon a question that is logically prior to legal practice, namely, what counts as 'law', or 'legal' argument? These questions must lie outside legal practice, it is thought, for they concern the general framework of ideas within which doctrinal questions are raised and debated. Jurisprudential theories are thus thought to involve the drawing of conceptual boundaries that identify the general subject-matter of 'law', without presupposing the validity or otherwise of ordinary doctrinal standpoints. For, in an obvious sense, each participant in a doctrinal debate articulates and advances *legal* concerns; and thus to incorporate the doctrinal lawyer's assumptions into one's theoretical concept of law is to confuse the idea of law with its particular manifestations, in a way that obscures the true nature of the practitioner's experience. Jurisprudential theories should instead seek to clarify the intellectual domain in which such debates take place, in order that the specifically doctrinal problems and disagreements, within which the lawyer moves, may be illuminated and revealed.

The modern jurisprudential writer therefore often views his task as that of describing the conditions that make legal practice possible and intelligible. This view of jurisprudential activity is premised on the assumption (widespread in analytical philosophy) that a focused regard for the detail of specific institutional arrangements, or of the moral understandings at work within ordinary practice, must either address sociological or empirical concerns that characterise specific types of legal practice, or else seek to attach particular moral significance to legal practices under the guise of revealing the essential 'nature' of those practices. Thus, in his 'Postscript' to *The Concept of Law*, H.L.A. Hart observes that the legal theory put forward in that work '… is morally neutral and has no justificatory aims: it does not seek to justify or commend on moral or other grounds the forms and structures which appear in my general account of law.'[1] The account is general 'in the sense that it is not tied to any particular legal system or legal culture, but seeks to give an explanatory and clarifying account of law as a complex social and political institution…'.[2] In a similar vein, Raz states that 'It is easy to explain in what sense legal philosophy is universal. Its theses, if true, apply universally, that is, they speak of all law, of all legal systems; of those that exist or will exist, and even of those that can exist or never will. Moreover, its theses are advanced as necessarily universal.'[3]

Yet we might wonder whether there are not manifold disadvantages to such a view. For it is far from obvious that the keys to a rich philosophical understanding of law lie in such strategies of detachment and abstraction from practical institutional arrangements. Why, after all, should we expect there to be informative or interesting points of comparison between systems of law such as the classical common law, civilian legal orders or aboriginal law? The legal philosopher is often thought to be engaged in the task of digging out the concepts and criteria presupposed in these otherwise different systems of law; criteria in virtue of which the various forms of legal order are manifestations of *law*. This form of conceptual archaeology occupies a rather curious place in the intellectual landscape: for, on the one hand, such activities purport to ascertain the necessary or 'essential' conditions for the existence of a legal system; but, on the other, the identification of *those* conditions (in place of some other list) serves to articulate a sociological judgment about the instances of legal order that actually exist.

Suppose we take the conditions necessary for the existence of a legal system to consist of the union of primary and secondary rules.[4] What would justify such

---

1   H.L.A. Hart, *The Concept of Law*, 2nd edn (Oxford, Clarendon Press, 1994), 240.

2   Hart, (above, note 1) 239. See also J. Raz, *The Authority of Law* (Oxford, Clarendon Press, 1979), 44. For some discussion of these claims, see S. Perry, 'Hart's Methodological Positivism', 4 *Legal Theory* (1998) 427–467, and S. Coyle, 'Two Concepts of Legal Analysis', in S. Coyle and G. Pavlakos (eds) *Jurisprudence or Legal Science?* (Oxford, Hart Publications, 2004), 16–32.

3   J. Raz, 'On the Nature of Law', *Archiv fur Rechts und Sozialphilosophie* (1996), 1–25, at 1–2.

4   Hart (note 1).

an assumption, rather than, say, the assumption that the step from the pre-legal into the legal world is effected where certain institutions or procedures (such as tribunals or boxing rings) are regularly used in the settlement of personal claims, or where the word 'law' (or some equivalent term) is used widely and reflectively to describe the body of standards that govern human conduct?[5] The response that these latter suggestions merely point to *contingent* forms of legal order is question-begging in this context, since there clearly exist forms of social order that do not embody recognised patterns of recognition for the identification of rules governing conduct, or contain the possibility for individuals or officials to vary the operation of such rules. Indeed, forms of social order might exist which recognise no categorical distinction between the powers of individuals and those of officials. (We might think of canon law in this context.)[6]

It is tempting to say, in such contexts, that our willingness to recognise forms of regulation as genuine instances of 'law' (or not) depends upon the extent to which they fulfil or resemble the criteria that constitute the central case. But it is unclear what is to be gained from pointing to the marginal nature of such judgments; for the recognition of an instance of legal order as a marginal rather than a clear one is premised purely on the adoption of the criteria that form the supposed central case. The status of the philosopher's 'necessary conditions' thus hovers uneasily between a stipulative definition and a sociological claim that a certain form of regulatory framework is *in fact* most prevalent among existing forms of social order. The possibility of fruitful inquiry into the moral nature of law is therefore obscured by the prevalence of disputes about the characteristics of the 'concept' of law, so that jurisprudential argument consists largely in advancing rival and incompatible versions of this concept, which jurists then assert and oppose to each other.[7]

These facts about modern jurisprudential argument perhaps go some way to explain the sense of remoteness and irrelevance that many students attach to the subject. For it is hard to suppress the feeling that in seeking to classify the variegated aspects of legal experience according to fixed conceptual boundaries (such as 'law' and 'morality'), legal philosophers have largely abandoned the traditional attempt to comprehend the ethical nature of that experience: instead, jurisprudential effort

---

5   Indeed it is possible to go further, for we might follow Fuller's suggestion that some authoritative form of publication of legal rules is necessary fully to instantiate the idea of law. Applying such a concept, the history of legal order would then be coterminous with the history of written law. (See L. Fuller, *The Morality of Law*, revised edition (Yale University Press, 1969) Chapter 2).

6   I refer here to the internal forum, where the exercise of legal authority is not cleanly separable from the possession of ecclesiastical authority generally.

7   According to Raz, the philosopher's theses 'do not determine the nature of law, they only affect its instantiation.' (above note 2, 3). Thus, the concept of law is said not to depend upon its instances, for legal institutions and practices are relevant to a society's self-understanding whereas concepts must transcend that self-understanding by addressing the 'essential features' of law (*ibid.*, 5–6). Raz admits that our ability to grasp the concept depends upon the manifestations of legality with which we are familiar; yet the independence of 'essential features' from actual contexts of legality renders the status of such essential features and their role in understanding deeply ambiguous.

focuses on the classification of the various elements of that experience as necessary or contingent aspects of a fixed concept.[8]

The implications of this approach can be seen quite clearly if we ponder the following example. Suppose someone advances the proposition that modern instances of legal order should be understood by reference to an organised body of rights rather than a system of black-letter rules. The prevalence of bills of rights within modern legal orders might be thought to lend weight to this assertion; yet it is unlikely that this realisation would lead to the rejection by legal positivists of a concept of law defined in terms of a union of primary and secondary rules. A bill of rights may after all be viewed as a posited instrument that lays down rules at a considerable level of generality and abstraction, leaving judges to fill in 'gaps' in legal understanding according to the policies or values the rules are intended to serve. A bill of rights might be taken in this way to expand greatly the realm in which rules of adjudication operate as a ground of legal validity in place of detailed practices of recognition. Pervasive reference to rights would then be conceived as a surface feature of legal argument, one that is grounded ultimately in a deeper understanding of legal order as a phenomenon based on rules. We might be forgiven for thinking, however, that there are important differences between the two conceptions of law which go beyond surface impressions: for whereas it is possible to see a body of imposed rules as the attempt to realise a stable social framework for the pursuit of private interests and goals where no common perspectives on social good exist, a legal order constituted by rights is naturally thought of as identifying shared ideals through the articulation of the boundaries between competing rights. These are not surface features of the legal order, but rather reflect deep and divergent understandings of the moral basis of the rule of law.[9]

Faced with such criticisms, the jurisprudential writer may seek to defend conceptual analysis in the following way. The jurisprudential concepts developed by legal philosophers (he may say) aim to establish a general body of insights that would assist in the analysis and description of all legal systems, real or imagined. The legal philosopher thus aims at the creation of a 'general jurisprudence', or legal science, distinct from the study of particular doctrinal systems or juridical arrangements. The philosopher's concepts might then be understood not as *necessary* conditions, in any

---

8   Perhaps with this in mind, Hart characterised his project in terms of 'identifying the *main* elements and organisation of elements which constitute a *standard* legal *system*' which would amount to 'an illuminating survey of "essential" features ... of a municipal legal system.' (Taken from Hart's notebook, quoted in N Lacey, *A Life of H.L.A. Hart: The Nightmare and the Noble Dream* (Oxford, Oxford University Press, 2004), 222.) Hart obviously experienced some doubt about the notion of 'essential' features: 'Why is the core essential? How much in core? ... What, after all, does this core explain?' (id. see Lacey, 223).

9   Positivists will typically respond to these suggestions by distinguishing between the concept of 'law' and various manifestations of the political ideal of 'the rule of law'. That is surely a fruitless view: the concept of 'law' (or 'right', or any other political concept) does not arise in isolation from human practices, but makes sense (and has a point) only within a body of human social practices. The attempt to produce a concept of law in abstraction from ordinary political contexts is thus unlikely to be informative in relation to that point or purpose.

straightforward sense, but as bringing into a common focus the principles and ideas required for the scientific analysis of systems of law linked by family resemblance. Austin, for example, understood such a general jurisprudence to consist of the elaboration of 'principles, notions and distinctions which are common to systems of law.'[10] By appealing to some such notion of legal theory, the jurisprudential writer might hope to avoid some of the criticisms that can be levelled against the idea of conceptual analysis: legal orders grounded in abstract rights require rational elucidation as much as do those premised on deliberately created rules, but a rational understanding (so it is thought) depends precisely upon the availability of a set of concepts that transcend the conceptual regimentations which represent the internalised viewpoints of participants within those systems.

In the end, however, reliance on the notion of 'family resemblance' as a focus for conceptual intuitions is no more illuminating of the legal philosopher's concepts and distinctions than the idea of 'necessary' or 'essential' conditions. For, even supposing a set of informative concepts exists to explain forms of legal order premised on basic ideas as diverse as rules and rights, the particular array of concepts and distinctions prized for their explanatory power will inevitably derive from the philosopher's judgment about which manifestations of social order count as central or paradigmatic, and which count as marginal or non-instances of law. The theorist's concepts thus cannot be presented as 'mere' clarifications or *neutral* standpoints (in Hart's terms), since the notions of clarity, neutrality, illumination etc. cannot be given sense apart from one's understanding of the central case.

Much of the attraction that is felt towards conceptual analysis is echoed by Wittgenstein's suggestion that philosophy exists to explain the mundane facets of ordinary experience. Insofar as philosophers have concerned themselves with metaphysical puzzles about the 'nature' or 'essence' of human experience and social institutions, they have been led astray by the capacity of ordinary language to produce nonsensical or meaningless questions: because of the similarity between expressions such as 'the nature of gravity' and 'the nature of legal rights', jurisprudential scholars can easily be fooled into thinking of legal rights as mysterious, incorporeal entities with a nature and properties of their own. Jurisprudence is then easily thought of as consisting in the scientific investigation of these properties. Wittgenstein viewed philosophical insight as the dispelling of such misunderstandings:

> Our investigation is a grammatical one. Such an investigation sheds light on our problem by clearing misunderstandings away. Misunderstandings concerning the use of words caused, among other things, by certain analogies between the forms of expression in different regions of language.[11]

---

10 J Austin, *The Province of Jurisprudence Determined*, H.L.A. Hart (ed.) (London, Weidenfeld & Nicholson, 1955) 367. A recent reappraisal of the character of general jurisprudence can be found in W. Twining, 'General Jurisprudence', in M. Escamilla and M. Savedra (eds), *Law and Justice in a Global Society* (Granada, 2005) 563–650, and *Globalisation and Legal Theory* (London, Butterworths, 2000).

11 L. Wittgenstein, *Philosophical Investigations*, trans. G.E.M. Anscombe (Oxford, Blackwell, 1963) s. 90.

Good philosophy, Wittgenstein thought, aims at 'the logical clarification of thoughts'[12] and is thus confined to the modest role of clarifying the conceptual structure of ordinary thought and speech. By focusing on the elucidation of basic concepts and distinctions, might we not claim to have uncovered the basic features and presuppositions of our practices in an illuminating and scientifically neutral way?

The supposition that our deepest questions about the nature of law arise from misunderstandings or confusion is in fact not easy to sustain: the effort to clarify our sense of the legal order most often springs from the desire to bring into intellectual focus the ideas and values that form the tacit underpinnings of our everyday practices, rather than the elimination of particular misunderstandings. But even if part of the motivation for jurisprudential analysis involves the dissolution of intellectual confusion, the resulting conceptual clarifications and distinctions could not claim to be *neutral* explanations in the appropriate sense. The motivations which precede the delineation of particular juristic concepts and analytical distinctions concern (on this view) the dispelling of doubts or puzzlement about certain social phenomena. But the features of juristic practice that we regard as standing in most need of clarification will in turn depend upon the prior entrenchment of certain basic premises or ideas, which form an implicit and unproblematic background to our understanding, and the assumption of others as problematic or confused.

We will thus regard certain concepts or distinctions as clarifications or illuminations *of law* only on the basis of some tacit set of assumptions about which forms of social practice are to count as 'law.' The notions of clarity, illumination, elucidation etc. can play no constitutive role in the making of such assumptions, since it is precisely in relation to the latter set of ideas that the former are rendered meaningful: any set of conceptual distinctions and ideas will have the effect of highlighting certain questions or features of the legal order as problematic or central, whilst dissolving or marginalising others. Our judgment in relation to forms of social practice is therefore more naturally explained by reference to the perceived point or purpose of those practices within a particular way of life.[13]

The theorist's concepts can thus be seen as suppressing (or presupposing) questions or ideas about the 'essential nature' of legal practice by reference to an intellectual dogma which presents those concepts as scientifically neutral analyses. Suppose instead, however, that the purpose of jurisprudential inquiry is to move

---

12 Wittgenstein, *Tractatus Logico-Philosophicus*, trans. D.F. Pears and B.F. McGuinness (London, Routledge, 1961) proposition 4.112. Wittgenstein's earlier and later thought is thus marked by a disagreement as to whether it is the logical structure or the 'grammar' of thought that is clarified; yet his general approach continued to exhibit the belief that philosophy consists primarily in conceptual clarification.

13 See J. Finnis, *Natural Law and Natural Rights* (Oxford, Clarendon Press, 1980) 3–4: '[Law] is constituted by human actions, practices, habits, dispositions and by human discourse ... But the actions, practices, etc., can be fully understood only by understanding their point, that is to say their objective, their value, their significance or importance, as conceived by the people who performed them, engaged in them, etc. And these conceptions of point, value, significance, and importance will be reflected in the discourse of those same people, in the conceptual distinctions they draw and fail or refuse to draw.'

varying understandings of the essence or point of legal practice from the implicit background of understanding into the foreground of juristic thought. By focusing directly upon our deepest assumptions about the nature of law, and by articulating the moral or practical ideals which underlie ordinary legal practice, we might come to see the legal order as itself a source of further moral insight and reflection. Our central questions will then concern the purpose or point of law within political and moral life, and the sense in which the legal order embodies the expression of a society's self-understanding and its views of human nature and the good life.

Much of modern jurisprudence seems designed to prevent fruitful engagement with questions such as these, by suggesting that the most fundamental theoretical disputes concern the proper conceptual space in which arguments about the nature of law must be framed. This lends overwhelming weight to the interpretation of jurisprudence as an intellectual domain in which different writers are most frequently talking past each other, without any real engagement between the rival views being possible. The present book is an attempt to reconnect with the traditional jurisprudential focus on the moral nature of law, in a way that opens up the possibility of substantial engagement between rival views of that nature.

Jurisprudence and the Moral Life

Any human society is likely to act *both* as a locus of human flourishing and collective endeavour *and* as a source of tensions and conflicts of interest. We might think of law as an attempt to foster and encourage institutions and modes of behaviour that promote human flourishing, and to deal with (and in some cases suppress) the existence of tensions and conflicts. Clearly, not every attempt to secure these goals will count as law (imagine, for example, a society that leaves dispute resolution to the bargaining powers of the respective parties rather than settled rules and principles); but it is clear that our understanding of law is not given by fixed conceptual boundaries here. Our idea of law is more likely to be guided by reflection upon a series of ideals through which we refine our understanding of law as a distinctive mode of governance. Differing jurisprudential accounts of the nature of law may then be viewed as differing suggestions as to how those ideals should be articulated and instantiated.[14]

---

14 This proposal has much in common with Lon Fuller's suggestion that the rule of law embodies a 'morality of aspiration': see *The Morality of Law* (above, note 5), Chapter 1. See also Nigel Simmonds's suggestion that law is a concept structured by an archetype rather than criteria: Simmonds, 'Law as a Moral Idea', 55 *Univ Toronto LJ* (2005) 61–92; and 'Jurisprudence as a Moral and Historical Inquiry', XVIII *Canadian J Law and Jurisprudence* (2005). The present suggestion avoids suggesting that law is an archetypal concept, since it leaves open the possibility that our comprehension of the ideals that guide legal understanding do not stand fully apart from our experience of the way in which such ideals are in fact instantiated by legal institutions. Indeed, it leaves open the possibility that our understanding of law might be shaped by conflicting but deeply-held ideals which prevent the emergence of a fully coherent legal understanding: the legal order would then be viewed as the complex product of various elements that exist in tension. (I discuss this point in more detail in Chapter 9.)

There is good reason to think of such guiding ideals as together embodying the rule of law. It becomes possible, in this way, to conceive of legal positivists and their intellectual rivals as expounding alternative visions of the rule of law. Positivism can be taken to represent (for example) the view that law must consist in an ordered and non-contradictory body of authoritative, determinate rules that have as their main goal the promotion and maintenance of stable social relations, and the creation of a framework of expectations regarding the limits of permissible conduct. Such a body of rules might be seen as having only an indirect relationship to ideals of justice: given that society is a locus of tensions between individuals who live in close and permanent relations (and who are thus to be expected to disagree about what is just), the law ought to consist as far as possible in precise and detailed rules that leave as little to the moral understanding of those who apply the rules as possible. The connection with justice, then, would appear most strongly in the context of the initial formulation of the rules, thereafter circumscribing as closely as possible the necessity for sustained moral introspection in relation to their application.

Such a view of the rule of law is most naturally combined with a view of the legal order as aiming for neutrality as between rival conceptions of the good, and as being concerned with the establishment and protection of restricted domains of liberty within which each individual can pursue his or her private interests and desires unimpeded by the actions of others. Where such moral neutrality proves to be impossible or unsustainable, the law can be thought of as an instrument for securing some reasonable compromise between the competing alternatives.

We might, alternatively, think of law as the attempt to realise a domain of value in human affairs, structured by the idea that important human goods can only be attained in common. A view of this kind inevitably presupposes or embodies a 'specific conception of the human person and of what is needed for the development of distinctive human powers.'[15] Law is then best understood as the domain in which concrete form is given to the search for the rational underpinnings of ethical thought. It is natural to regard the law (and other human social institutions and practices) as providing in this way a source of insight into moral rationality and the nature of the good, rather than a mere framework within which different forms of the good might be debated and pursued.

Posing the basic questions in this way has the advantage of focusing scholarly attention on the nature and purpose of law in human affairs, rather than on the possibility of drawing conceptual distinctions between law and morality. The latter possibility may, on this view, represent a manifestation of a general belief that the conditions necessary for the development of human powers and social institutions are independent of, or prior to, moral argument. But if that were true, law would seem to lose much of the centrality and importance with which the positivist conception of a basic framework of liberties imbues it. If each person's capacity for realising the good depends upon the establishment of basic liberties, law will seem to be of paramount importance in delineating with a reasonably high degree of comprehensiveness and precision those areas in which the individual is free to engage in enterprises of his own devising. Indeed, the higher the degree of pluralism exhibited in the views of

---

15 Hart, *Essays in Jurisprudence and Philosophy* (Oxford, Clarendon Press, 1983), 17.

legal officials and ordinary citizens, the more the legal order will come to be seen as a centrally important means of establishing boundaries to permissible conduct and the pursuit of value. In such circumstances, too, the appearance of moral neutrality in law will increasingly give way to an understanding of the legal order as effecting a *reasonable* ordering of competing interests and values.

By ascribing a 'nature' or intrinsic purpose to law, we do not foreclose on the possibility of positivistic understandings that seek to reveal categorical distinctions between 'established' or 'settled' legal rules and institutions, on the one hand, and the open-ended properties of moral debate, on the other. Rather, we open up potential and largely untapped lines of debate between theories where conventional ways of carving up the available positions forestall the possibility of interesting debate.

In the preceding section, I suggested that a good deal of modern jurisprudential argument consists of the construction and opposition of incommensurable 'concepts' of law. Much of this incommensurability derives from the fact that participants in those debates disagree with one another not only about the substantial content of the concept, but also about the correct way of evaluating or deriving that substance: does the truth of a concept of 'law' hinge upon its conformity to some characteristic of the moral good (which should therefore inform its construction), or in virtue of its accuracy in describing certain features of legal reasoning or institutions? Where disagreement extends not only to the propositions asserted in pursuit of an inquiry but also to the perspectives which underpin and give direction to that inquiry, the ensuing debate will of necessity exhibit a challenging subtlety and complexity. Yet there is much truth in the feeling that, in seeking to pin down or expose areas of common ground as a platform for genuine disagreement, adherents of the main rival theories have obscured virtually altogether the recognisable boundaries between the competing positions which previously governed and gave structure to the debate. Under the accumulated weight of these argumentative turns, traditional categories such as 'natural law' and 'positivism' become so kaleidoscopic as to defy real engagement with one another.

I do not mean to suggest that the categories of 'natural law' and 'positivism' are of no importance; for any philosophical debate presupposes some division into broad intellectual categories. My point is rather that when such positions have become distinguishable from one another only on the basis of the defence or rejection of subtly drawn conceptual necessities and contingencies, any shared sense of the significance of those positions is apt to be lost amid a chorus of conflicting claims about the 'nature' or scope of jurisprudential inquiry. An 'inclusive' positivist (for example) might seek to defend his position vis-à-vis natural law by entrenching a very weak version of the rule of recognition as a basic starting-point for engagement, and then offering an interpretation of natural law theory that demonstrates natural lawyers' acceptance of a basic rule of recognition *plus* the requirement that law serve the good. He will then argue that inclusive positivism takes account of this possibility whilst merely denying its *necessity*: conformity to the good may even emerge as a *practical* requirement of law's existence without determining the core of all imaginable systems of law. But then, what issue of practical significance turns on the distinction between inclusive positivism and natural law thus construed?[16] Faced with such obstacles to progress, might we not do better by challenging the existing framework, and re-imagining the philosophical possibilities we find within it?

How should the conceptual boundaries be re-drawn, if they are to retain their importance in jurisprudential thought? I propose the following approach as an enlightening way of proceeding: suppose we think of intellectual categories not as clarifying and distinguishing features of the intellectual landscape *prior* to engagement with substantive problems of justice, regulation and entitlement, but instead as reflecting differing or opposing ideas *within* legal thought as to how such problems are to be understood. The goal of legal theory would accordingly be to seek to reveal, through reflection on such categories, the internal structure and properties of legal order in the light of underlying beliefs about the point or purpose of a body of laws, and thus (at a more abstract level) to relate the idea of 'law' to wider understandings of a form of life. Where jurisprudential thinking embodies such concerns, the conceptual boundaries which define the inquiry are not likely to be driven by a direct focus on the law/morality connection, but by the question of how forms of juristic thought are related to the good, and of the role of law in realising the good. Such a move is naturally suggestive of a categorical division of the intellectual realm into those theories which perceive law as in some sense embodying and refining shared conceptions of the good, and those for which law is to be regarded as establishing a domain of priority and compromise between goods that are determined by private introspection (and which may therefore conflict).[17]

It is in fact not hard to strip away the concern with neutrality and conceptual clarification that pervades much of modern jurisprudential thought. In this way, we may reveal how familiar categories such as 'positivism' and 'natural law' relate to differing conceptions of law's ability to realise the good. In his introduction to *Essays on Bentham*,[18] Hart explains the importance of Bentham's conceptual approach to legal analysis by suggesting that Bentham's 'love of division and subdivision',

> ... was not mere, obsessive pedantry. Perhaps John Stuart Mill's essay on Bentham may have done something to convey the misleading impression that ... the novelty and value of what [Bentham] did 'lay not in his opinions but in his method' which Mill described as the 'method of detail'. My own view which I shall shortly attempt to substantiate is that this

---

16 See also J. Coleman and O. Simchen, 'Law', 9 *Legal Theory* (2003) 1–41: here the rule of recognition is said to be a necessary determinant of a legal system only as a metaphysical ground of legal validity, but acts as an epistemic guide to the content of legal rules only contingently. Perhaps there are some natural lawyers who might then subscribe to it. But if this is the case, the notion of 'recognition' seems to do no active work in determining 'validity': indeed, the rule of recognition in such a context has no obvious grounding in social practices at all (since practice, for Hart, determines content). The rule of recognition would have become nothing more than a purely formal requirement of legal validity in the manner of a Kelsenian Grundnorm, with the category of 'inclusive positivism' having few meaningful connections to Hart's original version of positivism.

17 Later in this book I shall suggest that this basic dichotomy stands in need of some refinement.

18 Hart, *Essays on Bentham* (Oxford, Clarendon Press, 1982).

is a misleading dichotomy between opinions and methods. Methods sufficiently novel, as some of Bentham's were, cannot be mere innovations of method. They presuppose too fundamental a reorientation of the direction of enquiry, and too radical a shift in the conception of what is to be considered an acceptable answer.[19]

Hart here demonstrates sensitivity to the symbiotic relationship that exists between the introduction of analytical distinctions and the refinement of concepts (on the one hand) and the presuppositions that underpin and drive our inquiry (on the other): the clarification of detail leads to 'bold and provocative reaffirmations of the general principles which gain in clarity and in a sense reveal more of their meaning when applied to small things';[20] such activity thus 'too often forces upon our attention new questions rather than new answers to old questions for its innovations to be considered as matters of method alone.' Mill's error, then, lay in the assumption that the method of refinement and clarification led merely to the accumulation of detail, without otherwise affecting our understanding of the subject-matter of the inquiry and of which questions are important or central in relation to it.

Hart later conceded that it was a 'general defect' in his earlier approach to jurisprudence that he had failed to understand the limitations of linguistic analysis, which is appropriate only in those cases in which we *share* criteria for the use of the concepts under investigation, not in cases where we diverge in our sense of which criteria are appropriate.[21] In view of the fact that the methods of linguistic philosophy purport to be neutral as between moral and political principles and 'silent about different points of view which might endow one feature rather than another of legal phenomena with significance',

> they are not suitable for resolving or clarifying those controversies which arise, as many of the central problems of legal philosophy do, from the divergence between partly overlapping concepts reflecting a divergence of basic point of view or values or background theory, or which arise from conflict or incompleteness of legal rules.[22]

In such cases, Hart argued, we must proceed from an 'identification of the latent conflicting points of view which led to the choice or formation of divergent concepts.' Hart's early jurisprudential work leaves little scope for such an enterprise, but we can see in *The Concept of Law* a (not wholly convincing) attempt to balance the claims of a descriptively neutral account of law with the need to identify a perspective from which the series of conceptual categories and definitions might flow. Hart seeks to describe the 'central case' of law in human affairs, and thus requires a perspective

---

19 *Ibid.*, 3–4 (the reference to Mill is to vol. 10 of the *Collected Works of John Stuart Mill*, 75).

20 *Ibid.*, 5.

21 See Hart, *Essays in Jurisprudence and Philosophy* (above, note 15), 5: 'an understanding, however sophisticated or profound, of the workings of language could only yield significant results for jurisprudence where difficulties had arisen from a failure to identify the way in which some particular use of language deviated from some tacitly accepted paradigm, or where radically different forms of expression were mistakenly assimilated to some familiar form.'

22 *Ibid.*, 6.

from which central cases can be distinguished from marginal or non-cases. Such a perspective will be (as argued above) inherently an evaluative one, and Hart therefore aims to preserve the neutrality of his theory with respect to competing conceptions of the good by basing his account on minimal or 'thin' assumptions, which all reasonable participants in debate over the good can accept.[23] The neutrality of the account is thus *relative* rather than *complete* neutrality, since any assumption may form the target for *some* person's criticism (from a perspective of radical scepticism or nihilism, say). Nevertheless, Hart's aim involves the balancing of the demands of evaluation with a general and widespread acceptance of the chosen evaluative standpoint.

Famously, Hart invokes the 'minimum content of natural law' as just such a minimal standpoint.[24] It is generally a part of human nature to prefer survival to extinction or death, and we can therefore view the existence and purpose of society as seeking the goal of human survival. We can do this on the basis of a few 'truisms' about the human condition (human beings are easily hurt, capable of limited altruism, etc.) without thereby presupposing a commitment to any moral values that are likely to form the subject of argument between different human beings bent on their own survival. Plausibly, the goal of survival hinges on the existence of a clear system of rules which restrain competition between individuals and which foster certain sorts of cooperative behaviour. But a primitive form of society may generate numerous informal, conduct-determining rules that curb threatening behaviour and demand the performance of social duties, and yet fall short of conformity to the characteristics of a society under the rule of law as we understand it. Thus, (in Hart's view) the step from the pre-legal, customary society into the society of laws is characterised by the presence of secondary rules that cure the obvious defects of a customary order, and which establish criteria for recognising the 'validity' of legal provisions.

Hart clearly recognised, in these passages, the necessity for our understanding of the central case to be grounded in some deeper perspective concerning human nature and the purpose of human society, even if it does not seek to justify the legal 'forms and structures' of a 'particular legal system or legal culture'.[25] It is in this sense that the idea of a union of primary and secondary rules might be said to constitute a basic foundation for legal understanding, independent at once of competing moral visions, and of the detailed disputes of the doctrinal lawyer. Yet it is impossible to maintain for long the suggestion that our 'basic understanding' or central case is determined prior to the contextual study of historically extended social practices and moral understandings: from the mere premise of 'human survival' it does not follow that law must take the form of a system of determinate rules subject to the exercise of secondary powers; nor that determination of the content of legal rules must proceed on the basis of 'recognition' by those who hold such powers.

The need for 'survival' may be traced out in different ways. On one view (resembling that of Grotius), human survival depends upon man's possession of an

---

23 For a similar, though to my mind more ambitious, claim see M.H. Kramer, *In Defence of Legal Positivism: Law Without Trimmings* (Oxford, Oxford University Press 1999).

24 See Hart, *The Concept of Law* (above note 1) 192ff.

25 *Ibid.*, 239–40.

intrinsically sociable nature, which both provides a foundation for mutual toleration and forbearance, and encourages the development of collective practices that stabilise and protect the interests and expectations of individuals who live in close proximity to one another. As human practices crystallise, the character of such forbearances and instances of toleration will naturally transform, over time, into a rudimentary system of rights and liberties. Since there need be no more to such a practice than a shared sense that certain basic liberties and rights are 'proper' to human beings, the goal of survival need not be tied to the development of positive law as the unique means by which social peace and stability are attained.

The idea that joint survival depends upon the realisation of positive law, in connection with powers of recognition and deliberate modification, is therefore naturally associated with an alternative, Hobbesian view of human nature as the individualistic pursuit of narrow self-interest in competition with others.[26] If human nature is intrinsically self-regarding rather than sociable, society is most naturally viewed as the product of artifice based on a clear body of positive laws, and customary practices will seem incapable of forming a stable and lasting basis for social order. Positivism therefore tends to accord law a predominant role within social life as the glue that prevents the various competing interests from spinning society apart into anarchic warfare; whereas the law of a customary society is typically viewed as an important, but less central underpinning for established social institutions such as the family, mercantile practice, and so on. The Hobbesian view of morality is not a 'minimalist' view in the sense of deriving a moral or political theory from the smallest possible number of assumptions, but in the sense that human nature alone is seen as implying and sustaining a minimal number of natural laws. It is therefore a substantial understanding of human nature and human powers, which stands as an important alternative to others.

Hart's argument for the central case makes it clear that he is contemplating a world fundamentally unlike that of the medieval period, in which important questions of collective survival (such as questions of property ownership, social status, liability etc.) were already to a high degree settled by religious belief or, in some cases, the inherited values of a shared pagan past: he addresses instead a modern world where rights are artificial creations of the human mind rather than attributes 'proper' to human beings. Hart's arguments are therefore to be seen as addressing a situation in which the erosion of shared standpoints has left in its wake an essentially Protestant and individualistic conception of the good, and of human society. But then in what sense is 'a purely analytical study of legal concepts' *separate* from 'historical or sociological studies' in coming to an understanding of the nature of law?[27]

The Protestant character of modern jurisprudential thought both grounds and encourages a perspective from which the study of legal concepts is detached from

---

26 Hart's minimum content theory does not fit neatly into any canon of natural law writing, since it has clear affinity with Hobbes, but also with elements of the thought of (for example) Grotius and Locke. But if Hart is seeking a *minimalist* foundation for legal understanding, he would naturally look to Hobbes rather than Locke for intellectual inspiration.

27 Hart, 'Positivism and the Separation of Law and Morals', in *Essays in Jurisprudence and Philosophy* (above, note 15), 57.

contextual study of the historical formation and development of social practices. The separation of these projects is not particular to positivism, for where morality and the good are viewed at a deep level as matters for individual judgment (in that each person's autonomy as a rational agent is dependent upon the ability to formulate his or her own conception of human flourishing), moral value itself becomes disconnected from custom and historical circumstance, and thus custom and history cease to be regarded as potent sources of moral reflection. The alternatives for those who wish to avoid a thesis of moral irrationalism will be to embrace a subjective picture of morality, as residing in the individual will, or else to ground moral values in abstract principles of justice or virtue, which are thought to transcend the variable facts of human experience. On the latter view, the common good emerges only to the extent that private interpretations converge on the basis of independently constituted grounds of reason, so that reason itself in some sense stands apart from the practices and institutions which are designed to promote or realise those goods.[28]

This separation of analytical projects from contextual historical study is unfortunate in that it unduly limits inquiry to those matters that are seen as being of pressing importance from the perspective of the prevailing viewpoint. It is this feature of modern jurisprudential debate that most encourages the entrenchment of a small number of rival positions, and which blinds participants in those debates to the possibility of formulating alternative perspectives that sit uneasily within the accepted categories and classifications imposed by the debate. Protestant political theory presupposes its own metaphysical picture of the world: a picture in which practice, will and abstract principle form separate starting-points for reflection. Rather than exhaustively exploring the alternative ways in which such a theory can be traced out, might not a more fruitful inquiry seek to *challenge* that picture, and to expose its limitations through the articulation of the theory's presuppositions, their origin, scope and intellectual commitments?

The Importance of a Historical Perspective

I have suggested that modern jurisprudence might be presented as a debate between two rival perspectives on law's capacity to realise the good. On one perspective, (which we may continue to call 'legal positivism') law facilitates pursuit of the good by establishing an organised body of relatively clear and precise rules on the basis of which individuals can exercise liberties to formulate and pursue projects that they deem to be constituents of a valuable way of life. On the other perspective, (which I shall refer to as 'idealism') the legal order consists of principles of justice, which define the extent of individual rights and which, taken together, embody a society's shared conceptions of the good.[29] I shall suggest, in the course of this book, that

---

28 See for example J. Rawls, *A Theory of Justice*, revised edn (Belknap Press, 1999), 114. As we will see in Chapter 2, these notions are also made to depend ultimately upon the will, although in a different way.

29 'Idealism' is therefore a wider idea than that of natural law, although it has an obvious basis in natural law theories. (See Chapter 2.) We might, I suggest later, see Ronald Dworkin as a liberal idealist for these purposes.

modern juristic thought is defined by a complex dialogue between these two basic perspectives.

Both of these perspectives, in different ways, seek to suppress the connection between jurisprudential analysis and historical reflection, by aligning moral values with the will, or by tracing out transcendent conceptions of justice as a basis for shared viewpoints in a world marked by moral disagreement. The suppression of historical reflection is a product of the progressive rejection of Aristotelian ethical thought in favour of a form of moral voluntarism which reached its high watermark in Kant's doctrine of Right.[30]

The jurisprudence of the present day can be regarded as a series of competing assertions about the way in which the assumptions of Protestant political theory may be traced out. The positivistic understanding of law as a framework of imposed rules designed to secure protected spheres of liberty and independence of will, is naturally thought of as attempting to realise conditions in which the joint pursuit of distinctive forms of the good is made possible. A perspective that seeks to present the legal order as a systematic body of rights, by contrast, serves Protestant autonomy in treating questions of individual entitlement and interest as matters for joint interpretation and concern. Both alternatives might be thought of as proposing some conceptual regimentation of the legal order on the basis of an implicit view of human nature which strives to reconcile Protestant autonomy with the demands of reason. The theory then seeks to explain law in terms of those features that most prominently reinforce and uphold that view.

By suppressing the historical perspective, which is essential to a proper understanding of the nature of law, modern versions of positivism and idealism place severe limitations on our ability to understand the present in terms of the past. For the pursuit of multiple and diverse goods, rather than the attempt to realise a harmoniously unified good or *telos*, is apt to suggest the need for a philosophical understanding of human choice and agency that is 'unconditioned' by involvement in historical contingencies. The detached perspective from which modern theorists view the objects of their inquiries encourages and heightens the sense of theory as an independent viewpoint capable of revealing permanent insights into the nature of our social practices, but it also serves to blind those theorists to the contingency and transience of their assumptions: treating the search for theoretical underpinnings as an exercise in the conceptual regimentation of our pre-theoretical 'intuitions', jurisprudence becomes 'wrapped in the mystery of its own familiarity.'[31] What is required is a perspective in which legal theory is not directed towards final resolutions or permanent ends, but rather the explanation of sources of moral and political tension and of law's role in responding to those tensions. Once we begin to

---

30 See Chapter 2. For some useful accounts, see Finnis, *Natural Law and Natural Rights* (above, note 13), 347–350; T.J. Hochstrasser, *Natural Law Theories of the Early Enlightenment* (Cambridge, Cambridge University Press, 2000), chapter 3, esp. 99–109; and S. Darwall, *British Moralists and the Internal 'Ought' 1640–1740* (New York, Cambridge University Press, 1995) 23–52 and 64–69.

31 I borrow this expression from James Murphy: see J. Murphy, *The Philosophy of Positive Law* (Yale University Press, 2005), 23.

appreciate morality as a form of reflective experience rather than an autonomously constituted body of moral laws, we will come to realise that the problems and frictions that inevitably arise whenever human beings live alongside one another in close and permanent relations should not be thought of as admitting of general solutions: morality and law supply ways of dealing with the effects of the problems of collective living, but do not finally resolve those problems.

The moral perspectives that develop within a society are therefore reflective of that society's attempt to have its say about political and social problems, which will continue to press on human beings even after present generations and civilisations have exited the mortal stage.[32] The moral nature of a society will, in consequence, be shaped and determined not just by the way it addresses questions of human social interaction, but also in the light of the aspects of human interaction that are considered to be worth addressing. A theory of law is thus one in which an understanding of ends is intrinsically bound up with our understanding of the concrete mechanisms through which we seek their establishment. The analysis of political concepts is accordingly shaped as much by our attempts to realise political ideals in social practice as it is about abstract theorising. Thus, if we wish to understand the nature of the relationship between Protestant autonomy and rationality, for example, we should pay attention to the historical development of social practices (such as 'right') which aim to instantiate or give joint effect to those ideas.

Ideas that are easily expressible within the confines of abstract theory frequently tend to alter and fragment when implemented in practice. For many modern theorists, this fact merely demonstrates the gap between theory and practice, and the propensity of theory to require or propose modification of the practice so that it may be more closely aligned to the abstract demands of justice.[33] Once our focus changes to historically developed practices as the forum in which political values are realised and articulated, we will become more attuned to the probability that constant revision and fragmentation are endemic to political ideals, rather than an unfortunate feature of current political life. The history of a political idea (such as autonomy) need not be one of convergence and increasing clarity and cohesion: it may just as easily reflect the deep tensions and contradictions in a shared social existence that the idea was meant to extinguish.

In the following chapters of this book, I aim to explore the intellectual and historical forces that underpin and sustain our current form of juristic thought. The powerful forces that place Protestant political assumptions at the centre of jurisprudence exhibit, so I shall argue, an intrinsic instability that causes jurisprudential thought to oscillate between versions of positivism (which emphasise the rule-based nature of law) and versions of idealism (which place emphasis on the systematic qualities of legal order, grounded in a conception of individual rights). By coming to an understanding of these tensions, we may hope to achieve a deeper and more reflective understanding of life under the rule of law in the British polity than

---

32 See L. Fuller, 'The Case of the Speluncean Explorers', 62 *Harvard Law Review* (1942), 616.

33 Or even, perhaps, merely those of integrity: see Dworkin, *Law's Empire* (London, Fontana, 1986).

modern analytical jurisprudence allows. For although positivism and idealism have made a deep and lasting impression on the English juridical consciousness, there are also permanent features of that moral consciousness[34] that are suppressed by the jurisprudential thought of modernity. These features of the English temperament are not themselves Protestant in form, but create an intellectual context in which Protestant forms of thought can exist: for they emphasise law as part of the fabric of civility which makes human beings ultimately comprehensible to one another. Such features of English juridical thought may in the end prove to be of greater importance to our self-understanding than the apparently progressive thought of modernity.

---

34 Gillian Rose has pointed out that fundamental forms of human judgment may be viewed as juridical in origin: see *The Dialectic of Nihilism: Post-Structuralism and Law* (Oxford, Blackwell, 1984).

Chapter 2

Reason, Will and Law

The legal system of every society constitutes a body of practices that extend through time. Obvious though that observation may seem, this fact about legal order is significant in determining jurisprudential perspectives because the patterns of legal reasoning and justification that develop in a society are themselves formed against the background of historically shifting political and moral concerns, and such concerns therefore provide the conditions of their intelligibility. This is because legal theory is not an investigation of abstract categories or concepts that are logically independent of doctrinal contexts of argument. The notions of 'law', 'right', 'power' and so on have significance outside the law as well as within it, and so we might expect the lawyer's doctrinal categories and justificationary practices to reflect changing beliefs about the political character of society.[1] Thus, for instance, the notion of 'right' within a feudal society informed by a tradition of belief in the divine law can be expected to differ in essential respects from the same notion held within the more limited deontological perspectives offered by mercantile capitalism.

The jurisprudential thinking of any era might be read as the effort to find some resonance between legal understandings and prevailing social concerns. If that is so, then the legal order need not be thought to exhibit coherence at the level of principle, for it may instead carry within itself tensions and contradictions produced by the coexistence of variant modes of thought within a single institutional structure of argument and justification.[2] The attempt to impose theoretical consistency upon legal practices via the operations of conceptual analysis is, in this way, apt to limit and distort understanding of the legal order rather than to increase it.

Because law is a historical practice, legal theory must itself seek an understanding of the social histories that are reflected in the concepts and categories of the modern legal order. The shifting forms of juristic understanding amount not merely to a history of ideas; they also embody a history of practices that have shaped the legal order in decisive ways and thus render it fully intelligible to modern understandings: an appreciation of the significance of 'rights' for juridical thinking requires, in part, sensitivity to the conceptual divisions of Roman law out of which our present legal conceptions evolved, and of the effect of changing social conditions upon the form

---

1   This observation is not limited to the main categories of legal thought, for a similar thesis holds true in respect of the categories of 'contract', 'property' etc. See A.W.B. Simpson, *A History of the Common Law of Contract: The Rise of the Action of Assumpsit* (Oxford, Clarendon Press, 1987). See also N.E. Simmonds, *The Decline of Juridical Reason: Doctrine and Theory in the Legal Order* (Manchester, Manchester University Press, 1984), 4.

2   See R. Geuss, *History and Illusion in Politics* (Cambridge, Cambridge University Press, 2001) chapter 3.

and purpose of rights within legal and political discourse. Fully to understand legal modes of reflection, one must comprehend the historic formation of moral and political understandings both within and outside the law. In the preceding chapter, I argued that such understandings presuppose differing ideas about human nature, and of law's capacity to realise the good. The present chapter will deepen and further elucidate this view.

Morality, History and the Will

Law and morality might be regarded as permanent features of the human condition, in that the notion of constraints upon human behaviour seems to exist in some form wherever human sociability has given rise to conceptual thought. The nature of morality is thus as important a question as that of the nature of legality as far as understandings of that condition are concerned. I suggested in Chapter 1 that there is little to be gained from the contemplation of associations or distinctions between conceptual categories of 'law' and 'morality'. Yet in one sense, modern jurisprudential argument is right to focus on the question of how law is connected to morality. I have suggested that much of modern jurisprudence might be thought of as a long-running battle between rival understandings of the rule of law.

Positivism, on the one hand, reflects a concern with a form of Protestant autonomy in which each person is free to develop and pursue his or her own conception of the good. For the exercise of autonomy to be meaningful, the law must do more than secure numerous limited opportunities for making choices: it must leave room for the establishment of significant spheres of liberty in which the individual is able to retain substantial control over his affairs in a way that allows for the pursuit of long-term objectives. Law, for the positivist, must therefore maintain a degree of neutrality between rival conceptions of the good, by sustaining some reasonable ordering amongst competing interests. Idealism (on the other hand) traces out the implications of Protestant autonomy in a different way, by supposing that law directly embodies an idea of justice that is thought to reflect shared conceptions of the good. The capacity for autonomous reflection is then thought to be captured by the idea that questions of individual interest are a matter for joint interpretation and concern.

By posing the question in this way, a little-noticed dimension of juristic thought is revealed to us: for the law can only be thought of as *manifesting* ideas of justice or morality where morality itself takes the form of essentially law-like standards and principles, capable of being understood systematically and in abstraction from particular cases and facts.[3] But this understanding leaves us with a problem, as the claim that the rule of law embodies a moral ideal does not concern the possession of moral qualities in *that* sense. The point of maintaining that the rule of law is an intrinsically moral idea concerns the centrality of law to the realisation of basic human

---

3   See Simmonds, (above, note 1), 39; and J.B. Schneewind, *The Invention of Autonomy* (New York, Cambridge University Press, 1998), chapter 7.

social goals, not the fulfilment of particular moral standards.[4] Law's possession of a moral nature should therefore alert us to other dimensions of morality aside from that which portrays morality as a body of juridical standards. Until we have freed ourselves of that picture, the forms of moral reflection within the law will remain opaque to us.

The common law is often represented as an intellectual domain that particularly lends itself to expression in terms of underlying moral principles and ideas of justice. We should not however make too much of this claim: for the grounds of decision in the majority of cases do not admit of formulation as general moral principles in abstraction from the particular context supplied by the judgment. It is often only with enormous difficulty that the *ratio decidendi* can be distilled from the rich brew of judicial discussion concerning the specific rights and obligations of the parties arising in the facts of each case. Such formulations are inevitably tentative, open to exceptions and revision in the light of application to particular circumstances, and the form of moral reasoning at common law is thus suggestive of an Aristotelian mode of ethical reflection in which moral understanding is achieved only in application, rather than in the contemplation of means and ends.

Unlike the moral philosophy of the post-Kantian era, which views morality as by-and-large a matter of ethical principles that must be grasped in the abstract and applied to the variable facts of experience, Aristotelian thought depicts moral knowledge as involving not only the theoretical understanding, but also the broader range of human capacities and experience. Within this picture, justice and moral nobility do not admit of neat formulation into rules and principles, but instead consist of the disposition of the rational man to act rightly in specific situations. The relevant image is that of 'our ability to internalise from a scattered range of particular cases a general evaluative attitude which is not reducible to rules or precepts.'[5] In becoming habituated to acting rightly and justly in a range of situations, we learn what is right or just. Aristotelian thought thus emphasises an aspect of moral reflection which modern, Protestant theories of moral understanding neglect: that of immersion within the contextual practices of a form of life as a source of moral knowledge and insight in its own right. Moral understanding, on this view, is arrived at not (as in modern moral philosophy) on the basis of induction, intuition or pure reason, but by comprehending certain actions as just or right in virtue of their justness or rightness. Aristotle speaks of our unreasoned evaluative responses as being initially guided towards the right objects (the purpose of law being to foster the inculcation of excellence-forming habits of behaviour), leading us eventually to a reasoned desire

---

4   See, for example, L. Fuller, *The Morality of Law*, chapter 1. Fuller was not the only writer to recognise this point: insofar as Bentham can be understood as rejecting a moral conception of the rule of law, his claim that law does not possess a moral nature is not that the law fails to embody particular moral ideals. See J. Bentham, *A Fragment on Government*, R. Harrison (ed.) (Cambridge, Cambridge University Press, 1988).

5   M.F. Burnyeat, 'Aristotle on Learning to be Good', in A.O. Rorty (ed.) *Essays on Aristotle's Ethics* (Berkeley, University of California Press, 1980) 69–92, 72. See Aristotle, *Nicomachean Ethics* (various eds), 1179b4–31: arguments alone are insufficient to make men good; the disposition towards and development of a virtuous character is required.

for virtue and knowledge of the good.[6] Aristotelian thought in this way represents a form of moral intellectualism, in opposition to the moral voluntarism of Kant and his intellectual heirs in the Protestant tradition.

It is no accident that the rise of voluntarist perspectives coincided with the gradual decline of Aristotelian modes of ethical reflection. The classical understanding of ethics had centred upon a unified object of practical contemplation ('the good') presupposed as an end in human nature and reality.[7] The emergence of deep divisions in the political and religious life of Europe in the 17th century cast doubt on the idea that rational deliberation is structured by a *summum bonum* located within the flourishing life of the agent; instead, rationality came to be seen as the logical fitting of means to desired ends in pursuit of one's own, private conception of the good in a world where plural notions of the good vie and compete for dominance.[8] Morality was gradually transformed through association with two separate yet related perspectives on the ethical life of the agent: one, in which morality was viewed as a set of demands or requirements of collective living, which were binding on people without any intrinsic connection to the agent's good; and another which tied morality to self-governance and freedom from interference by the state, the church and one's fellow citizens.

These two perspectives on morality exhibited an obvious dynamic tension in the political thought of the early modern era, and the wealth of philosophical classics produced in this period is perhaps a reflection of the intense energy that went into the attempt to reconcile them within a single framework of political thought. We might think of these efforts as effecting the transition from a Jurisprudence of Reason to a Jurisprudence of the Will. For in a world in which deep conflict is possible between individual forms of the good, the possibility of self-governance is attainable only through the imposition of fixed and determinate rules that *restrict* opportunities for self-expression in the name of the common good: some limitations on conduct (in order to prohibit violence, establish rules of property and so on) are inevitable if self-governance is to be meaningful, since wholly unrestrained freedom inevitably leads to insecurity and the impossibility of pursuing long-term projects. Where there is pervasive conflict amongst forms of the good, such rules must reflect some reasonable compromise between the competing interests, and are thus naturally looked upon as products of the will. The areas of liberty left open by the rules to the exercise of autonomy are then naturally interpreted as private spheres in which the individual will is free to determine its own moral course.

The transition to a Jurisprudence of the Will thus constitutes a form of moral thought in which the juridical domain of rights and justice comprises a separate

---

6   See Burnyeat, *ibid.*, 80.

7   One might distinguish 'ethics' from 'morality' in that the former is associated with the classical theme of the pursuit of excellence and virtue, whereas the latter tends to conjure up the image of law-like rules. The distinction is not in this way necessarily a firm one, but I shall employ the terms in roughly this way in order to convey more clearly the direction of argument and its underpinning intellectual sympathies.

8   For an insightful discussion, see S. Darwall, *British Moralists and the Internal 'Ought' 1640–1740* (Cambridge, Cambridge University Press, 1995), 2–9.

intellectual realm from that of virtue and the good. Law may *embody* moral values, but is not itself a source of insight into moral virtue or the good. Once moral values have become related to the will, the historical practices and forms of association which characterise the polity will no longer be viewed as possessing any intrinsic moral significance, and the intellectual basis of practical wisdom will be taken to express a contingent, rather than necessary, association between practice and virtue. The idea that ethical understanding is based on a capacity for moral discernment relating to one's experience will come to be treated with suspicion. This is because the exercise of practical reason is made possible by the social circumstances in which the *phronimos* lives. But what if the social and economic conditions of the state exhibit not virtue and enlightenment, but wickedness and injustice? Morality will then seem to constitute a body of truth more permanent than the contingencies of historical circumstance:

> ... we can contemplate the moral life in activity as well as the starry heaven above. It is only in a corrupt polity that the contemplative life need be other-worldly, and only in a corrupt polity that the policies promoting the development and exercise of contemplative activity would come into conflict with those establishing requirements for the best practical life.[9]

Does the idea of practical wisdom presuppose some *prior* familiarity with the good, independent of historical social practice? Faced with the possibility of the corrupt state, moral philosophers and jurists have tended to be sceptical of the rationalism inherent in the idea that experience can guide virtue, and have accordingly sought to separate social fact and institutions, on the one hand, from moral reflection, on the other. Such separation might be expressed in a number of different ways: by Austin's dictum that 'the existence of law is one thing; its merit or demerit is another'[10] (for example), or by the view that various interpretations of moral soundness must be 'fitted' to the facts of legal experience in order to present legal practice in a satisfactory light.[11] Where a moral interpretation of the legal order is viewed as a necessary component of a juristic point of view, moral insight is seen as deriving from reflective equilibrium between the various different sources which generate our intuitions. Once the notion of 'reflective equilibrium' is comprehended, earlier forms of moral inquiry, such as that of Aristotle, seem to involve a curious inattention to the dichotomy between facts and values, as made explicit in Hume.[12]

---

9   A.O. Rorty, 'The Place of Contemplation in Aristotle's *Nicomachean Ethics*', in Rorty (above, note 5), 377–94, 378. See also K.V. Wilkes, 'The Good Man and the Good For Man in Aristotle's Ethics', *ibid.*, 341–57.

10   J. Austin, *The Province of Jurisprudence Determined* (London, Weidenfeld & Nicholson, 1954), 184.

11   See R. Dworkin, *Law's Empire* (London, Fontana, 1986).

12   Arguably, Hume was merely offering a limited attack on rationalism by demonstrating that the possession by actions of moral properties could not of itself explain the motivating force that leads to those actions: a causal (or 'is' statement) is also needed. The inflation of this thesis into a general metaphysical picture of the world in which facts and values belong to separate logical 'kinds' is, in some ways, the product of later interpretations of Hume's work. Nevertheless, Hume's suggestion can be seen as a symptom, rather than a cause, of a world-

This has led to a perspective from which the generation of moral insights is regarded as separate from the historical examination of social institutions such as law. The dissociation of the sphere of moral insight and reflection from the juridical realm of right and duty is conjoined to this method explicitly in the writings of Henry Sidgwick.[13] Here, the correct method of reflection in political theory is said to be 'a method not primarily historical', in which historical reflection is employed 'either to confirm practical conclusions otherwise arrived at, or to suggest the limits of their applicability.'[14] The correct method for the political scientist is thus to 'assume certain general characteristics of social man – characteristics belonging not to mankind universally, but to civilised man in the most advanced stages of his development', and then to 'consider what laws and institutions are likely to conduce most to the welfare of an aggregate of such beings living in social relations.'[15]

Sidgwick suggests a picture in which the social nature of man is independent of, or prior to, the existence of social institutions. On this view, moral reflection is a matter for the theoretical intellect, seeking reflective equilibrium amid the variable facts of human experience and universal moral laws that exist in detachment from that experience.[16] Such a view depends for its attractiveness upon a metaphysical picture of the world in which the dichotomy of fact and value represents a distinction between natural kinds: a picture that both sustains, and is sustained by, a Protestant conception of moral reasoning. It is no accident that the political thinkers who developed and employed this method saw themselves as applying to the arena of moral philosophy the same standards of clarity and rigour as are to be found in mathematics and the natural sciences.[17] Yet this line of thinking ignores the sense in which the social nature of man is reflected and expressed in social institutions. For

---

view in which the classical association of fact and value is seen as resting on metaphysical error.

13 The phrase 'reflective equilibrium' itself derives from Rawls. Rawls cites Sidgwick's *Methods of Ethics* as an intellectual ancestor of his methodological project, and also (mistakenly, as I hope to explain), Aristotle's *Ethics*. See J. Rawls, *A Theory of Justice*, revised edn (Cambridge Mass, Belknap Press, 1999), 45n.

14 H. Sidgwick, *The Elements of Politics*, 2nd edn (London, Macmillan, 1897), 11.

15 *Ibid.*

16 Contemplation of the history of 'experience of civilised life' can thus be a *guide* to man's social nature and characteristics, which will produce conclusions not '*exactly* or *universally* true, even of contemporary civilised man; but only as sufficiently near the truth for practical purposes.' (Sidgwick, above, note 14, 11–12, emphasis in original).

17 What we might call the 'scientific tradition' of moral thinking emerges in the writings of Grotius: see for example *De Iure Belli ac Pacis* (various eds), Prolegomena, s.58: 'just as mathematicians treat their figures as abstracted from bodies, so in treating law I have withdrawn my mind from every particular fact.' Grotius inaugurated a line of thinking in which mathematical inquiries were seen as being of a not dissimilar kind to inquiries into morality, but merely as exhibiting a higher degree of certainty. Hume and, later, Bentham, would seek to provide certainty by grounding moral thinking in empirically ascertainable questions of utility. See also Prolegomena, s.30: 'For natural principles, being always the same, are easily put into a systematic form, whereas conventional principles, which often change and which vary from place to place, like other collections of particulars cannot be handled systematically.'

if we abstract moral thinking from the historical context of laws and institutions, with what do we structure our sense of the 'general characteristics of social man ... in the most advanced stage of his development'? The concern of science to detach a moral perspective from questions of prudence and wellbeing simply masks, and does not eliminate, the need for moral reflection to be grounded in a deep and textured understanding of human nature as expressed in historical forms of association.

The search for moral laws or principles of justice in detachment from the circumstances of their application places ethical inquiry on a path entirely divergent to that of classical thought. Aristotelians believe, of course, that it is possible to contemplate virtue as an object of thought distinct from the concept of virtuous action. But the process of refining one's understanding of an object through contemplation of both general and particular features is not a matter of constructing, from our considered moral judgments, a set of general moral principles existing in abstraction from our ordinary 'intuitions' about the arena in which they apply. Still less does it concern the attempt to find the best 'fit' between such judgments and the principles or general philosophical theories (such as a theory of procedural justice) which we 'construct' as starting-points for contemplation.[18] The relevant intellectual processes are not processes of abstraction or adjustment, but the situating of reflective judgments within a metaphysical framework, which is itself taken as an object of philosophical contemplation. The knowledge of the *phronimos* is directed to particular ends rather than some general scheme in which ends are related to higher values.[19] The absence of a general scheme of principle does not therefore signal a lack on the part of the *phronimos* of insight into or knowledge of the good, but is rather constitutive of the difference between practical wisdom and scientific inquiry as distinct forms of knowledge.

As long as we retain a sense of the importance of this insight, the appearance of a gap between the manifestation of practical wisdom, on the one hand, and the pursuit of abstract speculation directed at universals, on the other, will be revealed as resting on a failure to appreciate the way in which ethical thought represents, not a body of knowledge which is structured by our understanding of independently conceived ends, but one in which our ability to grasp the end or point in view is inseparable from the experience of reaching or aiming for that end. Scientific knowledge provides a misleading model for moral knowledge precisely because such detachment from concrete situations is a feature of physical and mathematical laws.

We can profitably conceive the transformation of the legal order, at the hands of the 17th century natural lawyers, from a loose collection of procedures and remedies into an organised body of rights, as an attempt to supply just this sort of detachment of legal principles from the particular situations in which they apply. But if the grasp of particular ends does not issue in a framework of general moral laws, we should not expect such an attempt to blossom into a fully coherent system (unless at a

---

18 See Rawls, 'The Independence of Moral Theory', 47 *Proceedings and Addresses of the American Philosophical Association* (1974–75), 8. Indeed, the view of virtue as an object of the understanding, rather than the will, precludes the use of 'construction' as the appropriate metaphor for comprehending such processes.

19 See Rorty (above, note 9), 384.

considerable level of abstraction from that of concrete application). Rather, such a system might be expected to exhibit internal tensions and the need for constant revision. The 'Protestant' character of post-Enlightenment jurisprudence accordingly embodies a peculiar dynamic tension of its own: for once moral insight is made to depend upon grounds of rationality which transcend contextual and historical concerns, it becomes unclear to what extent each person's pursuit of the good manifests genuine conditions of autonomy. To the extent that divergent, competing conceptions of the good are irreconcilable with universal moral laws, should not rationality be viewed as *incompatible* with genuine autonomy, rather than a ground of its realisation?

Natural Law and Protestant Autonomy

I have suggested that modern jurisprudence, in which ethical principles are seen as radically detached from the contingencies of historical experience, signals a move towards a voluntarist position which views moral principles as products of the will. Bound up with such a move is a changed conception of the nature and importance of law: for the inculcation of moral values will no longer be viewed as consisting of the cultivation of dispositions to act virtuously, but rather in obedience to moral *laws*:

> Since it is only the will of God which can be ascertained in the relation between God and man, man cannot possibly give his response to God through an act of thinking or perceiving, but only by his being obedient or disobedient, that is to say by his will.[20]

An important consequence of moral voluntarism was thus to detach law from the fabric of customary practices and social institutions, and to place it instead on the abstract juridical plane of rights and duties. Accordingly, law was thought of as possessing binding force not because it originated in the practices and social expectations of the people to whom it applied, but in virtue of its source in a superior will in conformity with independently given requirements of morality and justice. Law was viewed as having a 'natural' jurisdiction, which articulated the commands of the divine law, and an independently functioning 'civil' jurisdiction wherein the earthly ruler and the courts could create civic obligations and legislate rules for social conduct. Ultimately, this changed conception of the nature of law was to give rise to a form of moral Protestantism in which juristic understandings no longer addressed complex historical modes of resolution, practice, justification and judgment, but rather a body of abstract entitlements wherein the rational autonomy of diverse actors was reflected.

In viewing the legal order as an articulation of universal laws of morality, the early natural lawyers had before their eyes a powerful example of a detailed rational system of rules and entitlements in the Roman law. As the Roman mercantile class began to trade more frequently with outsiders, the Roman jurisprudence was forced to abandon much of the technical doctrine and complex procedure of Roman law,

---

20 A. Dilhe, *The Theory of Will in Classical Antiquity* (Berkeley, University of California Press, 1982), 15.

in favour of a simplified set of principles of honesty and fair dealing that could be readily grasped by those outside the Empire. Such principles could be regarded as a common basis for trade, it was believed, precisely because they formed a set of ideas reasonably imputable to all people.[21] The intellectual concepts and categories of Roman law were eventually to take on an additional significance for European jurists as the *ius gentium* gradually merged with the idea of *ius naturale*, in the sense of a law which is proper to people. The character of this natural law was at first associated with the intellect and understanding, rather than the will, for it consisted of a power or capacity for moral discernment in relation to a rationally intelligible universe which was imagined to be the product of God's nature rather than His arbitrary will. This created an intellectual context in which Aristotelian modes of ethical reflection could flourish alongside Christian theological perspectives: for even if God is taken to be a source of moral *laws*, ethical understanding and knowledge of such laws is possible only if goodness represents a dimension of morality distinguishable from the status of those laws as willed commands.[22] Suppose, for example, that the divine law demands the honouring of one's debts. The manifestation of a virtuous disposition demands not only knowledge of the wrongfulness of not complying with this rule, but also knowledge of *why* it is wrong: as how else am I to know how to act in difficult cases where the repayment of the debt will bring about some significant injury or wrong?

Theological perspectives upon the natural law were ultimately to threaten the coexistence of Christian and Aristotelian modes of thinking, eventually culminating in the decline of the latter. The treatment of ethical ideas as laws forced upon medieval theologians a juridical conception of morality in which such laws function, to some extent, as independently constituted ends for human action, rather than intrinsic dimensions of the human good. Once moral ideas are viewed as *laws*, the only theological source for such laws could be God's will; for the premise of divine omnipotence rendered impossible the suggestion that such a will could be governed by anything external to itself. Thus, Luther was to observe that 'What God wills is not right because He ought, or was bound, so to will; on the contrary, what takes place must be right, because He so wills it.'[23] So construed, the divine law must coincide with human interests only contingently, for the nature of such interests could not function as independent standards of goodness or rightness guiding or constraining an otherwise arbitrary will. A space thus opened up between the deontological force of ethical ideas (as laws), and the prudential advantages of conforming one's behaviour to that independently given order.

---

21 See Schneewind, (above, note 3), 17.

22 Grotius thus distinguishes between divine commands and 'counsels of perfection', both of which may have a Biblical source: see Prolegomena (above, note 17), LI.

23 M. Luther, 'The Bondage of the Will', in J. Dillenberger (ed.) *Martin Luther: Selections From His Writings* (New York, Doubleday, 1961), 196. See also J. Calvin, *Institutes of the Christian Religion*, III.xxiii.2: 'For if [God's will] has any cause, something must precede it, to which it is, as it were, bound; this is unlawful to imagine. For God's will is so much the highest rule of righteousness that whatever He wills, by the very act that He wills it, must be considered righteous.' See Schneewind, *Moral Philosophy from Montaigne to Kant* (New York, Cambridge University Press, 2003), 8.

By treating such rules as willed prescriptions, the medieval natural lawyers developed a theological perspective in which rationalistic modes of apprehension were not easily accommodated within a structure of moral knowledge. Ethical understanding was instead thought to consist in an attitude of pious acceptance of God's will, in which nature presents a context for moral reflection 'in its givenness, but not in its intrinsic orderliness or purposefulness.'[24] The visible world was viewed as being more or less corrupt and imperfect, with righteousness a matter of abstracting one's thoughts from material circumstances and contemplating the divine. The classical focus on historical reflection could exist only in tension with the voluntarist presuppositions of the natural law theory, for God's grace (as a source of virtue) was considered to be both outside and imperfectly realised within, the human social order:

> If His justice were such as could be adjudged just by human reckoning, it clearly would not be Divine; ... But inasmuch as He is the one true God, wholly incomprehensible and inaccessible to man's understanding, it is reasonable, indeed inevitable, that His justice should also be incomprehensible.[25]

It thus comes as little surprise to see Luther rejecting the study of Aristotle in the following terms: 'Yet this defunct pagan has attained supremacy [in the universities]; impeded, and almost suppressed, the Scriptures of the living God. When I think of this lamentable state of affairs, I cannot avoid believing that the Evil One introduced the study of Aristotle.'[26] The 18th century voluntarist English minister, William Law, gave some indication of the extent to which leading churchmen within the British polity viewed moral insight as essentially detached from experience: 'Nothing has a sufficient moral reason or fitness to be done, but because it is the will of God that it should be done.'[27]

The emergence of voluntarist perspectives on morality within the cultural polities of medieval Europe created lasting problems for moral and legal theory. Law came to be seen, not as an intrinsic foundation for social order, embodying the internalisation and reinforcement of shared understandings of justice and morality through their endless specification in particular cases.[28] Rather, it came increasingly to be viewed as a series of moral imperatives 'imposed on the formless contingencies of human

---

24 J. Porter, *Nature as Reason: A Thomistic Theory of the Natural Law* (Grand Rapids, William B. Eerdmans Publishing Company, 2005), 44. See Isaiah 55:8, 'For my thoughts are not your thoughts, saith the Lord.'

25 Luther, in Dillenberger (above, note 23), 200.

26 'Twenty-Seven Proposals for Improving the State of Christendom', *ibid.*, 470. In adopting a broadly Augustinian position, Luther and later John Calvin formed part of a tradition that viewed Aristotelianism as a source of the Pelagian heresy. For an interesting account of medieval heresies, see M. Lambert, *Medieval Heresy: Popular Movements from the Gregorian Reform to the Reformation*, 2nd edn (Oxford, Blackwell, 1992).

27 W. Law, 'The Case of Reason, or Natural Religion' [1731] in *The Works of the Reverend William Law* (Brockenhurst, G. Moreton, 1892), vol 2, 86–87. Quoted in Schneewind (above, note 23), xx.

28 See A. Brunder, *The Unity of the Common Law* (Berkeley, University of California Press, 1995), 3.

existence.'[29] This framework gave rise to a view of the individual as an autonomous being operating within the constraints of externally imposed obligations. But then how ought we to regard the relationship between morality and those externally imposed restraints? Should the moral good be associated with the individual's *own* good, so that an individual's self-understanding remains a source of moral insight; or does morality consist of rational standards or principles essentially unconnected with the agent's good? The political theory of the modern age thus paved the way for the recognition of diverse forms of the good, and the idea that the good of each person may deeply conflict with the good of others.

Such thoughts would have resonated powerfully with English thinkers of the 17th century. Wars of religion, which had shattered the shared cultural heritage of Europe, and the more immediate political crises occasioned by the civil war, had led to the gradual abandonment of the idea that morality concerns a complex but unified object of understanding, 'the good', through which human beings could pursue a harmonious flourishing. Instead, society was viewed as a loose association of individuals each striving to assert his own conception of the good over the rival views of others. Within this conception, each person represents a separate locus of interests and autonomous ideals. But if every such person is capable of refining a distinctive idea of the good, which conflicts with other such ideas, then it would appear that reason must be thought of in isolation from the good. Thus, rationality could no longer be regarded as that quality exhibited by the flourishing agent, but must be viewed instead as describing a set of external conditions (or laws) that allow for the possibility of joint pursuit of divergent goods.

Protestantism had provided a context within which the apparent rationality of the autonomous agent could be reconciled with the existence of a transcendent body of moral laws binding on all: for the agent's choices could be conceived as private determinations about the correct means of participating in and achieving a basic good (entry into the kingdom of Heaven) presupposed as an ultimate end. Thus, private 'conceptions of the good' functioned in reality as mere constituents of a unified, but complex ethical ideal. As morality became increasingly separated from moral theology, under the pressure of Protestant ideas, a secular concern with the individual began to emerge for which the capacity for autonomous reflection signalled genuinely distinct forms of the good, for we can think of each person's understanding of the means of achieving salvation as the adoption of a 'form of life'. It then becomes possible to view such understandings not simply as causal mechanisms for the realisation of some postponed good, but also as constituents of a good life in their own right. Protestantism thus allows scope for conflict amongst these differing forms of the good.

The emergence of Protestant ideas concerning morality largely spelled the end of the attempt to find within the law a systematic expression of human nature. Laws came instead to be viewed as the product of artifice, and thus as broadly aligned with the will rather than the ethical understanding. In the absence of such artificial constraints, men would be revealed as juridical equals, and thus the most pressing question for the modern polity became the derivation of social order and political

---

29 Porter (above, note 24), 50.

authority from an original position of fundamental equality.[30] Protestant thinkers such as Grotius sought to ground social order in a minimal set of understandings about the moral nature of human beings. Like Aristotle, Grotius viewed as the starting point of any ethical inquiry the realisation that human nature is essentially sociable. Unlike Aristotelians, however, Grotius did not draw the conclusion that a coherent impression of that nature might be gained by reflecting upon the character of the social institutions and arrangements in which it finds expression. Rather, he believed that the basic premise of sociability gave rise to numerous distinct forms of political society, in which the goal of human flourishing might be pursued in alternative and incompatible ways:

> But as there are several ways of living, some better than others, and everyone may choose which he pleases of all those sorts; so a people may choose what form of government they please: neither is the right which the sovereign has over his subjects to be measured by this or that form, of which divers men have divers opinions, but by the extent of the will of those who conferred it upon him.[31]

By setting aside the traditional notion of the *summum bonum*, how is one to arrive at an understanding of the justice of a body of laws, and of the measure of the sovereign's right? It is not at all clear why each person's autonomous reflections upon the nature of the good should result in the coherent expression of a collective 'will' by those upon whom the political order is settled. In the absence of any shared notion of the common good, which autonomous insights are to structure our understandings of justice, right, etc? Convergence upon a shared framework of ideas was explicable, within traditional philosophy, by the thought that ethical understandings are a matter not of will, but of reason and understanding. But where general ethical notions of justice and right have ceased to be regarded as products of reflective immersion within a form of life, and are instead viewed as in some sense constituting independently given points of convergence, it is difficult to see how reason can furnish a general framework of political ideas without undermining the autonomous capacity to formulate genuinely distinctive forms of the good. Such ideas of justice will have become, in effect, the limits within which autonomous agents may pursue their own understandings of the good life. The central question for Protestant political thought is, in a sense, how rationality may be reconciled with genuine autonomy.

In detaching individual conceptions of the good from a common or ultimate end (Christian salvation), secular forms of moral Protestantism undermined the synthesis between Protestant autonomy and rationality. The tension between rationality and Protestant autonomy might be expressed in terms of the motivating force of morality. Where morality addresses a unified good, the motivating force behind an individual's ethical decisions derives from the intrinsic association of moral values with the individual's own wellbeing. Even so, we might wonder whether some reference to the will of the moral agent is necessitated by the idea of an 'individual',

---

30 See N.E. Simmonds, 'Protestant Jurisprudence and Modern Doctrinal Scholarship', 60 *Cambridge LJ* (2001), 271–300, 274.

31 Grotius, *De Iure Belli ac Pacis*, 1.3.8.

and by the obvious propensity for human beings to choose narrow self-interest over virtue. Reliance upon the idiom of 'voluntary' conduct is unavoidable, for as Samuel Clarke wrote, 'Intelligence without liberty [is] no intelligence at all. It is indeed a consciousness, but it is merely a passive consciousness; a consciousness not of acting, but of being acted upon.'[32] We should not conceive of the classical ethical tradition, alive in the writings of the medieval jurists, as presupposing an idea of morality that leaves no room for voluntary action, however.

The origin of volition and desire, in classical thought, resided not in the 'will' but in the processes of cognition and deliberation through which the individual reflected upon his own experience as a source of moral understandings. The mode of choice facing the rationally deliberating agent is thus not *voluntas*, but *boulesis* (the rational desire for some good or benevolent end).[33] Pursuit of self-interest over virtue represented, then, not a 'free' choice of the agent but rather a form of intemperance or incontinence whereby reasonable desires (such as the need for food, or love) are distorted and become bent towards injustice. Such ideas retain sense where the ethical life is thought to relate to a notion of the good as an object of the understanding. Yet once the theological notion of a finally unified good is removed from this picture, it is hard to see how human choices can be other than 'free'.

The implications of 'free' choice for rational motivation were not lost on the political thinkers of the early modern period. Cudworth, for example, noted that:

> if the blind will ... remains indifferent to follow the last dictate of [the understanding] or not, and doth fortuitously determine itself either in compliance with the same or otherwise, then will liberty of the will be mere irrationality, and madness itself acting or determining all human actions.[34]

The recognition of diverse forms of the good undercut the traditional connection between the motivating force of morality and the good of the individual agent: for if moral goodness can potentially conflict with one's wellbeing, the mere 'goodness' of moral principles will provide insufficient reason for preferring virtue to self-interest. As long as the theocentric framework was retained, Protestant moralists could continue to locate the binding force of moral principles in the presence of divine sanctions that existed independently of the human will. Moral rules thus came to be seen as impositions of the divine will, backed by the threat of eternal punishment. The deontological force of moral rules was therefore separated, in Western moral thinking, from their motivating force in the agent's self-interest. Pufendorf's writings mark a watershed in this respect, for they are motivated by a distinction between physical and moral entities, in which only the former are deemed to possess causal properties. Moral entities, standing apart from that causal nexis, 'do not arise out of

---

32 S. Clarke, *A Discourse Concerning the Being and Attributes of God*, Lecture IX in *Works* (4 vols, London, 1738), vol 2, 548.

33 For an informative discussion, see C.H. Kahn, 'Discovering the Will: From Aristotle to Augustine', in J.M. Dillon and A.A. Long (eds) *The Question of 'Eclecticism': Studies in Later Greek Philosophy* (Berkeley, University of California Press, 1988), 239.

34 R. Cudworth, *A Treatise of Freewill* (London, John W. Parker, 1838), 23. Cf Darwall (above, note 8), 133.

the intrinsic nature of the physical properties of things, but they are superadded, at the will of intelligent entities, to things already existent and physically complete.'[35]

This separation of divine law from the causal order of nature presented a conception of morality as an autonomous outlook upon the world: 'That reason should be able to discover any morality in the actions of a man without reference to a law, is as impossible as for a man born blind to choose between colours.'[36] Once morality became cast adrift from its moorings in the divine will, some alternative explanation of its motivating or binding force became necessary. Faced with the problem of accounting for voluntary action in the face of a motivationally inert morality, on the one hand, and a motivationally inert reality, on the other, philosophers sought the causal mechanisms of individual action in the idea of the will. The Protestant ethical tradition which culminated in Kant's metaphysics of morals thus viewed it as a condition of the possibility of autonomous will that 'reason' take a purely practical form by legislating for oneself a normative judgment that is intrinsically motivating.[37]

For Kantians, obligation 'resides in the free, internal expression of rational choice by the agent himself.'[38] This involves a conception of the will as an aspect of personality which 'can rise above the emotional impulses of human nature through the purifying processes of choice': a choice that is 'free' in that it 'involves an act of independent will rather than a mere acquiescence in a goal set by nature... Reason paradoxically becomes practical by subjecting every maxim to the purely formal test of whether it can be redescribed as a universal law.'[39] It is no accident that the intellectual conditions that permit of reconciliation between freedom and rationality are described in purely formal terms. For a clearly defined understanding of terms such as 'rational', 'irrational', or 'objective' as qualitative indicators of argument tends to come about only within a context of practices involving deep *disagreement* about which arguments may be said to exhibit rationality. Only if we are prepared to ascribe moral disagreement to a significant degree of irrationality on the part of deliberating agents will rationality appear as a *ground* of freedom.

---

35 S. Pufendorf, *De Iure Naturae et Gentium*, trans. as *The Law of Nature and of Nations* (London, 1749), I.1.5–6.

36 *Ibid.*, I.2.6. This sentiment had once been a touchstone of scepticism in classical philosophy, as may be witnessed from Horace's maxim, 'For just from unjust, Nature cannot know.' (Horace, Bk 1.III.113). Indeed, voluntarist philosophers of the 17th century saw in the idea of divine will the only possible reply to scepticism, given acceptance of the truth of this proposition.

37 See Kant, *Groundwork of the Metaphysics of Morals*, trans. by H.J. Paton (New York, Harper & Row, 1964), 80: 'Everything in nature works in accordance with laws. Only a rational being has the power to act in accordance with his idea of laws ... and only so has he a will. Since *reason* is required to derive actions from laws, the will is nothing but practical reason.'

38 See T.J. Hochstrasser, *Natural Law Theories in the Early Enlightenment* (Cambridge, Cambridge University Press, 2000), 198.

39 *Ibid.* See also Schneewind, 'Kant and Natural Law Ethics', 104 *Ethics* (1993), 53–74.

Reason, for Kant, essentially boiled down to the law of non-contradiction: in willing a universal law to govern the conduct of others, one must also consider the law as binding on oneself. Inequality (considered as the practice of counting something as a reason in one case that one has discounted in a relevantly similar case) is 'the very same, in action, as ... contradiction, in theory.'[40] The development of coherent social moralities would seem to require richer standards of rationality than mere non-contradiction, however, for they presuppose a degree of convergence between the different possible views at which autonomous agents might arrive. But how is such convergence to come about, if the standards of rationality in moral thought are considered to be internal to the will itself?

The tension between the recognition of diverse forms of the good and the belief in historically and culturally transcendent principles of reason, is evident throughout the history of Protestant political thought. Dworkin, for example, emphasises the 'interpretive' character of law over its conventional, rule-based aspects in a way that would seem to reveal the law's nature as a source of moral insight and reflection: 'Integrity' is said to 'expand and deepen the role individual citizens can play in developing the public standards of their community', because it 'requires them to treat relations among themselves as characteristically, not just spasmodically, governed by those standards.' Political obligation thus 'becomes a more Protestant idea: fidelity to a scheme of principle each citizen has a responsibility to identify, ultimately for himself, as his community's scheme.'[41] Dworkin believes, of course, that the scheme of justice implicit within the law in fact uniquely determines the judgment that should be given in each case. Yet it is by no means easy to see why each person's 'Protestant' interpretation of the legal order should converge on right answers. We can think of each person's interpretation as establishing good reasons for supposing the existence of permissions, duties and entitlements of a particular kind. But what reason is there for believing that standards of rationality impose a hierarchy on such reasons? Each person's reasoned interpretations of shared practices and institutions are as likely to emphasise divergent conceptions of the significance of shared values and beliefs as they are to establish clear criteria by which the value of conflicting principles may be weighed and balanced. The conception of rationality at work in the notion of 'right answers' seemingly undercuts moral Protestantism rather than reinforcing it.

How might we seek to resolve this tension? Dworkin suggests that a shared language, as well as common interests and convictions, are necessary if we are to make sense of each other's behaviour and beliefs.[42] He *could* claim, therefore, that the intelligibility of 'fit' as a distinct determinant of legal decision (aside from the substance of interpretative judgments) testifies to the presence of settled interpretations that reflect shared insights into the nature of the good: the shared

---

40 Clarke (above, note 32), Lectures II.I, 619. See also Kant's view that one cannot will an impossible or self-contradictory idea: 'a will always presupposes the internal possibility of the thing itself'.

41 Dworkin, *Law's Empire* (above, note 11), 190. See also 413.

42 *Ibid.*, 63–64.

background of taken-for-granted assumptions establishes conditions that make possible widespread (even if defeasible) agreement on what the right answers are.

This suggestion is problematic, however, for it fails to realise that there is no basis to such shared interpretations *other than* the fact of agreement in judgments. By recognising the presence of common interests and convictions, we might hope to narrow the gap between rationality and Protestant autonomy. Since moral thought is rooted in shared convictions, it is then believed, such thought involves the recognition of common standards of rationality by which personal interpretations can be evaluated and compared. Yet there seems to be no intelligible distinction between standards of reason or rationality and good moral reasons. Since moral reasoning does not take place in complete abstraction from the circumstances to which moral values are applied, it is impossible to sustain a distinction between two different stages of reasoning: the determination of good or sound moral reasons, and the subjection of those reasons to further, independent tests of rationality which apply in abstraction from the variable circumstances in which moral convictions are formed. On the contrary, the rationality or otherwise of moral convictions is a matter of acceptance of, or convergence upon, good moral reasons.[43]

Where Protestantism remained rooted in a theological understanding of the nature of ultimate salvation, the divine law could continue to provide the standards of rationality against which autonomous wills might be measured. The removal of that intellectual framework left no obvious means of accommodating rationality within the conception of morality as a form of self-governance. The alternatives forced upon moral philosophy by modern Protestant understandings thus consist of a robust but inaccessible rationalism, and an unacceptably constraining moral subjectivism.

Historicism and Geist

To the majority of later thinkers, the Kantian framework of ethical speculation seemed inescapable. Morality could not be inferred from human nature, it was thought, for the presence of conflicting conceptions of the good ruled out the possibility of a single, unified end as a structuring principle for moral reasoning. Political and ethical thought, therefore, must aim at the delineation of principles of justice and equality that allow a degree of latitude for individuals to formulate and pursue their own conceptions of the good, free from the will of others. For the same reason, reflection upon the historical institutions and practices of human social life could not offer any lasting insights into the good, as this would seem to involve the ascription to human nature of some intelligible purpose or *telos*, and thus the presupposition of a form of metaphysical essentialism.

---

43 Reflective detachment from particular circumstances of social existence is always a possibility when those circumstances are contemplated (or confronted) one by one; the complete detachment from cultural circumstances *tout court*, as a condition of reflective equilibrium, on the other hand, seems to require the psychologically impossible insofar as it requires the manifestation of a general attitude of reflective detachment from the facts of experience.

In order to avoid the formality of the Kantian perspective, jurisprudential writers sought to give content to the ideas of justice and equality in one of two different ways. On the one hand, writers such as Hobbes, Bentham and Austin, in different ways, construed the legal order as establishing a reasonable ordering of competing interests through the imposition of clear rules considered as binding on all persons. Law could thereby provide a shared basis for social order even in the presence of widespread disagreement over the good. On the other hand, writers (such as Blackstone) drawing their inspiration from the tradition of 17th century natural law, viewed the legal order as an attempt to recast the unequal rights and privileges of ordinary people as the adventitious consequences of voluntary transaction and transfer: on the level of juridical principle, men stand as fundamental equals.[44] The legal order may then be viewed as a body of principles taken to encapsulate shared standards of justice, fairness etc. Law, on this view,

> becomes the benign precondition of a consensual transition to civil society in which everyone freely recognises the legitimate and sufficient constraint of a legal framework before the external exercise of free will can be successfully converted into rights.[45]

Both of these approaches, I have argued, can be construed as responses to the problems of Protestant political theory – for they concern the possibility of stable social order in a world characterised by basic disagreement over the nature of the good. In their recognition of distinctive forms of the good, positivism and idealism provide a context for juridical reasoning that departs fundamentally from that supplied by Aristotelian moral philosophy.[46] Grotius's Protestant successors retained and amplified the voluntarist underpinnings of his position, whilst making further significant departures from Aristotle. Grotius had remained an Aristotelian to the extent that the natural law was viewed as a prescriptive theory of human nature. Natural law functioned as a set of guides or 'promptings' through which men might achieve peace and social stability. Therefore, a great number of social forms might be 'patterned after nature's plan':[47] the liberal mercantile order as much as the feudal hierarchy of privileges or the totalitarian dictatorship. It followed that moral reflection requires the contemplation of the matrix of actual social institutions as nourishers of human potential, for only by doing so can the various social forms be considered as instantiations of an overarching plan or *telos*.

---

44 See R. Tuck, *The Rights of War and Peace: Political Thought and the International Order from Grotius to Kant* (Oxford, Oxford University Press, 1999), chapter 3. I ignore, in the present context, writers such as Marx who sought to highlight the legal order as a source of hierarchical privilege and inequality.

45 Hochstrasser, (above, note 38), 199.

46 For a fuller consideration of positivism, see Chapter 4, below.

47 Grotius, *De Iure Praedae Commentarius*, trans. G.L. Williams (Oxford, Oxford University Press, 1950), 229. Grotius's views embody rejections or modifications of Aristotelianism in numerous respects, but his writings remain broadly within the Aristotelian tradition: 'Our purpose is to set always a high value upon Aristotle, but so as to reserve to ourselves the same liberty which he himself took with his Masters, for the sake of finding truth.' Prolegomena (above, note 17), XLVI.

Neither Grotius nor his intellectual heirs accepted this view of the significance of human practices and institutions. The intellectual categories ushered into philosophy by the study of divine law recast morality as an independent standpoint for reflection, irreducible to a concern with mere facts and the detail of present arrangements. Moral values came to be thought of as products of the will, resulting from the adoption of a conscious attitude of reflection towards otherwise mute practices, and the search for equilibrium between the various 'intuitions' generated by that inquiry.[48] The central problem for moral Protestantism is thus an explanation of how such essentially subjective acts of autonomous willing can produce collective insights into virtue and the moral good.

Both the 'Protestant' *and* the classical Aristotelian modes of ethical thought, I wish to suggest, ultimately depend upon the manifestation in human affairs of some form of *Geist* (or 'benign guiding spirit') as the means by which the ideal of the good life is rendered intelligible and coherent. In the medieval world, Christian theology supplied the obvious framework through which individuals could abstract their reason from the harsh realities and injustices of earthly politics, and approach the divine. The schisms and internal conflicts that characterised the European Reformation rendered that framework itself the subject of disagreement, but insofar as entry into the Kingdom of Heaven remained central to ethical belief, the emergence of Protestantism signalled a breakdown in consensus about the means by which the ultimate good for man is to be realised, whilst leaving the intrinsic nature of the good intact. With the decline of religious belief as a central constituent of moral and political reflection, however, disagreement about the means of achieving the good readily transforms into recognition of plural forms of the good which exist in mutual tension. In such circumstances, belief in the rationality *and* autonomy of Protestant wills (i.e. convergence between transcendent rationality and Protestant autonomy) must be motivated and sustained by a set of beliefs that are of at least equivalent weight and significance as an underpinning theological perspective. Without such beliefs, there exists no reason for supposing that autonomy can be reconciled with rationality.

Although it does not exhibit the same tension between autonomy and rationality, the classical alignment of moral wisdom and experience also depends upon the assumption that the good is realised in ordinary life to some degree. But this basic assumption is more easily and fully integrated into the framework of Aristotelian thought, for in claiming that practical wisdom involves knowledge of the good through its realisation, Aristotle is addressing his remarks to those already possessed of good character and noble dispositions. Those who exhibit *akrasia*, or weakness of will, Aristotle says, require the imposition of rules to instil benevolent patterns of conduct.[49] The element of *Geist* in classical ethical thought is therefore a much clearer and more integrated part of the metaphysics of morals than is the case where facts and values are taken to denote separate logical or natural kinds – for, having

---

48 No social practice lacks its theorised element, and thus the alternative to the adoption of an attitude of 'constructive interpretation' is not one of 'runic traditionalism' or mere robotic observance: see Dworkin, (above, note 11), chapter 3.

49 See Aristotle, *Nicomachean Ethics* (above, note 5), 1152a6–7.

provided an extensive psychological underpinning for human nature as essentially benign,[50] Aristotle is then in a position to treat the human practices and forms of association that embody that nature as themselves providing a central source of insight into the nature of the good.

Do we find, in Protestant political thought, a similarly fully integrated and worked-out understanding of human nature? On the whole, we do not: for such theories tend to replace detailed investigations of the psychology of human nature with broad and general categories of autonomy, rationality, self-interest and freedom etc. as the basis of an account of moral thinking. As moral thinking becomes progressively detached from its foundation in the human character (and thus divorced from prudence and wellbeing),[51] abstract principles of reason are forced to supply the necessary element of *Geist* in leading those of suitable bearing towards the ultimate good. Such a manifestation of *Geist* inevitably operates in a much more detached and free-floating way in respect to human wills than is conceivable within classical ethical thought. This is because, being separated from both human *telos* and the supposition of external imposition by a divine will, the rational convergence of human wills upon common standards of justice and right becomes a matter of diffuse optimism concerning the 'objectivity' of moral values, and the ability of human minds to apprehend them.

I hope that these remarks go some way towards establishing the necessity of a metaphysical perspective as an essential background to an understanding of the nature of law. The intelligibility of human nature (or of morality, if viewed in detachment from human nature) implies purposiveness,[52] and we may rightly turn to the law as the social institution wherein human aims and purposes are most fully articulated. By studying the historical paths by which the present-day legal order is shaped and determined, we may seek to reveal important dimensions of law's place within political life, and of the moral character of the British polity.

---

50 See, inter alia, Aristotle, *De Anima*, D.W. Hamlyn (ed.) (Oxford, Clarendon Press, 1993).

51 If there exist diverse forms of the good, but a unique set of moral rules is necessary as the ground of social order and stability, it follows that morality may conflict with that which is good for a person.

52 See Porter (above, note 24), 72.

Chapter 3

Doctrinal Scholarship and the Science of Right

The modern legal order is in a process of transformation. Exhibiting for much of its modern existence the properties of a complex body of rules and precedents, the legal order is increasingly thought to be capable of exposition as an organised system of rights, underpinned by a general scheme of justice implicit in the rules that form its 'cutting-edge'. For many lawyers and jurists, this intellectual shift is of the greatest significance: the progressive realisation of basic human or constitutional rights as a framework for understanding precedents and rules is thought to represent the step into a more enlightened world, in which the connection between law and justice is greatly clarified.[1] The ideas explored in the previous chapter ought to incline us against lazy acceptance of historically linear trajectories of this kind; but the idea of linear development permeates the modern jurisprudential consciousness.

The idea that the law might admit of transformation into a body of protective rights is in fact not a new one. Roscoe Pound once observed that the trajectory of a mature legal order consists in the shift from a focus on remedies, to one rooted in a concern with duty, then right, and, eventually, interests; the latter (he believed) being logically basic and thus the proper focus of juristic science.[2] Pound's claim has the virtue of drawing attention to the various forms of juristic contemplation wherein our understanding of law is manifested; but do such forms of contemplation exhibit a *logical* ordering, each form constituting a mere stage of understanding to be jettisoned as legal thought develops? Or should we see them as revealing deep-rooted yet contradictory impulses that constitute recurring themes in the legal thought of different eras, or which exist in tension in legal thought within the *same* era? This question is to some extent the question of whether or not the dominant forms of juridical speculation in our own age should be viewed as significant stages in the achievement of juristic wisdom, on the way to some final end-point.

The intellectual form and structure of the legal order is in some measure determined by the wider political circumstances affecting the society of a given era. Where (for example) political and social structures derive their form from a theocentric outlook on the world, law is naturally seen as articulating and reinforcing the divine

---

1 See (for example) F. Klug, *Values for a Godless Age: The History of the Human Rights Act and its Political and Legal Consequences* (London, Penguin, 2000); I. Leigh and L. Lustgarten, 'Making Rights Real: The Courts, Remedies and the Human Rights Act', 58 *Cambridge LJ* (1999) 509–545; R. Dworkin, *A Bill of Rights for Britain* (Chatto & Windus, 1990).

2 R. Pound, *Jurisprudence* (Minnesota, West Publishing, 1959) vol I, 42.

ordinances that maintain those structures. The law of a market society, by contrast, is best understood, not as sustaining social hierarchies, but as to some extent levelling those hierarchies as part of the creation and maintenance of systemic liberties that enable competitive mercantile activity. But the law also possesses transformative powers that operate to change the features of the society in which it functions. It is in virtue of this that (as argued in the previous chapter) law is a valuable starting-point for reflection on the moral and political characteristics of a society: for it will embody not just a society's conscious attempts to bring about social or political change, but also its implicit currents of thought and understandings of the nature of the good, and of the relationship between collective and private attempts to realise the good. For this reason also, analysis of law must be regarded not simply as an exercise in clarifying a body of current practices and structures, but must also involve the study of a complex historical product whose past manifestations both contribute to and obscure the meaning of the present.

Rights and Forms of Justice

Pound's suggestion, that legal understanding logically proceeds from remedies to rights and interests (as the most logically basic concept), has much intuitive appeal. Legal order, in the most basic terms, exists to impose standards for human conduct, and we may reasonably expect those standards to display qualities of justice (or injustice) to varying degrees in a way that is open to rational understanding and quantification. A sustained focus on remedies is likely to impede such understanding if unsupported by underpinning notions of equity, juridical equality or entitlement, for it confines attention to the dynamics of particular situations in which harm must be redressed.

It has been the tendency of modern analytical philosophers to assume that the forms of moral contemplation and theoretical methodology that give structure to their activities are in some sense necessary, or else more reflexively aware than those of earlier historical periods. The philosophical achievements of earlier ages are, from this standpoint, to be viewed as a series of failed experiments and wrong turnings, and progress in philosophy is conceived as the gradual culmination of insights drawn from that history, coupled with an acute awareness of the failures of the past. This attitude has found an especially secure foothold in jurisprudential writings, and has often led to periods of boundless optimism. Much of Hart's work, for example, is permeated by a general sense of fresh beginnings and the rich potential of new methodologies; an attitude that (as N.E. Simmonds has observed) is also evident in Peter Laslett's famous announcement of the 'death' of tradition.[3] To philosophers raised on such understandings, the absence of ideas of 'right' within the legal order

---

3   See Hart, 'Definition and Theory in Jurisprudence', in *Essays in Jurisprudence and Philosophy*, 21–48; and P. Laslett, *Philosophy, Politics and Society: A Collection* (Oxford, Blackwell, 1962). Bertrand Russell's work on the foundations of mathematics displays the same self-conscious enthusiasm for the new vistas of opportunity provided by the development of set-theory and semantics: see for example B. Russell, *The Principles of Mathematics* (London, Routledge & K Paul, 1903). But the same general tendency is also to be found in

of the medieval and pre-modern periods will necessitate one of two alternative readings: either the interpretation of historical legal arrangements as 'primitive' and ethically unsophisticated, or else the presentation of earlier juristic understandings as unexplored potentialities within which deeper notions of right lie undiscovered.

The attitude of dismissiveness towards traditional forms of common law reasoning is a direct result of the decline of Aristotelianism amongst the writers of the early modern and Enlightenment periods. The political and intellectual climate of early modern Europe was such as to encourage the development of a 'rational science of morals', which sought to detach moral understanding from forms of historical reflection, and locate it in the will of the autonomous agent. The Protestant moral perspectives, which came to dominate 17th and 18th century legal science placed a high value on the *systematic* nature of moral thinking. Once recognition was given to the existence of distinct forms of the good, it became necessary to articulate the competing alternatives with specificity and precision. *Phronesis* (the exploration of ethical ideas embedded within human practices, to which no final speakable form can be given), then gave way to the need to formulate general principles of morality in abstraction from experience. For the jurists of the 17th and 18th centuries, law embodies morality at the level of doctrinal principle: particular legal decisions and rulings are moved by more general standards of justice, which require like cases to be treated alike. This demand is not one of mere formal equity (for *all* cases are capable of being treated alike in some respect), but rather involves substantive ideals of justice that receive expression within a context of asserted interests and moral ideas of considerable complexity.

Where law is viewed systematically in this way, the particular rulings and decisions of courts are thought to display a commitment to abstract moral ideas at the level of concrete fact. It will seem obvious to lawyers and jurists who operate within a context of doctrinal understandings to see earlier manifestations of juridical thought that focused upon the procedural context of particular rulings, as awaiting the development of systematic jurisprudence: the practice of earlier lawyers will resemble a wander in the dark, an attempt to 'do justice' in each case but without the guiding light of an idea of law as anything more than 'an unconnected series of decrees and ordinances'.[4] It may therefore seem as if the development of juristic thought must involve the progressive realisation that the legal remedies and governing standards derive from deeper principles of equity and justice, which admit of systematic regimentation.[5] Such reflections may indeed incline us to accept a view

---

the philosophical writings of earlier eras, such as those of the 'Enlightenment', the French *encyclopaedists*, and Jeremy Bentham.

4   Sir W. Jones, *An Essay on the Law of Bailment* [1781] (Garland Publications, 1978).

5   Certainly the natural lawyers of the late 17th century were of this opinion: Stair, for example, thought it 'both feasible and fit, that the law should be formed into a rational discipline', but 'regretted that it hath not been effected, yea scarce attempted by any': see *Institutions* (1681) 1.1.17. There is thus some evidence for Pound's claim, in that we can see in remarks such as this a dawning awareness of the limitations of the then dominant forms of legal writing, the glossary and the abridgment, in which systematic presentation of legal materials was confined to alphabetised compendia, or topical arrangements dictated by the needs of practice and convenience. Progress beyond the traditional categories was slow,

of rights and interests as logically prior to other possible conceptual understandings of the legal order. But we are immediately faced with a problem: for there is no universal agreement on what rights *are*, or of what effects or implications follow the ascription of rights to individuals.

The analysis of rights developed by the American jurist W.N. Hohfeld provides a convenient starting-point for reflection.[6] The term 'right' is to be understood as a complex idea that is ultimately reducible to four more basic notions: claim-right, liberty, power and immunity. These basic notions have distinctive logical properties which, in Hohfeld's view, make them more suitable for the exposition of legal submissions than the generic use of 'right', the internal complexity of which serves to obscure the juridical relationships and consequences implied by its ascription. Briefly, A's possession of a *claim-right* against some other person B entails the possession of a duty by B either to render assistance to A in some matter, or (depending on the content of the right) to refrain from interfering with A in relation to some matter. Possession of a *liberty*, by contrast, establishes the permissibility of some action of A's as against B, in the sense that B has no-right to prevent A from engaging in the action. 'Liberty' in Hohfeld's analysis thus signifies the mere absence of a duty in A to refrain from a particular action. Where A holds a *power*, A has the means to alter some feature of his or another's legal position: for example by waiving a contractual duty, or by transferring title to property.[7] B is then said to possess a 'liability' to have his legal position altered, relative to A's power. Finally, where B is 'disabled' from changing some feature of A's legal position (i.e. lacks the power to do so), A is said to enjoy a legal *immunity* from change.

Whilst Hohfeld's terminology does indeed facilitate more precise thinking about legal rights, it leaves open many of the most important questions concerning the nature of rights. For why should the more basic notions of claim-right, liberty, power and immunity be understood as notions *of right*? The utility of the analysis lies in pinpointing with greater accuracy the problems that must be faced by attempts to offer a unifying explanation of the concept of a 'right'. Two such responses in particular have become associated with the analytical jurisprudence of rights: the first seeks to explain the Hohfeldian notions as elements in a wider idea of 'right' by reference to their propensity to secure individual benefits to the right-holder; the other regards the uniting factor in those elements as being concerned with the protection of some aspect of the right-bearer's will (either negatively, by preventing the will from being overborne by outside determination, or positively, by securing

---

however, for both Blackstone and Bentham, writing in the 18th century, take as the starting-point of their own works the confused and unscientific state of common law scholarship. See further S. Coyle, 'Two Concepts of Legal Analysis', in Coyle and Pavlakos (eds) *Jurisprudence or Legal Science?* (Oxford, Hart Publications, 2005) esp at 17–28.

6   W.N. Hohfeld, *Fundamental Legal Conceptions as Applied in Judicial Reasoning*, Cook (ed.) (New Haven, Yale University Press, 1919).

7   More strictly, the exercise of a power will simultaneously alter *both* A's position *and* B's in that it changes some aspect of the legal relationship between them. The slightly looser formulation I adopt above might be permitted in order to indicate the focus of A's exercise of the power, i.e. his reason for exercising it in a given context.

to the right-bearer some legally significant choice). As is often observed, neither response is consistently reflected in the legal thought of this, or other eras.[8]

Whichever answer is preferred, lawyerly understandings of right are clearly not exhausted by the cataloguing of relational consequences. This is not to say that legal rights cannot be understood as complex combinations of claim-rights, powers, liberties and immunities (for such reductive explanations are always available); it is rather to point out that 'rights' in juridical discourse refer to more than an exhaustive enumeration of relations and consequences. Such relations guide reasoning where legal rights are ascribed to individuals, but they do not provide a reason for their ascription. Here, we are inevitably guided by the broader notions of benefit (or choice) that rights, in the more general sense, aim to secure: transmission of property, creation of contractual relations, the making of testamentary provisions, and so on. The more general notion of 'right' therefore '... gives an intelligible unity to a temporal series of the many and varying *sets* of Hohfeldian rights which at different times one and the same set of rules provides in order to secure and give substance to one *subsisting* objective.'[9] The Hohfeldian elements that operate within any given complex can thus be thought of as the procedural incidents of protection, whereby rights in this deeper sense are realised within the legal order.[10]

Our understanding of the temporal unity associated with 'rights' in the more general sense will often be driven by quite technical rules and doctrines: rights to property, for example, are created and exercised within a context of established ideas pertaining to title, possession, equity, the notion of an 'estate', real versus personal property, and so on. But the background of technical concepts and understandings do not exclude the need for moral reflection upon the underlying purposes for which a right is imposed, and the attempt to realise those purposes within the technical arguments and instruments of lawyers will require more or less concentration upon abstract ideals of equity and juridical equality, which are thought to serve and underpin the concrete rules and precedents. The notion of juridical equality is then seen as offering a further level of reflection, through which the scope of a right is determined vis-à-vis the protective instruments that secure it. The need for reflection will be most obvious where the rights concerned are judged to be of general political significance, or as supplying a 'fundamental' interpretative context for a body of laws: for which protective instruments are appropriate in the context of a right of a person 'to the peaceful enjoyment of his possessions', understood as constrained by notions of deprivation 'in the public interest', control 'in the general interest' and the securing of appropriate 'contributions or penalties'?[11]

---

8   See for example J. Finnis, *Natural Law and Natural Rights* (Oxford, Clarendon Press, 1980) 202–205.

9   *Ibid.*, 201.

10   As Finnis goes on to note, '... the procedural props and incidents can all be shifted more or less independently of each other without affecting the "right itself" which is the constant focus of the law's concern.' *Ibid.*, 202.

11   Art 1, Protocol 1 of the European Convention for the Protection of Fundamental Human Rights and Fundamental Freedoms (1952).

The subsumption of such broad political ideas within the institutional realities and potentialities of a legal system inevitably focuses attention on the realisation of sometimes complex benefits, or the establishment of areas of protected autonomy. For the purposes of the present discussion, however, it is not necessary to reach conclusions on the issue of whether rights principally convey benefits or whether they protect choices: the issues I intend to raise are largely independent of the choice/benefit dichotomy. Instead, let us proceed on the basis of the somewhat loose assumption that rights provide an intellectual framework in which general ideas of justice are applied to the concrete institutional structures and normative arrangements of the legal order. We may then think of rights as the juridical concepts wherein the law's rational, systematic qualities are most perspicuously revealed.

It is not difficult to see why Pound should have construed rights as intrinsic and logically basic within legal order, on the basis of such reflections. Yet although we may regard law as being intrinsically associated with ideas of justice, Pound's suggested ordering makes it easy to miss the fact that a jurisprudence of rights and interests embodies a particular *type* of vision of justice, one that is both contestable and of fairly recent historical pedigree.

Some indication of this may be seen in Hume's belief that the history of England embodies the gradual transition from a 'government of will' to a 'government of law'.[12] The legal writers of Hume's day would have associated this claim with the progressive limitation of the powers of the monarchy to intervene in the affairs of other 'Estates' of the realm, rather than the recognition of fundamental rights possessed by all. Governance by law was thus not conceived on the basis of a supposed principle of juridical equality, which limits interference by the strong in the dealings of the weak. It was rather premised upon the presence of entrenched privileges and specialised jurisdictions designed to sustain hierarchies and *inequalities*.[13] Informing such conceptions was the idea of Justice (as an ideal) as being inextricably linked to notions of property (i.e. propriety) rather than equality. John Locke, considered by contemporaries as a political radical, wrote that:

> Though I have said ... *that all men by nature are equal*, I cannot be supposed to understand all sorts of equality: age or virtue may give men a just precedency: excellency of parts and merit may place others above the common level: birth may subject some, and alliance or benefits others, to pay an observance to those to whom nature, gratitude or other respects may have made it due...[14]

Two traditions of thought would develop during the 18th century, however, which would ultimately detach justice from privilege and instead seek to locate it within

---

12 D. Hume, *The History of England* (6 vols), W.B. Todd (ed.) (Indianapolis, Liberty Fund, 1983). See especially vol 2, 434–442.

13 For a brief but insightful discussion of feudal privileges, see S.E. Finer, *The History of Government from the Earliest Times* (3 vols) (Oxford, Oxford University Press, 1997), vol 2, 864–874. See also M. Weber, *Economy and Society*, G. Roth and C. Wittich (eds) (Berkeley, University of California Press, 1978), 839–848.

14 J. Locke, Second Treatise of Government, s 54, in P. Laslett (ed.) *Two Treatises of Government* (Cambridge, Cambridge University Press, 1988).

a broader moral perspective informed by reason. The first of these was essentially positivistic in outlook, and regarded political stability and social order as a political achievement attainable only through articulated legal rules: as the system of ranked privileges gives way to the looser social structures of a mercantile society, inherited customs become a doubtful focus for collective understandings of the good, and a system of deliberately created, authoritative rules comes to be seen as the unique means of bringing about harmony and certainty in the interpersonal relationships on which social order rests. This is because each person will begin to perceive the good, not as a complex thing to be realised in common, but as something to be achieved through the exercise of one's private talents and ingenuity. Justice thus consists not in maintaining disparities and lordships, but rather in the removal of inequalities that constitute barriers to free exchange and dealing, and the realisation of one's personality.

The other tradition of thought embodied a form of moral idealism, for which rights, rather than posited rules, supply the basic elements of legal order. The intellectual shift from a body of evolved practices to a system of intersecting patterns of entitlement required the development of a systematic jurisprudence: an individual's rights were seen as deriving from universal principles that applied *mutatis mutandis* to all citizens, giving rise to a conception of law as the concrete expression of those principles. Private law thus came to be represented as the domain in which the boundaries of competing entitlements are worked out on the basis of ever more specific articulations of the requirements of justice. Emphasis was placed not on the removal of outward barriers for the realisation of an external goal (the facilitating of free market interaction), but rather on the recognition of fundamental equality between individuals who may, through their voluntary actions, alter their situation vis-à-vis others for better or for worse.

We can see in these differing understandings two rival traditions of juristic contemplation. Starting from a concern for the removal of unequal privileges, they spell out the consequences of a Protestant, free-market society in different ways. Within the positivistic tradition, the association of justice and reason is based on the notion of *rules* (*regula*), for it is only through the establishment of regularity in human affairs that any sense can be given to the idea of juridical equality. The intellectual progenitors of this tradition are Hobbes and Samuel Pufendorf. Pufendorf had observed that, whilst nothing has value as of nature, civil society is characterised by the ascription of values to things through rules: actions, things and events have value only when related to a norm, and this relationship is forged by beings whose intellect allows for the understanding of *regular* connections. It follows, for Pufendorf, that one human can offer guidance to another only by *legislating* for it.[15] Though not himself a positivist, Pufendorf thereby provided a basis for later positivist thought concerning the nature of equality and justice. As Hart was to observe, the idea of juridical equality, although 'a central element in the idea of justice', is but

---

15 See S. Pufendorf, *Of the Law of Nature and of Nations* [1672] (London, Basil Kennett, 1729), I.2.vi. For an informative discussion, see K. Haakonssen, 'Natural Law and the Scottish Enlightenment', in Jory *et al.*, *Man and Nature IV* (1985) 47–80.

an incomplete expression of the idea of justice.[16] This is so, Hart says, 'because any set of human beings will resemble each other in some respects and differ from each other in others'; and until we offer some further account of which points of resemblance, and which differences, are relevant in determining equal treatment, the idea of equality remains 'an empty form'.

Formal equality, on this view, is made manifest through political choices: the extension or withholding of privileges or burdens to dark-haired individuals as well as light-haired individuals, or to those with university degrees as well as those without formal qualifications, reflects a decision not to treat hair colour, education, etc., as relevant grounds for treating otherwise similar cases differently. At the same time, mental incapacity, minority or past criminality might, in some circumstances, be thought to constitute relevant grounds for singling out certain individuals for different treatment. The drawing of such distinctions, Hart observed, highlights an important connection between the idea of justice and the notion of proceeding by rules:

> Indeed, it might be said that to apply a law justly to different cases is simply to take seriously the assertion that what is to be applied in different cases is the same general rule, without prejudice, interest or caprice.[17]

The recognition that juridical equality hinges upon rule-based distinctions is readily suggestive of a utilitarian understanding of justice: for it leads to the thought that certain, basic inequalities are inevitable between persons in a large and complex society, and that justice in the end depends upon the removal only of *irrational* inequalities, understood in relation to some anterior goal. Since the goal of each person is, at a reasonable level of abstraction, pursuit and realisation of 'the good', understood as a personal idea rather than a collective aim, justice and law are seen to concern 'utility' and the structuring of human conduct in ways that maximise the potential for its realisation.

For idealists too, the political thinking of the post-medieval world is shaped by the notion of individuals as both a focus for moral and political concern, and as sources of moral insight and reflection in relation to the good life. The erosion of religious belief as a source of shared insights and understandings, as well as the decline of the feudal order as a framework for the regulation of narrow and inherited social roles, forced the idea of conflicting individual claims into the limelight of political thought. The realm of politics was thus connected with morality in a much more complex way than medieval thought supposed: natural law came to be regarded not as a set of unchanging moral prescriptions identifying the good independently of concrete social arrangements, but as a body of broad principles capable of grounding agreement on general matters such as the desirability of social coexistence, whatever form such arrangements might take. More concrete moral insights arose, in Hume's words, 'from the circumstances and necessities of mankind' about which different individuals might disagree.[18]

---

16 H.L.A. Hart, *The Concept of Law*, 2nd edn (Oxford, Clarendon Press, 1994) 159.

17 *Ibid.*, 161.

18 D. Hume, *A Treatise of Human Nature*, P.H. Nidditch trans. (New York, Oxford University Press 1978) 477.

The collapse of medieval beliefs, which linked governance and authority with the divine order, thus left in its wake a series of assumptions about human equality. Natural lawyers such as Grotius argued that long-established social roles were not the reflection of some higher natural order, but rather one of a number of social forms that might be 'patterned after nature's plan'.[19] Forms of political authority were thus to be construed as productions of the human will, which attempted to give expression to mankind's essentially social nature: in the absence of such social forms, individuals confronted one another as fundamental equals. The legal life of the polity consisted, for those jurists, in tracing out the structure of an ideal body of rights in terms of which individual interests are articulated, and the legitimate bounds of individuals' entitlements discovered. Individual rights were therefore conceived as essentially public standards, a matter for collective determination in the light of a shared conception of justice rather than for private choice.[20]

Modern forms of juristic consciousness, which follow Pound in giving a dominant place to rights in the idea of justice may be thought of as giving expression to liberal forms of idealism. The basic insight that plural visions of social and political good might coexist in a single social setting is thus recast as a concern with equality among individuals who realise that 'the issues of principle affecting them – the people – should be settled, ultimately, by them and only them on a basis that paid tribute to their fundamental equality.'[21] Liberal idealism may thus be understood as an attempt to tackle the consequences of moral Protestantism by displaying a concern with the general framework within which different individuals formulate and argue about their interests. Rather than mapping out areas within which the exercise of distinctive visions is possible, rights come to be understood as the general, public standards that result from collective deliberation over differing moral visions: 'It becomes a more Protestant idea: fidelity to a scheme of principle each citizen has a responsibility to identify, ultimately for himself, as his community's scheme.'[22]

The foregoing reflections hopefully give some sense of the intellectual context in which Pound's claims about the priority of rights are situated. For neither Protestantism, nor the idea of rights, is inevitable wherever law emerges as a distinctive force in the political realm. But if rights do not represent advanced stages or end-points on some trajectory of juristic contemplation, what is their significance in legal thought? In the remainder of this chapter, I propose to shed some light on this question through an exploration of the intellectual origins of idealism, and its relationship to forms of doctrinal scholarship.

---

19 H. Grotius, *De Iure Praedae Commentarius* [1604], (Oxford, Clarendon Press, 1950) 229.

20 Idealism, then, reflected Hume's belief that 'Tho' rules of justice be artificial, they are not arbitrary.' Hume, (above note 18) 484. 'Artificial', in Hume's sense, referred to the adventitious conditions in which justice emerges, rather than to any sense of justice as determined by purely positive stipulation.

21 J. Waldron, *Law and Disagreement* (Oxford, Clarendon Press, 1999) 249.

22 R. Dworkin, *Law's Empire* (London, Fontana, 1986) 190.

Natural Right and Political Authority

The 17th century marks an important turning-point in political theory. Declining interest in Aristotelianism and a general suspicion of ethical theories structured around a common good or human *telos*, had led writers to abandon the idea of government as a source of guidance concerning salvation or the good life, and to embrace instead some notion of governmental authority as a necessary means for the protection of each person's capacity to formulate and pursue their own, contentious conceptions of the good. The notion of a 'right' thus came to occupy a central place within political theory: for then the laws of a state will be justified insofar as they reinforce or demarcate areas of liberty wherein individuals may autonomously pursue and realise diverse goals in common. Rules designed to secure autonomy in this way will, of course, reduce the scope for autonomous action in other ways; and thus we may come to think of a person's 'rights' as consisting of those private domains in which the individual enjoys a certain freedom from the will of others. Reconciling the possession of 'subjective' rights with the need for collectively binding rules and practices can be seen as the defining problem for modern political theory.

We might demarcate two divergent understandings of the nature and significance of such private domains in the juridical thought of modernity. The first of these, finding its source in Hobbes, viewed rights as the adventitious or contingent products of the state, as defined in positive law. The other can be viewed as originating in the work of Grotius, and forms the main subject of this chapter. It perceived rights as intrinsic dimensions of human nature which are in origin independent of state power. The possessive quality of such rights was not lost on Grotius and his intellectual heirs, for whom rights define the sphere of 'one's own' (the *suum*), or that which is proper to a person, and thus an individual was understood to be 'free inasmuch as he is the proprietor of his own person and capacities.'[23] Men are, for Grotius, thus no longer *zoa politika*, owing nothing to society for the possession of such traits and basic entitlements.[24]

The notion of a 'right' retains its fundamental centrality in political thought only against the background of Protestant conceptions of social life as a form of 'perpetual motion of things and minds' wherein diverse interests must be secured through collective practices and institutions.[25] The laws of ancient Greece, for example, were geared towards the pursuit of excellence and of conditions that make excellent, valuable lives possible. Consequently, the notion of a 'right' as a private entitlement allowing an individual scope to order his interests in ways not aligned with a common good, is almost wholly absent from classical Greek jurisprudence. Even within medieval common law scholarship, the law was conceived in terms of the reasoned settlement of wrongs, without any parallel notion of individual *rights* as we have come to understand the term.

---

23 C.B. MacPherson, *The Political Theory of Possessive Individualism: Hobbes to Locke* (Oxford, Clarendon Press, 1962), 3.

24 Contrast Aristotle, *Politics*, I.ii: '... man is by nature a political animal. [*zoon politikon*]'

25 Grotius, *De Republica Emendada* [c. 1600], 5 *Grotiana* (New Series, 1984), 524.

The language of rights itself derives from Roman law, and its origins lie in the word *ius*.[26] The term '*ius*' had been an established category in legal writing within the common law for many centuries prior to the emergence of Protestantism. Doctrinal legal science did not emerge, therefore, at a stroke, but came about partly as the result of the accumulation of small shifts within juridical thought, the significance of which became fully apparent only in retrospect.

The dominant usage among the Roman jurists treated *ius* as signifying something objectively right or just. In this way it had functioned as a synonym for 'law' as long as the dominant legal treatises were composed in Latin. At the same time, the term was essential to claims about the way two disputants should behave towards one another, and was thus confined to the description of private, bilateral relationships.[27] Within such relationships, the notion of 'what was due' to one related as much to the assignment of burdens or obligations as to the recognition of benefits. It is therefore not uncommon to find references in Roman texts where *ius* refers to both sides of the juridical relationship between litigating parties, so that the plaintiff's *ius* of stillicide, or eavesdrop onto neighbouring land, is coupled to the defendant's *ius* of not obstructing overflow onto his land.[28] The disputational context forced upon the Roman jurists an elusive distinction that was never fully articulated within the Roman law tradition. Outside that context, right denoted a conception of that which is the right thing for a just man to do. When functioning as an instrument of disputation, however, the logic of Roman pleading suggested that 'right belongs to the recipient of the action. It is *his* right, *suum ius*…'[29]

The emergence of a modern history of legal rights is often said to involve the recognition of a distinction between 'objective' and 'subjective' rights. Once the category of *ius* came to be seen as something a person could *own*, it became possible to interpret the mechanics of legal pleading in a new and powerful way. For suppose someone wished to claim *dominium* over some object or person: since *dominium* was in essence a relationship of power or control over other things capable of being defended in law, it signified a form of legal standing. But to have one's *dominium* upheld was to be granted a *ius*; and thus such actions seemed to involve the ownership or control of aspects of one's legal position. Rights thus signalled the presence of a domain in which individuals were able 'to constitute themselves as their own object, or to be self-determining.'[30] The consequence of such developments was to suggest a distinction between 'subjective' right (denoting moral licence or freedom), and

---

26 More particularly, the origins of the notion of a 'right' lie in the complex and shifting relationship that existed between the concepts of *ius*, *dominium* and *res*. I do not propose to examine this relationship in any detail, but a brief yet informative account can be found in R. Tuck, *Natural Rights Theories: Their Origin and Development* (Cambridge, Cambridge University Press, 1979), chapter 1.

27 *Ibid.*, 8.

28 See for example *The Digest of Justinian*, A. Watson (ed.) (University of Pennsylvania Press, 1997) VII.2.2. The passage also mentions the *ius* of not building so as to obscure one's neighbour's light.

29 A. Brett, *Liberty, Right and Nature: Individual Rights in Later Scholastic Thought* (Cambridge, Cambridge University Press, 1997), 92.

30 See Brett (above, note 29), 12–14. The words quoted are those of Augustine.

'objective' right (denoting obligation or one's 'due'), which was to prove congenial to voluntaristic understandings of morality – for the presence of domains of self-ownership pointed to the existence of areas of autonomy and liberty in which individuals exercise moral powers, finding their source in the will, rather than in the intrinsic structure of a universal order. A conception of law thus slowly emerged for which the notion of a 'right' would play a central role: for having grasped the notion of a sphere of individual liberty, might we not seek to recast the legal order as a *systematic* ordering of such liberties, structured by general doctrinal principles of justice?[31]

The natural lawyers of the 17th and early 18th centuries were conscious of these various dimensions to the word 'right': for both Grotius and his later English counterpart, Thomas Rutherford, 'right' was said to signify, first and foremost, what is right and just; but it can also carry the sense of 'law', and it could also denote an individual moral faculty or power.[32] The political writers of the 17th century displayed a greater awareness of the distinctions between the various meanings of 'right' than had their intellectual predecessors in the Roman law tradition; but such meanings continued to structure the approach of the natural lawyers to the central questions of political theory. Yet the notion of a right was to undergo an important shift in the period extending from Grotius to Pufendorf and Hume.

Grotius is often credited with having offered the first 'modern' account of rights within legal and political thought. This judgment partly derives from the supposed fact that Grotius recognises a purely 'subjective' form of right, and partly because modern writers have found in Grotius the origins of a secular account of rights which formed the basis for the eventual removal of the theological framework of natural law from legal and political thought. Such interpretations are reinforced by passages in which Grotius apparently detaches the content of rights from the divine will: 'And indeed, all that we have now said [concerning rights] would take place, though we should even grant, what without the greatest wickedness cannot be granted, that there is no God, or that human affairs are of no concern to him...'[33] The 'secular' interpretation of this passage is in large part the result of some polemical passages in Pufendorf's hugely influential *De Iure Naturae et Gentium*, in which Pufendorf castigates Grotius for his 'horrid impiety': 'For should any wretch be so horribly

---

31　The clearest expression of this view is to be found in Hobbes, who famously contrasts 'right' and 'law': *Leviathan*, R. Tuck (ed.) (Cambridge, Cambridge University Press, 1996), I.14.91. Brett rightly observes that medieval voluntarists did not share this conception of law: for them, rights were faculties or powers exercised in accordance with law, rather than liberties exercised outside the law. (See Brett, above, note 29, 3–6). Yet there can be no doubt that the emergence of subjective right was immensely *congenial* to voluntaristic understandings of morality.

32　See Grotius, *De Iure Belli ac Pacis* [1625] I.1.iii–ix. Rutherford echoes Grotius in his *Institutes of Natural Law* [1754] Book 1, chapter 2, 25–33.

33　Grotius, *De Iure Belli ac Pacis*, Prolegomena, XI. The passage goes on: '...the contrary of which on the one hand is borne in upon us (however unwilling we may be) by an innate light in our soul, and on the other is confirmed by many arguments and miracles witnessed down the ages. It follows that without exception we should obey God as our creator to whom we owe everything...'

senseless as to maintain that wicked and absurd hypothesis in the rankest way, and so hold men to have derived their Being wholly from themselves; according to them the edicts of Reason could not rise so high as to pass into the condition of laws...'[34] The point of Grotius's hypothesis was not to suggest that God was irrelevant to morality, however, for the divine will continued to supply the deontic force of the natural law, and it thus played a key role in elevating what would otherwise be merely prudential prescriptions for a fulfilling life to the status of moral duties. Moreover, passages hypothesising God's inexistence were a commonplace of voluntarist theology throughout the history of medieval and early modern thought, and in repeating the argument Grotius was doing little more than rehearsing a piece of orthodoxy.[35]

Pufendorf's reaction to Grotius is nevertheless revealing of the extent to which juridical ideas in the 18th century embodied voluntarist perspectives on ethics, for in denying that any moral significance attaches to human actions in themselves, Pufendorf removed the possibility of inferring any moral knowledge from the historical facts of human associations: moral understanding requires 'reference to a law', and 'all law presupposes a superior Power.'[36] Although it is undoubtedly true that Pufendorf took a decisive, further step away from Aristotelianism than had any previous writer, he would in fact have found little in Grotius to trouble his theological suppositions. For Grotius, knowledge of morality did not derive from externally intelligible practices, but from an internal source in the human will. God, according to Grotius, has implanted in man a desire for *intellectus modo ordinatae* (rational order), and thus man is distinct from other animals that seek their own interests on the basis of 'some extrinsic principle of intelligence.' Human actions and choices rather 'stem from some internal principle, which is associated with qualities belonging not to all animals but to human nature alone.' The human *telos* is thus 'care for society, in accordance with the human intellect, which [as] we have roughly sketched, is the source of *ius* ...'[37]

These more limited departures from Aristotle were not made with the aim of ushering in a new age of secular reasoning in relation to morality, but with preserving the traditional theological premises of moral philosophy within a context of religious disagreement that had seen a near-complete erosion of shared standpoints. Voluntarism represented an accepted and long-established means of securing this aim, for it enabled Grotius to discover a minimal perspective for the human *telos* in the notions of self-preservation and sociability. Rights and principles of justice could then find a source in the *suum*, considered as an internal domain of self-ownership in which one's interests and goals become clear through a process of *inward* reflection, rather than a search for outward meaning and intelligibility in the natural order of the external world:

> Indeed, to borrow Aristotle's admirable explanation, 'Whatever each person's understanding has ruled for him regarding a given matter, that to him is good.' For God created Man ... 'free and *sui iuris*', so that the actions of each individual and the use of

---

34 Pufendorf, *De Iure Naturae et Gentium*, II.3.19.
35 See for example Finnis (above, note 8), 43.
36 Pufendorf, *De Iure Naturae et Gentium*, I.2.6, II.3.19.
37 Grotius, *De Iure Belli ac Pacis*, Prolegomena, VII–VIII.

his possessions were made subject not to another's will, but to his own ... For what is
that well-known concept 'natural liberty' other than the power of an individual to act in
accordance with his own will?[38]

Such views exemplify the attempt of Grotius and his successors to ground moral
theory in a theologically uncontentious perspective. By basing natural rights in general
postulates of wellbeing acceptable to all Christians, it was hoped that such theories
could avoid involvement in the sectarian complexities of ecclesiastical politics.[39]
From this point of view, Grotius's arguments presented a context of reflection for
later writers who sought to detach the juridical framework of rights and duties from
the theological moorings of natural law – for, in common with Pufendorf, it seemed
to such writers that Grotius had offered a perspective in which the motivating or
prudential aspect of natural rights derived entirely from their convergence with basic
elements of human utility:

> nature can be termed the grandmother of civil law. But utility is annexed to the natural
> law ... and utility is the occasion of civil law, since what I have termed association or
> subjection originally came into existence for the sake of some interest [*utilitatis*]. It is also
> the case that anyone who prescribes laws for other people usually does so with a view to
> increasing utility, or at least ought to do so.[40]

Grotius was still a central text in England (and in Europe generally) until well into
the 18th century, and it was therefore natural for writers such as Hume to draw upon
the authority of the work in support of their own utilitarian arguments: 'Examine
the writers on the law of nature, and you will always find, that, whatever principles
they set out with, they are sure ... to assign, as the ultimate reason for every rule
which they establish, the convenience and necessities of mankind.'[41] Bentham, too,
sought to detach utility from the notion of divine will as it featured in Blackstone's
influential *Commentaries*:

> Besides, if we lay it down as a fixed principle that whatever laws have been given by
> the author of revelation were meant by Him to be laws subservient to the happiness of
> present life, that this subserviency is an indisputable evidence of the authenticity of what
> are given for such laws, that is, of their really coming from Him, [then] to know whether a

---

38 Grotius, *De Iure Praedae Commentarius*, (above, note 19), 18.

39 'My prime concern,' Grotius stated, 'was to base my proofs of what belongs to the
laws of nature on ideas which are so certain that nobody can deny them without doing violence
to their fundamental being.' Prolegomena, XL.

40 Grotius, *De Iure Belli ac Pacis*, Prolegomena to the first edition. The first edition
prologue can be found in the Liberty Fund edition of 'The Rights of War and Peace', R. Tuck
(ed.) (Indianapolis, Liberty Fund, 2005), vol 3, 1749. Grotius made significant revisions to
later editions of the book in order to appease the authorities in the United Provinces who had
earlier imprisoned him and caused his exile. For an account of some of these changes, see
Tuck, 'Introduction', vol 1, xxv–xxvi.

41 D. Hume, *Enquiry Concerning the Principles of Morals*, T.L. Beauchamp (ed.)
(Oxford, Oxford University Press, 1998), III.ii.156. See also Hume, *A Treatise of Human
Nature*, D.F. Norton (ed.) (Oxford, Oxford University Press, 2000), 3.2.2.8.

measure is conformable to the dictates of the principle of utility is at once the readiest and surest way of knowing whether it is conformable to the dictates of revelation.[42]

There is an important divergence between the arguments of Bentham, and those of Grotius and Hume, however. For neither the Grotian nor the Humean accounts were intended to *remove* God from the picture of morality, and thus to present morality in terms of an ungrounded exercise of secular will. Grotius *contrasts* his position with that of the ancient sceptics, pointing out that the view of utility as the mother of justice and equity 'is not true, if we speak accurately.'[43] The source of rights is instead thought to lie in man's social nature, as willed by God. The correspondence between human interests and the natural law was seen as revealing a further dimension of God's benevolence. Having created a being with these particular characteristics, God's will could be interpreted through the suitability of natural law to sustain prosperous human societies. Utility is then revealed as a ground of right and law only within a complex metaphysical framework of reflection upon God's will and upon the human *telos*.[44]

The deontological underpinnings of the Grotian theory nevertheless muted the significance of teleology in cultivating human understanding of morality and the good life. It therefore became increasingly common for political writers to locate the foundations of moral knowledge, as Grotius had, in the internal properties of the will. One result of these ideas was to detach governance from its capacity to realise or foster some aspect of the human *telos*, and to locate it instead in a juridical system of abstract rights. The structure of such a system of rights could not itself derive from insights into a common good, but must (it was thought) depend upon specifically *legal* considerations that distinguished 'perfect' or genuine entitlements from 'imperfect' rights that depend upon a 'law of love': only the former are rights properly so called, for they consist of a 'moral quality of a person, making it possible to have or do something lawfully',[45] and thus give rise to distinct obligations; whereas the latter signal a mere aptitude or worthiness to receive some benefit, and thus properly correlate not with obligations but with compassion, generosity etc. In this way, a juridical science of morals came to be detached from the older tradition of enquiry into virtues and excellences.[46] Governance

---

42 J. Bentham, *A Comment on the Commentaries*, I.3, in J. Burns and H.L.A. Hart (eds) *A Comment on the Commentaries and A Fragment on Government* (London, Athlone Press, 1977), 27–28.

43 Grotius (above, note 40), 1749. The sceptical interlocutor is Carneades. See also Prolegomena, LVIII: 'I have forborne [in the main work] from discussing questions of utility, which are appropriate to some other work; for they properly belong to the science of politics … – unlike Bodin, who has confounded this science with the kind of legal analysis I have undertaken.'

44 This line of thought can also be found in Locke: 'That which we call Good, which is apt to cause or increase pleasure, or diminish pain in us … and on the contrary we name that Evil which is apt to produce or increase in us any pain' Yet, Locke goes on, 'Pleasure and pain, *and that which cause them*, Good and Evil, are the things on which our passions turn.' *Essay on Human Understanding*, P.H. Nidditch (ed.) (Oxford, Clarendon Press, 1989), II.20 (emphasis added).

45 *De Iure Belli ac Pacis*, I.1.iv.

46 The same distinction was reflected in the writings of all the major philosophers, as with Kant's dichotomy between artificial and natural virtues: natural virtues do not admit of

of the polity was then thought to depend solely upon conformity to a body of rights which logically precedes social order.

English politics at the close of the 17th century provided a context in which Grotian ideas resonated strongly with the concerns of the educated classes. The most pressing questions facing the British polity centred on the nature of hereditary rights to the throne. Such questions were intimately bound up with questions of divine right, and were raised squarely by the crisis surrounding the attempts to exclude James, Duke of York from the throne on grounds of his open Catholicism. The central issue of the 'Exclusion Crisis' hinged on whether monarchical power was an inherent form of privilege, or whether Parliament was a trustee of the basic rights of individuals from which a more limited, consensual right of governance had been carved out. Scholarly assessments of Grotius's historical importance have thus largely mirrored the fortunes of the so-called Whig interpretation of history. That interpretation has tended to associate Grotius with a 'natural liberty school' of writers, of whom the most prominent was Locke, and whose work led gradually to the transformation of English society into more liberal and democratic patterns of governance. In this way, Grotius has been presented as a powerful advocate of the connection between natural rights and limited government. Grotius's social background lends some plausibility to this suggestion, for the presence of such a connection had been a touchstone of the Calvinist Protestantism of Grotius's homeland since the 16th century. Protestantism was thus associated with belief in a hypothetical 'right of resistance' against a monarch who exceeded his constitutional authority, by (for example) interfering with established rights of worship.

It is not difficult to find passages in *De Iure Belli ac Pacis* that would seem to support the cause of English radicalism. Near the beginning of the book, Grotius endorses the proposition that society is not the product of 'divine precept', but of human will. Thus, all legitimate political power is said to be exercised through an original agreement that establishes that power and the social institutions in which it is manifested.[47] The royalist Robert Filmer found enough disturbing material in Grotius's book to devote passages of his work, the *Patriarcha* of 1628, to a rebuttal of the work.[48] It is by no means clear that Grotius did support limited constitutionalism, however. Grotius had indeed stated in one passage that 'By nature all men have the right of resisting in order to ward off injury.' But he immediately qualifies this assertion, displaying his clear intention to limit the radical implications of his own theory of natural rights:

> But as civil society was instituted to maintain public tranquillity, the State forthwith acquires over us and our possessions a greater right, to the extent necessary to accomplish this end. The State therefore in the interests of public peace and order can limit that

---

clear and precise definition, and thus run into one another, whereas artificial virtues depend upon clear and definite formulation, which renders them capable of legal protection.

47 *De Iure Belli ac Pacis*, I.3.viii; see also I.4.vii.

48 Filmer's book, not published until 1680, had as its principal targets Francisco Suarez and the Jesuit Cardinal Robert Bellarmine.

common right of resistance. That such was the purpose of the State we cannot doubt, since it could not in any other way achieve its end.[49]

Grotius also expresses his intention to 'reject their opinion who will have the supreme power to be always and without exception in the people, so that they may restrain and punish their Kings as often as they abuse their power.'[50] Indeed, it was Grotius's arguments in the same passage that led many Whig radicals to renounce Grotius, for his theory was viewed (not altogether unreasonably) as justifying absolutism. Such passages give some substance to Rousseau's later claim that the theories of Grotius and Hobbes were essentially similar. Richard Tuck's claim, that 'Grotius was both the first conservative rights theorist in Protestant Europe and also, in a sense, the first radical rights theorist' is at least partly true.[51]

Grotian ideas of natural right had a considerable impact on the future direction of English political thought. Yet important though the idea of rights would become to political argument, it is not possible to view Grotius as the standard-bearer of a modern, liberal tradition of English thought. All sides in the Exclusion Crisis drew on his arguments, and it is perhaps because those arguments were so pliant and adaptable that they were to make no lasting impression upon the political life of the polity. For the majority of Whig political thinkers in the late 17th and early 18th century, radicalism of any kind was to be rejected (as being too closely associated with the currents of political thought that had led to the execution of James's father Charles I, and the ruinous political instabilities that followed). Locke's writings, in particular, which refined and extended the more radical of Grotius's ideas, gained little popularity amongst serious thinkers until almost the beginning of the 19th century, and thus did not herald the acceptance of a more modern, liberal society after 1688. Arguments concerning natural liberty and 'equality' were treated with suspicion by Whigs as leading to revolutionary social policies of redistribution and 'levelling'. Whigs, as much as establishment Tories, wished to settle political differences whilst leaving intact the traditional property, privileges and hierarchy of the British classes.[52] The aim of most Whigs was deeply conservative, for they wished to bring about a traditional form of English monarchy, as a legally limited institution with a degree of Parliamentary control over the succession. These ideas were presented by the Whigs as a deeply ingrained feature of English Protestantism; Catholicism (especially amongst monarchs) being linked with absolutist notions of government and threats to national sovereignty.[53]

---

49 *De Iure Belli ac Pacis*, I.4.xxi.

50 *Ibid.*, I.3.viii.

51 See R. Tuck, *Natural Rights Theories: Their Origin and Development* (Cambridge, Cambridge University Press, 1979), 71.

52 See O.W. Furley, 'The Whig Exclusionists: Pamphlet Literature in the Exclusion Crisis 1679–81', 13 *Cambridge Historical Journal* (1957), 35, and the flawed but interesting discussion of the impact of Grotian ideas on English thought in L. Ward, *The Politics of Liberty in England and Revolutionary America* (Cambridge, Cambridge University Press, 2004), chapters 3–11.

53 See the excellent discussion in H.T. Dickinson, *Liberty and Property: Political Ideology in Eighteenth Century Britain* (London, Weidenfield & Nicholson, 1977).

The idealistic theories of natural rights were therefore not a simple stepping-stone towards a liberal conception of the polity. Notwithstanding the failure of Grotian ideas to institute a modern political order based on the recognition of fundamental rights, Grotius remains an important figure in European legal thought. Despite their similarities, Grotius offers a vision of juridical scholarship that differs in significant respects to that of Hobbes and his legal positivist successors. Out of these theories was to emerge a new form of doctrinal legal scholarship, the philosophical implications of which are still a central concern of jurisprudence.

There is an important connection between doctrinal scholarship and the idea of rights, for it is through the notion of abstract rights that a deeper idea of the systematic nature of law can be given expression. The political instabilities that afflicted England during the course of the 17th century had led to a situation in which it was impossible to maintain the image of the common law as an expression of a shared conception of the good. For much of its history, the common law had operated around a limited number of technical categories, which gave structure to the complex process of pleading. The bulk of the medieval practitioner's experience was not informed by any deeper theoretical perspective concerning the nature of law, however, nor was there general agreement amongst lawyers on the basic conceptual categories and ideas through which they reflected upon the substance of points of law: the categories of custom (*consuetudo*), *lex non scripta*, reason, *ius* and *ley* formed the basis for lawyerly deliberation and legal explication, but no settled interpretations of the significance of those concepts, or of the relationship between them, emerged in medieval legal writing.

The lack of a systematic theory of the nature of law did not appear to trouble the classical common lawyers. One prevalent attitude amongst common lawyers, for example, asserted the dominance of statute over custom, in virtue of the constitutionally higher status of the former. A more-or-less equally well-entrenched attitude, however, held custom to be more fundamental than statute, since the detailed application of statute must involve elaboration through existing legal and customary understandings, considered as an oral tradition of the court.[54] The point to bear in mind, however, is that it is in many cases *the same* lawyers who advocated the former position who also gave expression to the latter. Therefore, the basic terms and categories of legal thought cannot represent a fixed and stable intellectual framework of legal thought.

Such an unfocused attitude could not survive the political controversies that surrounded the status of hereditary right and sovereign powers, for such debates demanded the clarification of a hierarchy amongst the sources of law (particularly statute and custom). The theories of Grotius and Hobbes sought to discover system and coherence within the law in different ways. Whereas Hobbes gave centrality to authoritatively formulated posited rules as the basis for legal reflection, Grotius emphasised the dependency of legal thought upon a system of natural obligations and entitlements which precedes and guides the interpretation of the rules. As I hope

---

54 See N. Doe, *Fundamental Authority in Late Medieval English Law* (Cambridge, Cambridge University Press, 1990).

to make clear in this and the next chapter, we can see these theories as different ways for working out the implications of a Jurisprudence of the Will.

Natural Right, Juridical Reason and Legal Doctrine

The views of the natural rights theorists had a pronounced effect on juristic understandings of the nature of law. Medieval jurisprudence had considered law to be a rational product, the perceived rationality amongst legal rules being grounded in divine law. Voluntarism, which regarded the divine will as permanently inscrutable to man, therefore afforded only a limited context for juridical reasoning, for knowledge of law would then seem to depend upon an ability to form direct intuitions of moral laws. Legal science is accordingly limited to the articulation of 'innate ideas' and the tracing of their consequences in particular cases. Systematic forms of legal writing could not flourish against this background. The leading treatises of the common law in the medieval period thus tended to be practitioners' texts designed to serve the needs of practising lawyers. The form of such writings consisted almost entirely of abridgments, indices and glossaries (that is, commentaries on individual laws) arranged either according to procedural considerations, or in alphabetical order. Having confined the significance of the divine will to a deontological role, the 'reason' of the common law could no longer be thought to find a source *either* in teleological understandings of the good life *or* in a structure of innate ideas. Instead, law came to be viewed as rational to the extent that the various rules, actions and entitlements could be presented as instances of more general principles of justice in which the fundamental equality of self-determining agents is reflected.

Grotius was conscious of the significance of this enterprise: 'I wanted,' he said, 'to advance the study of jurisprudence.'[55] The attempt to discover rationality and coherence within the law, at the level of general principle, necessitated a distinction between natural and artificial or 'adventitious' rights: for a systematic jurisprudence depended upon the possibility of presenting the holders of manifestly unequal rights and privileges as enjoying basic equality at the level of their *fundamental* rights. Such a jurisprudence must be a Jurisprudence of the Will: for then the unequal status of individuals could be demonstrated as flowing from their own choices and transactions:

> Many people have already tried to put [jurisprudence] into a systematic form, but no one has succeeded; nor will they, until there is a proper distinction made between what is conventional and what is natural ... For natural principles, being always the same, are easily put into systematic form, whereas conventional principles, which often change and which vary from place to place, like other collections of particulars, cannot be handled systematically.[56]

---

55 Grotius, (above, note 40), 1753. Later versions of the Prolegomena carried a marginal summary noting the author's 'endeavour to promote the Knowledge of Law, by giving an example of a Method for it.' (See Prolegomena, XXXI.)

56 *Ibid.*, 1753–1754.

Legal experts must therefore 'first set to one side everything which derives from the free will.' The effect of Grotius's theory was to transform juristic understandings of the legal order from a loose collection of procedures and remedies into an organised system of principles and rights. The English common law tradition might have been expected to provide an excellent seed-bed for Grotian ideas, for here was a legal order purportedly grounded in the national *Volksgeist*, yet situated in a context of ideological conflict and political instability. Might the legal writer not seek to expose such conflicts as the result of conventional arrangements, and thereby reveal the law as resting on underlying general principles that make the exercise of opposing wills possible?

The emergence of doctrinal writing is often thought to stem directly from Grotian perspectives on natural law, for the aim of the doctrinal writer lies precisely in the systematic exposition of a principled context for the resolution of particular disputes. Legal writing in England during the 17th century did indeed begin to exhibit systematic qualities, and was ultimately to blossom into a rich tradition of authorship of legal treatises, which had as their aim the presentation of law 'in a strictly deductive framework, with the implication that in the beginning there were principles, and that in the end those principles were found to cover a large multitude of cases deducible from them.'[57]

The legal treatise, as a form of legal literature, is closely tied to an underlying theory that emphasises the nature of law as the product of natural law. Yet its origins lie in more basic practical concerns: common lawyers throughout the medieval period had insisted that the apparently chaotic nature of English law was merely due to its superficial appearance. Beneath the disordered and unmethodical arrangement of technical prescriptions and forms of action, the law was thought to consist of fundamental principles or 'maxims', which gave structure and rational coherence to legal practice. Close involvement and long study were prerequisites to an understanding of this deeper order, and thus the ordinary layman was dependent on the emergent professional class of lawyers to guide him through the mystifying complexities of litigation.[58] The problem facing lawyers was that legal education itself failed to manifest the properties of rational coherence and systematicity, which were the alleged province of educated jurists. Viscount Stair confirmed the general impression of the confused state of the common law, writing in 1681 that 'there are not wanting of late of the learnedest lawyers, who have thought it both feasible and fit, that the law should be formed into a rational discipline, and have much regretted that it hath not been effected, yea scarce attempted by any.'[59]

---

57 T.F.T. Plunkett, *Early English Legal Literature* (Cambridge, Cambridge University Press, 1958), 19.

58 See W. Prest, 'The Dialectical Origins of Finch's *Law*', 36 *Cambridge LJ* (1977), 326–352, at 327–328. The inaccessibility of law to the layman is also partly explicable by the tendency for legal proceedings to be conducted in a mixture of English, Latin and French: see G. Postema, 'Classical Common Law Jurisprudence (Part I)', 2 *Oxford University Commonwealth LJ* (2002), 155–180.

59 Stair (above, note 5). Stair's own work was, of course, institutional rather than doctrinal as such, yet he shared with the treatise writers the aim of introducing rational order to the complex array of statutes and cases confronted by the ordinary lawyer.

The dominant forms of legal writing reflected the lack of overall coherence and system. Rudimentary forms of order could be found in the various abridgments of cases and statutes and procedural texts which aimed to steer the law student through the daunting bulk of disordered materials; yet the clarificatory intentions of such works were essentially modest: William Sheppard's prefatory remarks to his own abridgment, the *Actions upon the Case* of 1663, inform the reader that '... you will find [herein] nothing of mine, but the method, or labour of putting together, and setting out the grave and learned judgments, resolutions and opinions of the eminent and learned judges, ... where perhaps you may find some repetitions of the same things.'[60] By the act of 'bringing together' the judgments and actions relating to a given subject, then, the legal writer aims to elucidate connections and common concepts; but he does not pretend to originality, nor the discovery of underlying principles in the light of which a body of law as a whole might be presented.

The practical need for some methodical statement of the cases, however, raised an issue that was not squarely confronted by the medieval jurists: if concepts and connections can be 'formed' in this way, then why could not the compiler of the abridgment, or the writer of the gloss, not state them directly? The intellectual unity of the common law might then be thought to consist of the possibility of stating the recognised branches of law (contract, property, etc.) as systematic bodies of principles, definitions and distinctions. Having admitted this possibility, jurists were confronted with a problem – legal writers themselves possess no *auctoritas*, or rule-based authority; what status, then, attaches to their pronouncements? Littleton's *Tenures*, the only medieval tract to have exhibited the law as a system of principles, had by the 16th century itself attained the status of law, so that later jurists produced their own glosses of the work.[61] But what intellectual processes had led to this position? Natural law provided an obvious solution, as coherence in the law could be explained according to a body of rational principles that derive their substance from human reason, finding an ultimate source in the divine will. Anticipating Grotius by over a decade, the English jurist John Dodderidge had argued that all legal systems (including the common law) comprised a series of derivations from a body of rational principles directly apprehended by:

> the light of natural reason tried and sifted upon disputation and argument ... not that every man can comprehend the same; but it is artificial reason, the reason of such as by their wisdom, learning, and long experience are skilful to the affairs of men, and know what is fit and convenient to be held and observed for the appealing of controversies and debates among men...[62]

The ideas of Grotius and his contemporaries mingled with the efforts of common lawyers to make systematic sense of their complex and disordered procedures. Amongst the English jurists, the idea had long existed that the common law rested on 'maxims', said to constitute 'a foundation in Law, upon whose reason the structure

---

60 W. Sheppard, *Actions upon the Case for Deeds*, [1663], iii.

61 Notably that of Sir Edward Coke: see *Coke Upon Littleton* [1628]. T Littleton, *Tenores Novelli* [c1481].

62 J. Dodderidge, *The English Lawyer* [c1590], 242.

of many particular cases doth stand.'[63] The common law thus appeared to English lawyers as a reasoning process or 'market in ideas',[64] rather than a body of rights or rules: the principles or maxims exhibiting rationality in relation to their ability to make structural sense of the legal order (as a complex arrangement of specific pleading procedures) rather than their embodiment of substantive moral and political ideals. It was in this sense that the reason of the common law was 'artificial', being comprehensible only to those who had long pondered the deeper systematic connections between the seemingly haphazard rules and procedures. If legal principles were not, as such, products of artifice, then they were nonetheless products of the will. In this way, the form of reasoning at common law moved away from its traditional association with *phronesis*, and instead came to take on the appearance of a Ramist logic (or *techne*), in which the emphasis lay on the organisation of a body of knowledge by reference to distinctions, definitions, divisions and systematising principles. Collections of 'maxims' began to appear that attempted to lay bare the law's rational structure in just this way.[65]

The decline of Aristotelian perspectives on divine law provided a context in which Ramist ideas could coexist easily with traditional assumptions about the character of natural rights. This is because the identification of systematic connections between the various rules and decisions of the courts were naturally expressible in the form of substantive doctrines (*caveat emptor, quod legis constructio mon facit injuriam,* and so forth), capable of being understood as giving protection to basic interests and entitlements. In this way, juristic scholarship could go beyond the mere collecting and reporting of rules and decisions, involving instead quite sophisticated processes of reasoning and contemplation, and the discovery of coherence and unity within the law. The comments of Stair and other 18th century jurists attest to a desire amongst lawyers to provide a comprehensive theoretical framework for legal practice. Scientific method, the reduction of complex bodies of observable phenomena to a few rational postulates, was the main source of inspiration for jurists who wished to develop a 'science' of pleading within the common law. The combination of such views with ideas of natural right formed a rich brew indeed.

The legal texts and institutional works that began to appear during the 18th and early 19th centuries, in which the law was presented systematically with little reference being made to the procedural incidents of enforcement, clearly separate the juristic scholarship of the period from that of earlier times – for it is in works such as William Jones's *Essay on the Law of Bailment* and Blackstone's *Commentaries of the Law of England* that we can perceive most clearly the attempt to work out the detail of contract law, tort, property law, etc., from an initial starting-point in abstract principles of justice, equality and right. The legal treatise, as a literary form, represents in many

---

63 M. Hawke, *The Grounds of the Lawes of England*, [1657], iv. Quoted in A.W.B. Simpson, 'The Rise and Fall of the Legal Treatise: Legal Principles and the Forms of Legal Literature', 48 *University of Chicago LR* (1981) 632–679, at 650n.

64 S.F.C. Milsom, 'The Nature of Blackstone's Achievement', 1 *Oxford Journal of Legal Studies* (1981) 1–11, at 1.

65 The earliest of these was Bacon's *Elements of Law* [1597], first published in 1630; see Prest (above, note 58), 328.

ways the high watermark of attempts to provide a richly articulated jurisprudential underpinning for common law. Yet if Grotian ideas inspired the development of doctrinal scholarship, they also proved to be its undoing, for it became apparent to most jurists, through the same works, that the common law could not be derived from a limited number of abstract rights or principles of justice. Blackstone's multi-volume work, the *Commentaries*, was both the most impressive attempt to present the law as a coherent expression of justice, and the clearest failure to carry through such a project. Blackstone's natural law theory offered little explanation of the way in which lawyers could use general principles of justice to find the law, and it thus remained an abstract and free-floating adjunct to his substantive explanation of law as a set of remedies.[66]

The explanation of law in terms of substantive doctrinal principles would remain a central feature of legal treatises until their eventual demise in the late 19th century; but the attempt to ground the various doctrines, rules and principles in broader theories of justice and natural right steadily declined to the point where they occupied the place of mere introductory or prefatory remarks to the general substantive work. In this respect, the modern legal textbook resembles the classical treatise most strongly. Such works typically contain an opening 'conceptual' chapter designed to set the study of technical, black-letter law within its social, historical or theoretical context, but thereafter little attempt is made to present the huge volume of rules and decisions as elements of a systematic theory of justice.[67] Doctrinal scholarship thus came to serve the more limited aim of explaining the goals, principles and policies thought to underlie the specific cases and statutes, without any attempt being made to ground those values in a deeper jurisprudential perspective or theory of the good. Such ideas were hence to be understood as of interest to philosophers, but of limited relevance to a knowledge of lawyers' law.

The later history of jurisprudential thought consists roughly of two perspectives on the significance of legal doctrine. Positivists, unsurprisingly, have tended to be dismissive of legal doctrine, regarding it either as the misleading product of a failure to distinguish sufficiently between the activity of reporting the law's content and that of evaluating it, or else as a general term for the various rules, distinctions and definitions to be extracted from the cases, considered as a 'source' of law. There can, on the positivist view, be no interesting disagreements about legal doctrine, for all such disagreements are at best the result of a curious feature of judicial judgment, in which the grounds of decision are not precisely set out in abstraction from the concrete facts and circumstances of the instant case. Because principles and rules may be abstracted from the judgments in different ways, the goal of the doctrinal scholar is both to exhibit accuracy and skill in articulating the rules, and 'to arrange

---

66 For an excellent discussion, see M. Lobban, *The Common Law and English Jurisprudence 1760–1850* (Oxford, Clarendon Press, 1991), chapter 3.

67 See, for example, G.H. Treitel, *The Law of Contract*, 11th edn (London, Sweet & Maxwell, 2003); J. Beatson, *Anson's Law of Contract*, 28th edn (Oxford, Oxford University Press, 2002); W.V.H. Rogers, *Winfield and Jolowicz on Tort*, (London, Sweet & Maxwell, 2002). See also K. Gray, *Elements of Land Law* 1st edn (London, Butterworth, 1987), chapter 1. (The chapter does not appear in later editions.)

yesterday's results in whatever way will be most convenient for those working on today's problems.'[68] Those jurists whom I have called 'idealists', by contrast, sought to retain a sense of the importance of legal doctrine through the association with legal rights. Doctrinal principle was to be explained as deriving from a systematic vision of justice running through the law, and thus the doctrinal writer's mission was to interpret the law in such a way as to reveal the underlying coherence of a body of rules found in statutes and judicial decisions in terms of that vision. The law, on this view, 'does not consist in particular cases, but in general principles which run through the cases and govern the decision of them.'[69] Specific legal rules, then, invited consideration as partial or fragmentary statements of more inclusive legal obligations and entitlements. Positivists, on the other hand, viewed rights as enjoying legal protection insofar as established rules identified a remedy or duty connected with them.

The intimate connection between rights and these more limited doctrinal perspectives encouraged a view of rights as 'subjective' legal instruments or claims, in a way that muted the association of rights with 'objective' notions of justice. Rights were no longer viewed as the direct expression of a basic human equality, but rather of *law*:

> For 'tis ridiculous trifling to call that power a *right* which, should we attempt to exercise, all other men have an *equal right* to obstruct or prevent us ... because all men being naturally equal, one cannot fairly exclude the rest from possessing any such advantage, unless by their consent, either express or presumptive, he has obtained the particular and sole disposal or enjoyment of it. And when this is once done, he may then truly say he has a *right* to such a thing.[70]

The more limited notion of a right as a legal instrument gained a central place in the juridical thought of common lawyers. Thomas Starkie in his Inner Temple lectures of 1834 was to remark that '[t]he first and great business of the law is, to define rights and correlative duties of all kinds, whether they be public or private,'[71] adding that 'in our law, the extent of the right is limited and defined by the extent of the wrong.'

Starkie's remarks exhibit the characteristic tension found in modern legal orders: for how is the extent of legal 'wrongs' to be discovered? Having placed rights at the centre of legal thought, should we seek to delimit their scope by reference to formal rules, or through a conception of justice said to underlie and inform the rules? The jurisprudence of the modern age might be presented, therefore, as an argument about the possibility of reconciling the 'subjective' notion of legal rights with the objective conception found in Grotius and his intellectual ancestors. For once we are in possession of the distinction between objective and subjective *ius*, it becomes easy to imagine that the ordinary, subjective claims individuals make in relation to

---

68 Milsom (above, note 64), 1.

69 *Rust v Cooper* [1774] 2 Cowp, at 632 per Lord Mansfield.

70 Pufendorf, *De Iure Naturae*, III.5.3.

71 *Law Examiner and Law Chronicle III*, 172–173. Quoted in Lobban (above, note 66), 187.

their rights are ultimately governed by an objective order of moral rightness. In this way the notion of objective right can be conceived as a fixed standard against which the inequalities and imperfections of ordinary life can be measured. We might then hope that the constantly shifting pattern of uncoordinated and competing claims can be rationalised in a way that reflects that ideal moral order: then we may claim to have simultaneously reconciled those clashing interests and delineated the scope of individuals' *legitimate* interests.

However, for one who dismisses the possibility of reconciling the notions of objective and subjective right, the political life of the state will come to be regarded as a matter of achieving a reasonable and stable balancing of those interests. Rights will then take on a different role: where no stable perspective exists against which the irregularities and conflicts of everyday life can be evaluated and resolved, individual rights will come to play a central role in the delineation of protected spheres of interest and choice distinct from the aggregative and distributive policies of the state. The laws of the polity will accordingly resemble less a body of principles aiming at the establishment and protection of equal rights, and more a framework of social rules for dealing with the effects of manifest inequalities. To that extent, the law can be seen as displaying a concern with the needs and wants of individuals, and as securing a framework of stable expectations in which those needs and wants can be pursued and fulfilled. Such a view might then be expected to emphasise the essentially different nature of the lawyer's and the philosopher's enterprises; or else it may result in a theoretical perspective that aims to account for law and morality as separate concepts, and to explain the presence of moral ideals within the law as contingent features of legal experience.

The possibility of reconciling objective and subjective right, by contrast, depends upon the tracing out of an intimate relationship between black-letter law and legal theory. The common law tradition has, throughout its history, proved resistant to the development of general theoretical perspectives, with the result that such general perspectives as have emerged tend to be looked upon (at least by lawyers) as intellectual reconstructions of the legal order rather than articulations of immanent truths. I have argued, in this book, that modern understandings of the legal order as conceptually separable from such wider concerns, themselves depend upon a theoretical standpoint concerning the moral nature of law, the character of moral knowledge, etc. The decline of Grotian ideas about the significance of doctrinal legal scholarship is in part the product of a rival intellectual tradition originating with Hobbes, and continuing with Jeremy Bentham, which sought to separate law from wider notions of right. It is to this tradition that we now turn.

Chapter 4

Legal Positivism, Doctrinal Science and Statist Conceptions of Law

The form of juridical consciousness explored in Chapter 3 embodies many of the philosophical assumptions and motivations that lie behind the legal doctrinal scholarship of the present day. Yet, increasingly, lawyers regard doctrinal reasoning less as an autonomous domain of juristic concepts aside from those of positive law, and more as a set of intellectual processes that determine the application of technical rules. Law is viewed instead as a product of human artifice and the expression of deliberately chosen goals and policies. The classical idea of protected domains of privacy thereby come to be detached from their moorings in human nature and capacities, and are instead viewed as areas of personal discretion established or left open by the state. We may use the term 'legal positivism' to refer to this view.

In this chapter, I aim to explore some of the intellectual conditions that led to the emergence of legal positivism. I shall suggest that positivism was made possible, in part, by a changing conception of the moral basis of a system of laws. Once seen as a rational reflection of human nature, law gradually came to be viewed as an artificial product of the state.

A statist view of law creates an immediate problem for the relationship between legal authority and political legitimacy: how can a body of imposed rules provide a legitimate basis for the rule of law? Legal positivists have tended to respond to this problem by drawing a distinction between the law's formal, rule-based authority and moral questions pertaining to its legitimacy, concentrating on the former as the proper domain for jurisprudential enquiry. The statism apparent in the writings of Hobbes and his intellectual descendants makes such conceptual distinctions largely inescapable. The form of legal science developed by Grotius and his intellectual heirs does not sit well with these ideas, for it seems to embody a conception of law in which the moral dimension of social life grounds the truth of legal propositions. Where law is understood overwhelmingly in terms of deliberately formulated rules, however, the systematic properties of the legal order are revealed as expressions of policy rather than of human nature; thus, legal doctrine comes to play a shadowy part in legal understanding. For, lacking determinate form, how can doctrinal propositions claim to possess authority? My discussion in this chapter, and the one following, will consider the implications of the positivist view for our understanding of the nature of law and of legal authority.

Doctrinal Science and Posited Rules

The emergence of doctrinal legal science represents an intellectual achievement of considerable importance and sophistication. Legal doctrine presents an especially valuable context for theoretical reflection, for it is the aspect of modern legal order in which the moral dimension of law is most apparent. Yet it is – for the same reason – also that aspect of law wherein an understanding of law's relationship to morality proves most elusive. The question of law's relationship to morality is most *clearly* addressed in the context of adjudication, for it is here that questions relating to the law's legitimacy and binding authority arise in their most distinctive forms: if it is sometimes necessary for a judge to reach beyond the settled law in order to produce judgment in a difficult case, then how can the authority of legal decisions be considered an aspect of their legitimacy?[1] The authority of judicial decisions would then seem to be associated with the official powers of a judge (conferred by rules of adjudication) rather than the reasons underpinning judicial opinions. This forces us to confront the possibility that judicial deliberations must focus on conventionally constructed rules and standards that might conflict with general principles of justice.

Yet a focus on adjudication, although it allows the basic questions to be posed in a clear-cut way, also considerably narrows the scope for informative answers: general questions pertaining to law's authority are unhelpfully bound up with the more specific rule-based authority of judges to render decisions. The question becomes whether the law can be said to exhibit principles of justice that are interpreted and expounded as they are applied; or whether legal judgments should be recognised as entailing moral choices about the applicability of legal rules and principles *in place of* general considerations of justice. However, if we turn our attention away from the adjudicative context in which the law is applied, and focus instead upon the context in which the law is expounded and studied, the basic questions imposed by the concern with authority and legitimacy are much less clearly posed and responded to.

When we consider the law from the perspective of the jurist rather than the judge, it becomes manifestly less easy to separate the formal authority of law from its perceived legitimacy. The common law system of doctrinal precedent is one in which scholarly exposition has generally involved the exploration of received ideas and concepts rather than the enumeration of settled rules. Hence it is difficult to separate the humanly-created aspect of law from the thought that doctrinal scholarship consists of the tracing out of principles and entitlements that need to be 'dug out' and interpreted from the mass of existing writings and ideas rather than consciously laid down or invented. Because the jurist aims to shed light on the whole mass of legislative rules and decided cases, his writings reveal perspectives on (and hence raise questions about) the principled aspects of law that are not evident from

---

1   On the relationship between authority and legitimacy generally see M. Weber, *Economy and Society*, G. Roth and C. Wittich (eds) (Berkeley, University of California Press, 1968), 31–38. Weber's notion of legitimacy is one of collective belief in the 'validity' (*Geltung*) or binding quality of a system of social order. It is in this sense that I use the term here.

a mere familiarity with statutes and cases.[2] Legal theory, then, might be viewed as the attempt to reconcile the posited, rule-based character of law with its principled, systematic qualities.

Doctrinal scholarship embodies both the human face of law *and* its moral, principled character: the activity of the legal scholar in interpreting and expounding the law preserves the intuition that law derives from intellectual endeavour, finding an ultimate source in the will, without forcing us to see it as the product of conscious decision. Legal theory in the present day is often considered to stand somewhat apart from doctrinal scholarship. The immediate concerns of the legal scholar are quite obviously not those of the philosopher, for the philosopher can be viewed as offering theoretical 'reconstructions' of the legal order rather than seeking the resolution of particular doctrinal controversies. Lawyers, in this view, apparently employ relatively settled ideas of what counts as sound doctrinal legal scholarship; the task of the legal philosopher is then to explore deep philosophical problems concerning the basis and significance of the ordinary lawyer's assumptions. By isolating and articulating the philosophical principles that underpin the ordinary lawyer's concepts and criteria, the legal philosopher attempts to reconstruct the legal order in terms of the moral and philosophical theory presupposed in the application of its rules, principles and doctrines. Such questions do not arise in legal practice: the ordinary lawyer confronts the legal order as a body of highly technical rules, definitions and distinctions, which require specialised techniques of interpretation and application. By applying these techniques, the lawyer can ply his or her trade without raising any of the deeper questions uncovered by the legal philosopher.

Where perspectives of this kind exist, the goal of legal theory consists not in the resolution of doctrinal disputes, but in uncovering their significance. The obvious bearing of law on our moral lives gives impetus to the formulation of philosophical accounts of the lawyer's assumptions. Accounts of legitimacy and authority are then revealed as having little to do with the substance of rules and doctrines, for it is the *form* of such arrangements which matters. This distinction between legal practice and the theory of law is perhaps most starkly evident in the writings of Jeremy Bentham.

In a long footnote to his discussion of common law, Bentham claims that '[a] rule of law must be predicated of some certain assemblage of words – it can never be predicated of a bare assemblage of naked ideas.'[3] The reason for this, he says, is that only a verbally formulated rule possesses the certainty associated with binding legal standards. The suggestion is that only posited rules, and not ideas that may be formed from them, can claim to be an authoritative statement of the law. One would struggle to find a view more remote from the model of legal science found in Grotius and the later doctrinal writers. In due course, Bentham recast this distinction as a distinction between 'authoritative' and 'unauthoritative' propositions of law: the former consist of the express declaration of a legislator; the latter express 'either

---

2   See in particular Blackstone's remarks on the virtues of a common legal education: *Commentaries of the Law of England* I, 32 (various editions).

3   J. Bentham, 'A Comment on the Commentaries', II.10 in *A Comment on the Commentaries and a Fragment on Government* (London, Athlone, 1977), 259n.

(first) the will of certain judges acting as such, or else, secondly, inferences drawn from what is supposed to have been such will, or thirdly, what is supposed to have been the will of a legislator.'[4]

Bentham apparently experienced considerable difficulty in articulating his exact meaning in regard to this distinction. Yet it is clear that much of its significance, for him, lay in the distinction between stipulated rules, on the one hand, and reports or explanations of those rules, on the other. Whereas stipulated rules consist of certain words, purported explanations or attempted interpretations of the written rules do not: here, the form of words used depends upon the commentator's subjective idea of the rule, and thus no part of his or her explanation or gloss can claim to be an authoritative proposition of law. At best, we have 'the shadow of the shadow of a shade' which is nevertheless 'worshipped as the substance.'[5] The natural law theories to be found in the writings of Grotius and his intellectual heirs (Locke and Blackstone especially) were then the product of a tendency to conflate the distinction between authoritative and unauthoritative legal propositions. For they incline us towards a view of the legal order as a systematic and internally coherent body of rules and principles underpinned by more general values, in a way that disguises the true form of law as a series of particular commands. The distinction between authoritative and unauthoritative propositions thus reflects a more general division between the projects of expository and censorial jurisprudence. The attempt to delineate the content of law beyond that stated by authoritative words will become the construction of justifications for applying a rule in a particular way according to 'underpinning' moral values. Hence, Bentham thought,

> ... it would have been better, had [unauthoritative propositions] never been characterised by the name of Law: had [they] never been characterised by any other name than that of Jurisprudence...[6]

Bentham's distinction between 'law' and 'jurisprudence' might be viewed as an apt characterisation of the lawyerly belief that black-letter rules are conceptually distinct from the justifying arguments and commentaries typically found in textbook accounts of the law. We think of textbooks as *describing* a particular area of the law, but not as an authoritative *source* of law: any authority possessed by the textbook is entirely derivative from the rules it purports to describe. At the same time, the attempt to give expression to the rules of the common law is seen as an intellectually challenging task, relying on complex and elusive considerations demanding great skill on the part of the legal scholar. Judgments of the court seldom embody a sharply delineated and definitive statement of the law, clearly distinguished from the various justificatory arguments and findings of fact present in the reported case. How, then, are such dimensions to doctrinal scholarship to be explained?

In the preceding chapter, I sought to explain the rise of doctrinal legal science as the product of a convergence between the classical forms of common law argument and the ideas of 'right' that can be found in the natural law theories of Grotius and

---

4   *Ibid.*, 260.
5   Bentham, *Of Laws in General* (London, Athlone, 1970), XV, 188.
6   Bentham (above, note 3), 261.

his intellectual successors. Because the common lawyers had focused on the forms and methods by which pleas were brought before the courts, the power of the court to provide a ruling on whether an alleged wrong was illegal received little sustained theoretical attention. The categories of *lex*, *ius*, *consuetudo curiae*, etc., represented an open-ended and shifting body of sources by reference to which lawyers could ground their legal arguments in relation to correctly presented pleas, as structured by the system of writs. The dominance of the writ system, both in practice and in legal education, ensured the long survival of the view of common law as a reasoning process rather than a body of established rights or rules.[7] It was through the influence of natural law that the categorical understandings of the common lawyers gradually coalesced into substantive doctrinal principles, thought of as establishing and protecting concrete rights. Such ideas encouraged the conception of law, not as a mere collection of procedural rules and remedies, but as a system of interlocking rights.

This intellectual shift required the development of a systematic jurisprudence: law came to be viewed, at least in ideal terms, as a system of horizontal and vertical patterns of entitlement in which every individual is portrayed as formally equal. The notion of formal equality entailed the assumption of universal postulates beyond the specific rules that outlined each person's *actual* entitlements. Once law is presented as a body of rational principles in this way, the black-letter rules cease to be thought of as customary ideas that come into focus only gradually and incompletely. They come instead to be regarded as being related to those principles deductively, and thus as possessing a definite content. Since the general principles can be interpreted in different ways according to the moral values and purposes they are held to serve, the idea of *canonical* rules becomes important. We will then be led to adopt something like Bentham's distinction between authoritative and unauthoritative legal propositions: for legal rules, we are tempted to think, are set apart from open-ended moral debate precisely in that they are ascertainable and final.

Political Stability and 'Top-Down' Authority

Views of this kind are often traced to a source in the writings of Thomas Hobbes. Hobbes is usually regarded as standing at the head of a 'positivist' tradition of juridical reflection in contrast to the 'natural law' tradition of Grotius. In a sense, it is wrong to *contrast* Hobbes's 'positivism' with natural law, since Hobbes also viewed municipal law as deriving from the 'law of nature'. Yet there is an important sense in which Hobbes and Grotius stand on opposite sides of a debate about the character and significance of doctrinal legal reasoning. The natural lawyers of the 17th century focused on *rights* first and foremost, devoting little theoretical attention to rules as the distinctive means by which a society might give effect to abstract entitlements, or regulate competing rights. Hobbes's philosophy, by contrast, articulates a jurisprudence based on posited rules as the principal means by which social life is regulated.

---

7 See M. Lobban, *The Common Law and English Jurisprudence*, 62–78; and my discussion in Chapter 3, above.

Writers before Hobbes had placed weight upon the idea of law as a body of rules for restraining human conduct. The Catholic natural lawyer Suarez, for example, had maintained that 'Binding and coercing [the will] is the chief, or very nearly the sole effect, of law.'[8] The same view was also reflected in the writings of English jurists intent on challenging the constitutional claims of Sir Edward Coke. John Selden, in his *History of Tythes* [1618], thus argued that the common law is merely a set of rules that govern 'things and persons, as they have reference to a common, not sacred, use or society established in a commonwealth.' These facts, coupled with the fact that Hobbes's arguments broadly concern the *character* of natural law rather than its existence, should serve to highlight that positivist understandings transcended the issue of natural law.

The distinguishing feature that separates Suarez and Grotius, on the one hand, from Selden and Hobbes, on the other, is the position and significance accorded to natural rights. Their opposing views on this subject stand as an effective definition of the two dominant attitudes to legality and politics in the jurisprudence of the present day. Whereas Grotius had viewed the natural state of mankind as one governed by an interlocking system of rights and duties established by the natural law, Hobbes (building on the work of Selden) famously contrasted right and law: 'For though they that speak of this subject use to confound *Ius* and *Lex*, *Right* and *Law*, yet they ought to be distinguished; because RIGHT consisteth in the liberty to do or to forebear, whereas LAW determineth and bindeth to one of them: so that Law and Right differ as much as Obligation and Liberty, which in one and the same matter are inconsistent.'[9] Grotian thought was characterised by a belief that, by abstracting from or removing the positive content of the legal order, one would discover an underlying rational framework organised around individual *sua*. For Hobbes, the absence of concrete legal rules and principles signalled a chaotic world of competing wills in which everyone has a right to everything, 'even to one another's body.'[10] For Selden, too, 'the law was inherently mutable and in some sense uncertain – it could never reflect an underlying set of rational principles.'[11] His activities as a Parliamentary MP demonstrate the different direction in which Selden's thoughts were moving vis-à-vis Grotius: in the course of a debate concerning the legality of the imposition of martial law by the king, Selden argued against Coke's position, which held that such an action was prevented by the common law, by asserting that questions of legality pertained only to the interpretation of statutes currently in force:

> We are not now to consider what shall be, but to state the question as the law is ... The same power that establishes the common law must establish martial law, and were it established here by act of parliament, it would be most lawful...[12]

---

8   F Suarez, *De Legibus* [1612], II.9.1.

9   T. Hobbes, *Leviathan* [1651], R. Tuck (ed.) (Cambridge, Cambridge University Press, 1991), I.14, 91.

10   *Ibid.*

11   R. Tuck, *Philosophy and Government*, 209.

12   W. Bidwell (ed.) *Proceedings in Parliament* (New Haven, Yale University Press, 1997), vol 2 (17 March–19 April), 574–576. See also Tuck (above, note 11), 211.

The political disagreement between Coke and Selden reflected a deeper jurisprudential disagreement concerning the nature of common law and legal certainty. Coke, like other jurists of his generation, expressed the hope that the disorganised appearance of the common law was a mere surface phenomenon, concealing a deeper order and coherence at the level of abstract principle: 'I affirm it constantly, that the law is not uncertain *in abstracto* but *in concreto*, and that the uncertainty thereof is *hominis vitium*, not *professionis* ... [A proper report] doth set open the windows of the law to let in that gladsome light whereby the right reason of the rule (the beauty of the law) may be clearly discerned.'[13] Selden (in the course of an attack on Aristotle) argued on the contrary that there are no universal principles of morality that are accessible to all men in the light of their natural reason: the only principle capable of universal acceptance was the need for men to obey a superior will with the ability to make laws and inflict punishments for transgression.[14] Legal certainty could only come about through *posited* laws.

The thoughts of Grotius (on the one hand) and of Selden and Hobbes (on the other) can be conceived as opposing tendencies within a modernist juridical outlook. Modernism, in this context, refers to the intellectual shift towards a descending model of legal authority. Classical juristic understandings rested on the assumption that the possibility of governance through law was dependent upon that law being, in some sense, *our* law; that is, as embodying shared standards of conduct that emerge, not from 'above' by the arbitrary fiat of a political overlord, but from the shared attitudes and understandings of the people to whom the laws apply. The rejection of Aristotelian moral philosophy in favour of a form of moral voluntarism rendered such views deeply problematic, for the voluntarist understandings placed human beings with diverse interests and agendas at the centre of the moral universe. Law ceased to be regarded as the expression of universally accepted moral truths, and instead came to be seen as an instrument through which the activities of individuals with competing interests and needs might be regulated and coordinated. The foundations of legal authority were instead sought elsewhere: either in the system of rights and principles that derive from the natural law, or else from the state itself, in the form of legislated commands emanating from a sovereign will. Political and social life had come to be regarded as something governed *by* law rather than *through* law.

Hobbes, like Grotius and other natural law writers, based his account of political origins on the thought that human beings possess natural rights to their own preservation and survival. Despite this common starting point, Hobbes was to view the presence of natural rights as giving rise, not to doctrinal legal science, but to a conception of legal authority as the product of artifice, and of law as the creature of the state. 'The Right of Nature', Hobbes proclaimed,

> is the Liberty each man hath, to use his own power, as he will himself, for the preservation of his own Nature; that is to say, of his own Life; and consequently of doing any thing, which in his own Judgment, and Reason, he shall conceive to be the aptest means thereunto.[15]

---

13 E. Coke, *9th Repts.*
14 See Tuck (above, note 11), 215.
15 T. Hobbes, *Leviathan* (above, note 9) I.14, 91.

This way of understanding natural rights suggested a very different underpinning for civil authority from that proposed by Grotius and his intellectual heirs. Grotius's own theory was based on the view that the law of nature demanded the mutual recognition of basic rights possessed by human beings, both to self-preservation and to the material means to sustain life. Natural laws thus simultaneously permit human action and set limits to permissible action in ways that allow for collective flourishing.[16] Insofar as the natural law reflected man's social nature, the means by which lasting forms of social order could be achieved were not thought to be fully distinct from the ends in view: many forms of social order, from primitive customary orders to complex totalitarian or market societies, might develop as manifestations of this nature as long as basic rights continued to receive recognition and forms of human flourishing remained possible. But although human sociability might be given expression in different ways, the Grotian theory clearly presupposed the existence of basic agreement (through rational reflection) on a framework of moral ideas by which peaceful forms of association could develop.

The philosophical standpoint developed by Hobbes had no place for such a suggestion; for, although he shared with Grotius the idea that everybody would recognise a basic right of each person to preserve and defend themselves, he argued that such a recognition could do nothing to prevent fundamental conflicts of belief about the actual circumstances in which defensive actions are justified.[17] Accordingly, Hobbes interpreted such conflicts as creating conditions of permanent and pervasive conflict in which each person must rely on their own judgments as to how their preservation is to be secured. The recognition of this necessity can thus be interpreted as the possession by every person of 'a Right to every thing; even to one another's body.'[18]

This use of the language of rights is in some ways misleading, for Hobbes's assertion that 'right' signifies an area of liberty wholly outside that of 'law' makes it unclear whether he intended to describe a juridical situation at all. The conflicts Hobbes has in mind are those of belief. Our moral judgments, he believed, were rooted not in any external moral qualities of actions or events, but in desire itself, and thus claims about the good (or evil) 'are ever used with relation to the person that useth them', there being 'no common Rule of Good or Evil, to be taken from the nature of the objects themselves…'.[19] It followed that specific implementations of the right of self-preservation are incapable of being characterised as 'just' or 'unjust' in any significant sense: 'To this war of every man against every man, this also is consequent; that nothing can be Unjust. The notions of Right and Wrong, Justice and Injustice have there no place. Where there is no common Power, there is no Law; where no Law, no Injustice.'[20]

---

16 See H. Grotius, *De Iure Belli ac Pacis*, Prolegomena, 8–9, and the discussion in Chapter 3, above.

17 See R. Tuck 'Introduction' in *Leviathan* (above n 9) xxix; also Hobbes, *Leviathan* I.13, 89–90.

18 Hobbes, *Leviathan* I.14, 91.

19 *Leviathan* I.6, 39.

20 See *Leviathan* I.13, 90. I have suggested elsewhere that this reading of Hobbes needs some qualification: see S. Coyle and K. Morrow, *The Philosophical Foundations of Environmental Law – Property, Rights and Nature* (Hart Publications, 2004) chapter 2.

Hobbes believed that the sole means of escape from the conditions of boundless conflict lay in the realisation that each person's beliefs about the morality of their actions are products of the imagination and possess no foundation in reality. His thought is thus underpinned by a form of moral voluntarism more extreme than that of Grotius. The fact that each person holds different and opposing beliefs about justice and the good should indicate to the wise that their assumptions are no more secure than anyone else's. The possibility of stable social relations in such conditions depends upon the joint relinquishing of powers of moral judgment, and the passing of those powers onto a judge or arbiter 'whom men disagreeing shall by consent set up, and make his sentence the Rule thereof.'[21] Hobbes's proposed understanding of political authority is based on the priority of form over content. Since there is no secure basis for ethical reflection from which shared moral perspectives might emerge, law must take the form of explicitly prescribed rules laid down by some recognised authority. 'It is not Wisdom, but Authority that makes a law.'[22]

This approach to the problem of political origins suggests a different, more formal understanding of legal authority from that proposed by Grotius. By viewing natural rights as belonging to individuals *prior* to the emergence of a stable social existence, Grotius had encouraged a view of rights as an intrinsic part of human nature independently of their propensity to foster or subvert the good. The Grotian picture was one in which rights do not *derive* from law, but rather *ground* law.[23] Yet the theological premises of Grotius's argument, which aligned human utility with the good, give substance and direction to law insofar as the legal order must promote and sustain basic rights. The humanly-created aspect of law was thus explained as one facet of a natural jurisprudence grounded in substantive moral principles and understandings of the good. Hobbes essentially detaches the legal order from these theological underpinnings, for Hobbes viewed 'the good' in terms of desire: by being 'moved towards' certain objects (that is, desiring them) we are led to view them as 'good'. Thus, it is wrong to think of our desires as inclining us towards that which is good for us (as in Grotius); instead, we think of objects as 'good' *because* we are moved towards them.[24]

The 'unceasing motion' of human minds had been a commonplace of moral philosophy from the medieval period through to Grotius; yet this was explained by human striving for an ultimate good (communion with God) that could not be fully realised in this world. For Hobbes, on the other hand, the absence of motion meant, not the attainment of a state of wisdom or ultimate good, but rather inexistence: thus 'there is no such *finis ultimis* (utmost aim) or *summum bonum* (greatest good)' upon which the laws of the polity can be structured. Instead, we are invited to think of the binding force of legal rules as being a matter of their origin and of the fact of their constituting authoritative, clear-edged propositions that each person consents to

---

21 *Leviathan* I.6.39.

22 Hobbes, *Dialogue Between a Philosopher and a Student, Of the Common Laws of England*, in A. Cromartie and Q. Skinner (eds) *Thomas Hobbes: Writings on Common Law and Hereditary Right* (Clarendon Press, 2005), 10.

23 See Schneewind, *The Invention of Autonomy*, 80.

24 *Leviathan*, I.6, 39.

accept as a shared basis for social order in the absence of agreed moral perspectives. Law might then be viewed, not as a body of ideas expressive of shared conceptions of justice, but instead as a framework of imposed rules, entitlements and permissions which make the joint pursuit of competing conceptions of the good life possible.

Hobbes's political philosophy is thus the intellectual ancestor of positivist theories of law in which the humanly-created aspect of the legal order represents a distinct dimension to that of systematic doctrinal understandings.

Posited Rules and Formal Authority

Both Hobbes and Grotius viewed the law, in different ways, as the product of artifice. Recognition of the law's humanly-created character places questions of legal authority and legitimacy at the heart of political thought, for we are then forced to explain how the inequalities of power implicit in the idea of 'law' (and sustained by legal institutions) are derivable from an initial postulate of human equality. Jurisprudential writers have accordingly tended to place Hobbes's views within an 'authoritarian' tradition of political thought, which is opposed to the 'liberal' writings of the Grotian tradition. As we have seen, such views are somewhat misleading: Grotius was viewed by many as an apologist of absolutist or unlimited government, whereas the notion of a 'liberal' society or tradition of thought did not fully emerge until the 19th century. It is in differing visions of the *form* of the legal order, rather than in understandings of law's instrumental significance, that Hobbes's views are most clearly distinguished from those of Grotius.

The juristic thought of the 17th century marked a significant departure from medieval understandings of human nature, which derived their form from the doctrines of Aristotle. Aristotelian moral science sought to explain human beings in terms of the possession of a rational nature. One might then expect that nature to be reflected in that set of social institutions and practices (the law) that embody the most theorised and fully articulated understandings of human social life. The formality of Hobbes's conception of legal authority may then be presented as a consequence of his more thoroughgoing rejection of Aristotelian thought. The juridical character of 17th century moral thought had given rise to a conception of human nature that was independent of particular times, places and circumstances. Grotius had grounded the basic properties of human nature in natural rights: the individual is defined by the *suum*, and the sociable character of human beings is explained in terms of the rational desire to sustain and protect basic interests. The human character is then a product, not of one's predetermined place in an externally determined order, but of one's *choices*. A person's choices must of course be exercised against the background of existing arrangements, which are themselves the outcome of social choice, and which may limit one's capacity for autonomous decision in various ways. Thus, the law, as the outcome of a complex history of collective choices, may be viewed as the expression of a society's collective understandings of justice and the common good. Although law might take various forms, it could nevertheless be said to 'reflect' aspects of human social nature. Hobbes derived his understanding of human nature from an initial hypothesis of absolute freedom rather than from natural rights.[25] A science of law could then only hope to determine the *formal* characteristics of legal order, for the substance of legal rules must, in this view, derive entirely from conventional agreement: the 'rationality' exhibited by human nature being no longer determined according to some ultimate end, but becoming simply a matter of the instrumental connecting of means to practically desired ends.

By viewing natural law in essentially instrumental terms, Hobbes was to give expression to a form of juristic scholarship in which the *form* of legal rules, as willed commands, is distinct from their substantive embodiment of certain interests or social goals. The significance of legal doctrine was thereby diminished, for doctrinal propositions consisted of mere general impressions or ideas formed from the legislated rules. From the existence of legal rules of a given kind nothing could be inferred about human nature, as the law consists of rules that are *imposed* upon human beings in order to create or maintain social order where otherwise there would exist merely a chaos of conflicting moral intuitions and claims.

The view of law as a body of formal, source-based rules is not without problems, however. We need such rules, on this view, because of the nature and characteristics of the modern state. Modern society consists of large and relatively mobile populations engaged in economic and social relationships demanding complex modes of governance. Large societies are incapable of otherwise reaching agreement on basic norms that could serve as a foundation for social order. Each person pursues his own narrow self-interests, and the endless diversity that exists between personal conceptions of the good would exclude the possibility of developing settled rules for addressing shared moral concerns in abstraction from the circumstances of particular conflicts. Suppose we accept the view that, in the absence of authoritative, black-letter rules, the social world would be characterised by a chaotic struggle between subjective understandings and intentions. How can precisely stated posited rules bring about social order in such conditions?

There are two distinct senses in which explicitly formulated rules might be said to offer precision. The rules could be 'precise' in the sense of possessing an authoritative verbal form, or they could exhibit precision in *applying* in a fully determined and unambiguous way to the particular circumstances of each disagreement of a certain kind. No realistic set of imposed rules could be said to exhibit precision in the latter sense: the legal rules of a large or complex society inevitably focus on types of behaviour rather than specific actions, so that the application of a rule depends not upon 'matching' a set of facts to precisely worded descriptions enshrined in the rule, but proceeds instead from understandings and appraisals of action in the light of the purposes or policies the rule is thought to serve. Yet, for this reason, the possession of an authoritative verbal form is in itself insufficient for reconciling divergent points of view about the demands of justice in specific situations. Because no two situations are entirely identical, the application of general rules to particular circumstances involves the tracing out of quite fine differences between otherwise similar sets of facts in the light of the values that the rule promotes. But it is precisely

---

25 The 'right of nature' described by Hobbes, as previously noted, signified mere liberty rather than entitlement.

these differences that disputing parties will seize upon to justify their divergent understandings of the rule, for their argument can be represented as one concerning the *relevant* respects in which one case can be distinguished from others in the light of the rule's purpose. Verbally formulated rules are thus just as likely to amplify interpretative disagreements as to resolve them.

The Hobbesian state of nature is often taken to exhibit these difficulties in an especially potent form. Outside the artificial bonds of civil society, Hobbes argued, men stand in relationships of 'continual jealousies, and in the state and position of gladiators; having their weapons pointing, and their eyes fixed on one another.'[26] In a world where each person poses an immediate threat to everyone else, shared interests and beliefs cannot establish themselves; for how could we communicate basic desires to one another when the only occasions for human contact involve tense face-offs and fights for survival? People in such circumstances would remain unreadable to each other, for our grasp of the beliefs and motivations of others would be forever formed from our private interpretations and the struggle for survival at all costs. The very possibility of men setting up by consent a ruler or judge, whose sentence will become a source of rules for governing conduct, is undercut by the very conditions that make such rules necessary.[27]

Suppose such an authority laid down rules for regulating conduct in this way. Shared interpretations depend upon a reasonable degree of uniformity in experience and attitudes, which allow for the possibility of shared understandings of how human beings adapt their conduct to the world around them. Without some measure of convergence on basic concerns, rules seeking to regulate conduct in specific ways would remain completely unintelligible. We can see this if we contemplate a rule forbidding children from smoking tobacco. In the absence of shared understandings, how might such a rule be regarded? Does it, for example, mean that children are allowed to chew cigars, since chewing is different from smoking? Does 'smoking' refer to inhaling, or does it merely imply setting fire to something – so that children are free to purchase cigarettes and inhale their fumes so long as they do not themselves light the cigarette? By 'tobacco' does the rule mean to refer only to actual tobacco leaves, so that children are forbidden from setting fire to tobacco plants (perhaps out of a concern for those plants) but are otherwise permitted to light and consume tobacco products? Does 'smoking' include the ingestion of the smoke from *other* people's cigarettes, so that infringements of the rule may occur accidentally? Indeed, does the rule apply only where *more than one child* smokes tobacco at a given time?

---

26 *Leviathan* I.13, 90.

27 For one thing, it is entirely unclear how the denizens of the state of nature could evolve a shared language through which such sentences would be understood. Shared interpretations of vocal sounds and utterances also depend upon some collective sense of how human beings perceive and understand the world around them. Without a shared language, of course, it would seem that human beings lack the ability to formulate reasoned propositions about what the laws of nature demand. See Hobbes, *Leviathan* I.13, 89.

There is, in principle, no limit to the number of conflicting interpretations we could make of rules such as this one.[28] The reason why we are able to disregard such interpretations lies in the shared background of understandings and concerns within which individuals in a stable community think and move: although we will inevitably differ from one another to a degree over the moral status of children, issues relating to liberty etc., we share enough in the way of ordinary concerns and ideas so as to make the moral conceptions at work in the rule intelligible. We know, for example, that the rule serves to protect children from the consequences of a reduced decision-making capacity, and to promote their health and wellbeing in the face of avoidable harm. We know this, because we share basic understandings of what children are like, and because we value health and recognise that a free choice is not always appropriate or desirable. Without such understandings, expressly created rules contribute nothing to an orderly social existence.

The failure of authoritative, deliberately posited rules to bring about stable social relations by virtue of their supposed 'precision' may lead us to contemplate another way in which expressly created rules might supply grounds of social order in a morally divided world, for instead of bringing about a convergence in attitudes and concerns, such rules might be seen as offering neutral standpoints within which various, possibly conflicting visions of the good life can be formulated and pursued. Law, in this view, consists of a framework of rules and principles that prescribe no particular form for the good life, but instead establish pockets of right and liberty within which individuals are free to engage in their own projects and pursuits.

This proposal initially seems more promising than one that focuses on the precision with which deliberately created rules are expressed. Whereas the latter approach conceives of legal rules as bringing interpretative disagreements about the good to an end, the former seeks instead to contain such disagreements within the reasonable boundaries set by the rules. Indeed, the rule-based neutrality view need not be premised on a view of law as consisting of *posited* rules at all: we might, if we wished, think of morality or reason as suggesting an ideal distribution of entitlement and liberty under which each person can freely pursue his or her own ends without undermining the efforts of others.[29] The circumstances of disagreement from which the need for positive rules of law arises, nevertheless reveal rule-based neutrality as a particularly attractive ideal in which to enfold a positivist view of law. A chaos of competing views and ideas would prevent any widespread recognition of neutral standpoints; yet the explicit creation of formal rules for peaceful social interaction would both furnish such standpoints *and* reveal the law's moral neutrality.

We might wonder whether, in the end, rule-based neutrality provides any better reasons for embracing legal positivism than the view that deliberately imposed rules create 'precision'. For rule-based neutrality to work, the rules of the legal order must not be constitutive of any particular form of the good, but must instead bring about conditions that facilitate the pursuit of diverse conceptions of the good by individuals

---

28 For further discussion, see N.E. Simmonds, 'Between Positivism and Idealism', 50 *Cambridge LJ* (1991) 311–318.

29 See, for example, Kant's 'Metaphysical Principles of the Science of Right', in Kant, *Philosophy of Law*, W. Hastie trans. (T & T Clarke, 1887).

who disagree about what the moral good requires. Suppose we think of a conception of the good life as being a matter of what each individual rationally prefers. Since there are no obvious means of establishing which set of rational preferences are the best, the laws of the polity must ensure that each person remains free and unmolested in their pursuit of their own preferences in their own way.

There are at least two difficulties with this suggestion. It is, first of all, unclear whether this ideal is really any different from one of 'precision': saying that legal rules must not allow any one conception of the good life to dominate over others is *the same* as saying that the rules must not be capable of interpretation in the light of subjective conceptions of the good. As we have seen, however, the application of general rules to specific circumstances of disagreement is precisely an occasion for the emergence of rival interpretations of the rules in the light of the moral conceptions and experiences of disputing parties. The ideal of 'neutrality' is thus of no more use than the ideal of 'precision' in bringing such disputes within a firm regulatory framework.

Suppose it were possible for legal rules to establish precise, determinate standards, which would allow them to express moral neutrality in this way. The ideal of rule-based neutrality would then face a second, and seemingly insurmountable, objection. Each person, on this view, formulates and pursues their private conception of the good life within the boundaries permitted by the rules. The formulation of each person's rational preferences therefore takes place within constraints and limits imposed by authority. Neutrality demands that the formulation of preferences remains independent of the content of legal rules, for the presence of causal links between rules and preferences would undermine moral neutrality. Yet we do not think of individuals as plucking preferences out of thin air: rather, we think of preferences as making sense only within the concrete possibilities established by a way of life. Since the framework of legal rules is instrumental in determining the form of life within the polity, a person's preferences are never fully independent of the rules that make a shared social existence possible.[30]

The rule-based neutrality view overlooks the constitutive role played by legal rules in shaping the social life of the polity. A person's preferences relate to the choices that can be made about different paths in life. Law inevitably shapes such choices, by establishing limits to permissible conduct. Consider the rule banning children from smoking: even if we share enough in the way of cultural understandings to comprehend the meaning of such an injunction, how can it be presented as a neutral standpoint in a world in which concerned welfarists live alongside radical libertines? In such a world, disagreements about the positive rules would force the jurist to seek out 'neutral' interpretations in ever more abstract and recondite forms. An image of rationality in which each individual adopts a free-floating attitude of 'preferring', within the constraints established by posited rules, is thus of no value to an understanding of the complex relationship between law and the web of social life. This is because we think of each person as formulating and making choices from a

---

30 Hobbes's philosophy is thus underpinned by the idea that I shall come to desire things only to the extent that my desires allow me 'to exist with others who have a similarly limited set of preferences'; see Schneewind, (above, note 23), 90.

position of immersion *within* the ordinary meanings and shared understandings that the rules perpetuate.[31]

Positivism and Statism

The attempt to understand law in terms of formal authority was a response to the circumstances of disagreement that characterise the modern world. The problem of peaceful coexistence in such a world was the problem of identifying neutral standpoints that could serve as a basis for social order. Hobbes, and later legal positivists, conceived of deliberately created standards as the unique means by which a peaceful and stable coexistence could be achieved. Law, for such thinkers, could not embody a source of reflection on human nature; the substance of law must instead derive from a 'logic of the will'.[32] Moral philosophy was thus increasingly conceived by such writers in terms of the search for 'scientific' principles of human society in which the 'logic' of human choices is explained by reference to general motivating forces, such as pleasure and pain.[33]

It is in the writings of the Utilitarians that the most sustained attempt to carry out this project can be found. Yet our sense of the importance of figures such as Bentham and James Mill is in large part a consequence of histories of morality written in the 19th century: the monumental three-volume work by Sir Leslie Stephen on *The English Utilitarians*, devoted to Bentham, James Mill and John Stuart Mill, providing just one example. Stephen begins the work by expressing his intention to give an account of the work of 'a group of men who for three generations had a conspicuous influence upon English thought and political action.'[34] He then goes on to state that 'Jeremy Bentham, James Mill and John Stuart Mill were successively their leaders...' It is unlikely that the intellectual contemporaries of those writers would have agreed with Stephen's assessment. During the 18th century it was not Bentham, but the influential Anglican divine William Paley who was the dominant figure in English Utilitarianism.[35] Paley did not view the principle of utility as providing a purely secular basis for a science of legislation, but rather as a central element of a metaphysical defence of contemporary political and clerical arrangements as reflective of divine law.[36]

The idea that human nature could be reduced to metaphysically ungrounded principles deriving from a 'science' of motivation, and that such principles could

---

31 A similar argument can be levelled at Ronald Dworkin's interpretivism: see Simmonds, 'Between Positivism and Idealism' (above, note 28), 325.

32 J. Bentham, *An Introduction to the Principles of Morals and Legislation* [1789] J.H. Burns and H.L.A. Hart (eds) (Oxford, Clarendon Press, 1970), 8.

33 Bentham, 'A Table of the Springs of Action', in *Deontology*, A. Goldworth (ed.) (Oxford, Clarendon Press, 1983).

34 L. Stephen, *The English Utilitarians* (London, 1900), vol 1, Introductory.

35 See T.P. Schofield, 'A Comparison of the Moral Theories of William Paley and Jeremy Bentham', 11 *The Bentham Newsletter* (1987), 4–22.

36 See W. Paley, *The Principles of Moral and Political Philosophy* (London, 1785), esp 402ff.

then be used as a basis for understanding legal and political life, was rejected in Bentham's own lifetime. Writers such as T.B. Macaulay perceived clearly the philosophical method of the Utilitarians: 'Certain propensities of human nature are assumed; and from these premises the whole science of politics is synthetically deduced!' Such a method was 'utterly unfit for moral and political discussions', being occasionally serviceable for philosophical truth only 'by accident'.[37] In his review of Mill's *Essays*, Macaulay concluded that 'it is utterly impossible to deduce the science of government from the principles of human nature.'

Macaulay's own remarks demonstrate the extent to which classical ethical ideas had declined as a basis for moral philosophy by the 19th century, for – in rejecting principles of human nature as a foundation for political reflection – he neglects the possibility that human nature may itself be reflected in the dominant practices and institutions of the polity. Both Utilitarians and their rivals moved within a positivistic conception of legal science, in which the laws and institutions of the polity are conceived in terms of a descending model of political authority. The concept of the 'state' itself became more formal, coming to be regarded as a set of institutions with law-making power distinct from the private 'Estates' of the monarch, aristocracy and clerisy. In the political life of earlier ages,

> the agencies of 'the state' did not simply impose themselves on 'society' ... In [the 18th century], 'the state' had more presence as a nexus of shared experience, history, culture, and language rather than as the automatic, predictable functioning of bureaucratic agencies.[38]

The moral historians of Stephen's age no longer sought to explain a form of political life in which 'the effectiveness of central government agencies depended on, as much as it caused, the internalisation of values in the localities.'[39] Instead, the views of the 19th century philosophers increasingly gave expression to a polity in which legal rules embody the attempt to impose a degree of order on an otherwise formless social void.

Despite the problems with that suggestion, we may feel reluctant to give up altogether the idea that posited rules are in some sense necessary for the coordination and regulation of conflicting desires and interests. In conditions of prolonged controversy about the moral good, customary practices and local understandings will seem to offer too thin a basis for stable social relations, and the idea of natural rights will fail to stabilise expectations significantly in the absence of broad agreement as to how such rights should be traced out. Positive law might then be thought of not as a creative force, bringing about agreement through the imposition of rigid prescriptions on an otherwise shapeless social void, but as an instrument through which existing expectations and interpretations are reflected and refined.

---

37 T.B. Macaulay, Review of James Mill's *Essays on Government*, quoted in J.C.D. Clarke, *English Society 1660–1832*, 2nd edn (Cambridge, Cambridge University Press, 2000), 161.

38 Clarke (above, note 37), 42.

39 *Ibid.*

A proposal of this kind requires substantial revisions to the positivist notion of formal authority. Suppose we were to turn the Hobbesian argument around: black-letter rules do not forge social consensus out of the chaos of competing moral visions, but instead prevent the breakdown of shared beliefs to the point where a chaotic anarchy of subjective claims threatens to engulf us all. Such rules cannot exist *apart* from shared understandings and beliefs, but they provide a focal point through which beliefs and understandings can be articulated and reinforced. This necessitates the recognition of the social world as something other than an anarchy of conflicting subjective visions. But such a recognition renders a purely *formal* conception of legal authority impossible: for it demands that we view many ordinary legal rules as being tied to underlying practices that treat the rules as expressive of the broad moral ideals that are implicit in our social relationships and dealings. Some degree of convergence in ethical judgments is a prerequisite for social relations of any kind. We might then think of the rules as offering further stability and refinement to ordinary expectations where reasonable people disagree about the precise implications of informal understandings.

Legal positivism of this latter kind is captured neither by the thought that posited rules establish rigid and precise standards, nor by the idea that legal rules exhibit moral neutrality. Positivism of this kind is best understood as the suggestion that the law of a complex and morally diverse society must consist largely of rules articulated by 'the state': either in the form of general legislative frameworks devised to secure some collective advantage or goal, or through the binding judgments of courts in the adjudication of private interests and claims. A statist conception of law is thus indicative of a changing conception of the function of law. Law is no longer viewed simply as a collection of received procedures and remedies for redressing private wrongs, but as an instrument for the general regulation of private life and for the pursuit and realisation of social goals. As the possibilities of law's regulatory function manifest themselves within the scholarly imagination, doctrinal legal rules are less easily presented as crystallised judicial customs, their content increasingly seen instead as determined by official practices of recognition.

The shift towards a statist conception of law entails certain assumptions about official determinations of the content of legal rules. One persistent source of philosophical debate in modern jurisprudence is thus the notion of a 'rule of recognition'. In some respects, the rule of recognition offers a means of clarifying the legal order's place in intellectual life, which is not vastly different in scope and purpose from the attempts of Bentham and earlier positivists to *define* 'law': exercises of political power constitute a permanent source of moral disagreement among the members of a polity, but (the positivist argues) our moral deliberations are considerably clarified by an understanding of which forms of political interference have the force of law.

What begins as a concern to clarify procedures and forms of action may then lead to a more general concern to distinguish 'law' and 'morality'. If a rule of recognition is to produce such clarity, it might be thought, then it must establish criteria of legal validity that do not *inevitably* appeal to moral values: the criteria of validity that determine the law within a jurisdiction *may* include reference to moral criteria, but do not *necessarily* so refer. Hence, many legal philosophers have sought to clarify the nature of law not by sustained reflection on the role of law within the political life of the polity, but through argument about the properties of the rule of recognition itself. Jurisprudential reflection has thus come to centre on the issue of whether or not the process of 'recognising' the validity of legal rules is inherently a moral one.

Concern about law's moral nature is of course hardly a modern invention. The political writers and jurists of the Exclusion era constantly feared the development of 'arbitrary' or absolute government: the fear that the monarch, as the supreme source of legal and political power, would seek to rule without Parliament and institute political and religious reforms fundamentally at odds with the established customs and moral life of the realm. Opposition to the idea of arbitrary rule received expression through the belief that the country was governed by an ancient constitution that safeguarded individual rights and established limits to the use of political power throughout the polity. Jurists such as Coke and Sir John Davies thus famously argued that the common law derives not from monarchical authority but from 'immemorial custom.'[40] Such works embodied the idea that the binding quality and ruling force of law in some sense emerge from the characteristics and practices of the people to whom it applies.[41] The possibility of law was thus thought to depend upon the positive law being underpinned by practices that treat those rules as expressive of a moral position drawn from the social life and customs of the realm.

Within modern legal philosophy, the fears of the Exclusion-era writers might be thought to demonstrate the contingency of the association between law and morality: by deliberating and opposing the idea of arbitrary government, early-modern thinkers displayed their awareness of absolutist rule as a *possible* form of social order. Hence (we might be led to suppose), the rule of law does not inevitably depend upon conformity to certain moral values, but may just as easily rest upon the shoulders of a powerful monarch whose very word is law. There are at least two good reasons for denying the validity of such suppositions.

In the first place, it is far from clear that arbitrary government in the intended sense *is* a possible source of stable social order. Where repressive, totalitarian or absolutist forms of government exist, they generally have to be sustained by a significant ruling class to whose values and interests the laws appeal. Not only will laws require interpretation in the light of those values and preferences, the legal order must also continue to regulate the wider moral, political and economic life of the polity. A system of laws is thus dependent upon the maintenance of existing social ties in respect of commerce, labour, religion, the recognition of property and familial relationships, and so on. An authoritarian regime with an aggressive agenda

---

40 See Coke, *Institutes ii*, 7. See also Davies, *Irish Reports* (London, 1674). For a classic study of ancient constitutionalism, see J.G.A. Pocock, *The Ancient Constitution and the Feudal Law: A Study of English Historical Thought in the Seventeenth Century* (Cambridge, Cambridge University Press, 1987).

41 This belief constituted the main strand of Whig opposition thought throughout the late 17th and early 18th centuries. Parallel notions of social contract and popular sovereignty were sharply distinguished from it, and were largely confined to the margins of British political life. For a useful, although not wholly reliable, account of Exclusion-era political thought, see L. Ward, *The Politics of Liberty in England and Revolutionary America* (Cambridge, Cambridge University Press, 2004). For a rather different take, see Clark (above, note 37).

for social change will inevitably modify *some* established ties, but it must ensure basic continuity with previous patterns of social practice if it is to create a lasting form of social order. A system of posited laws (even under 'arbitrary government') must therefore be rooted in widely acknowledged social practices that treat those laws as expressive of certain moral ideals. Lasting forms of social order thus do not invite classification as 'law' *because* they conform to certain semantic criteria, but because they foster or perpetuate certain social and political practices which, in the case of absolutist regimes, allow the ruling caste to maintain dominance over the repressed majority.

The second point is that the forms of arbitrary government to which the legal philosopher may appeal in support of the law/morality distinction do not represent the typical form of governance in the real world. The goal of jurisprudential reflection is to understand the role of law *within* the political life of the polity. The proper focus for philosophical inquiry is thus upon the forms of legal order most central to that life.[42] Since it is typically *governance* rather than 'repression' as such, which constitutes the point of law, philosophical reflection is best aided by concentration on instances of legal order which seek to promote stability and peaceful forms of human flourishing rather than those that undermine or suppress them. Analytical philosophers may, of course, develop and pursue conceptions of 'law' in ways that are independent of particular political goals and ideals; but they do not thereby clarify law's role within political life: rather they obscure it. Notions such as 'law', 'right', 'justice', etc., do not constitute self-standing ideas but form part of the canon of political ideas through which we understand and reflect upon our form of life. The idea that we can achieve an enlightening understanding of law prior to immersion in substantive moral and political forms, is a chimera indeed.[43]

Statism and its Limits

The statist idea of law came about as a means of addressing the problem of coordination and stability in conditions of moral pluralism and social disagreement. Early positivists such as Hobbes and Bentham are best understood as proposing a conception of law as an instrument for stabilising and securing moral consensus rather than suggesting the legal order's complete separation from morality. Nevertheless, the move towards a more formal conception of law's authority is bound to invite progression beyond a view of the law's refining function, to one in which legal rules are viewed as modifying and supplanting existing moral practices (as is the case in Bentham's jurisprudence). Law accordingly comes to be regarded as an instrument for the pursuit and realisation of social goals, not a reflection of the moral nature

---

42 Typical or central, that is, as opposed to merely most prevalent; although one would obviously expect forms of governance that are most central to the realisation of a form of social life to be also most prevalent among instances of that form of life.

43 See my discussion in Chapter 1, above. One is reminded of Jeremy Waldron's suggestion that many latter-day legal theorists seem intent on defending a position *called* 'legal positivism', no matter what that position turns out to be. See J. Waldron, *Law and Disagreement* (Oxford, Oxford University Press, 1999), 166.

of human beings. Lacking a fixed moral 'essence', the law instead seems to consist of technical rules of variable content. The central problem of jurisprudence then becomes that of explaining how law can be both reflective and at the same time constitutive of social order. I propose to defer a full discussion of this problem to Chapter 5; but I shall offer here some initial thoughts as a background to that later discussion.

The same circumstances of disagreement that propel the idea of posited black-letter rules into the centre of legal thought also render accounts of law's binding authority deeply problematic. It is not easy to offer systematic answers to these contradictory features of the legal order without presupposing either a narrow and constraining positivism or increasingly abstract versions of moral idealism. It is nonetheless possible to offer the following tentative suggestions.

(1) The law of a complex market society is no longer capable of being viewed as a body of customs reflecting shared practices and expectations; rather, law inevitably comes to be seen as consisting largely in a system of imposed rules which *restructure* expectations. A statist conception of law thus makes it impossible to understand legitimacy as deriving from the thought that the law is in some sense 'our' law. Instead (in the absence of any other obvious expedient), legitimacy becomes a matter of the law's conformity to standards of fairness, equality and the protection of individual rights etc., which exist in abstraction from the ordinary contexts of clashing understandings in which they figure.

This is inclined to suggest a picture in which the law is *either* seen as serving universal moral values which lie beyond the expressly formulated rules; or else as establishing conventions to which each person is subject in the same way, no matter what their personal status: the legal rules that apply to young hooligans are the same as those that apply to little old ladies.

The former view encourages the legal scholar to seek out the meaning of equality and fairness at ever-increasing levels of abstraction from the black-letter rules that are said to exhibit those virtues. Legal rules are then conceived as giving no more than partial expression to moral ideas that stand in need of elaboration in the light of more general ethical understandings and ideas of justice. Accordingly, the jurist's task is seen as that of offering an account of the general theory of justice which underpins a body of black-letter rules. Unfortunately, the corpus of legal rules in some area of law (say, property law) is not usually thought to serve this or that specific moral purpose, but rather to regulate a whole range of social relations in the absence of shared moral perspectives on the questions to which the rules apply. Doctrinal principles relating to the transfer of property can be viewed as expressing *the same* underlying principles of justice as rules relating to the operation of trusts only by espousing ideals of justice in the most glib and uninformative terms. The quest for unifying explanations of a body of rules is thus often wont to suggest the picture of an ideal order of moral principles quite at odds with the mundane reality of clashing interests and interpretations.

The second suggestion lately set out does not, however, fit with ordinary legal practice much more successfully, for the common law is not easily viewed as consisting of the application of fixed standards to abstract bearers of rights and duties, but instead displays sensitivity to circumstance and to the peculiarities of the dealings between the litigating parties (we can think about the kinds of circumstances that affect a person's status as a *bona fide* purchaser, for example). Jurisprudential writers who favour this second understanding are then forced to resort to the pernicious idiom of distinguishing rigidly between 'applications' of the rules versus formulated 'exceptions' to those rules.

The formalistic conception of legal authority encouraged by the statist view is unfortunate in making abstraction at one of these points – either in the interpretation of rules, or in their application – seem inescapable.

(2) The conception of formal authority proposed by the statist idea of law is best viewed as a response to the problem of clashing moral visions, which characterises the modern polity. It is then possible to understand a positivist outlook on law as a symptom of the erosion of shared understandings, and of the realisation that customary practices alone are incapable of providing a stable basis for social order in the modern world. We have seen that a body of posited rules (as much as a putative body of natural rights) can offer no final way of resolving the conflict of interests that defines modern social existence. Much of the law thus exists to impose a level of order and regulation upon a body of interests and expectations which will continue to conflict even in the presence of deliberately posited rules. It is not immediately clear how such an understanding of law's role is connected to questions of authority and legitimacy, and it is possible to see a good deal of analytical jurisprudence as responding to this question via a series of attempts to locate moral understandings either within legal practice itself or else in the regulatory interstices created by the focus on deliberately formulated rules.

In fact, the presence or absence of conceptual connections between law and morality shed little light on an understanding of the contribution of deliberate black-letter rules to social order. Even if the application of legal rules does not presuppose some general commitment to the moral value of those rules (or to law generally), such rules inevitably need interpreting in the light of their perceived point or purpose: except in extremely mundane contexts involving the application of precise technical rules to well-understood situations, this interpretative activity will amount to the tracing out of conceptions of morality or justice taken to be implicit within the express verbal form of the rules. Theoretical attempts to place such moral understandings outside the formal boundaries of the law are, in the end, of little significance to our ability to comprehend these interpretative activities.

(3) Modern outlooks on the legal order depend in some measure upon an understanding of the law's coordinating function. We might think of an official

practice of recognition in this context as supplying an additional dimension of precision and stability to ordinary understandings. The harmonisation of divergent outlooks and interests in a large and complex society cannot, however, be achieved simply on the basis of imposed solutions, but instead implies compromise between a range of conflicting interests. For suppose the legal order embodied an arbitrary preference for one set of interests over another: those whose interests are trammelled and systematically overridden would have little motive for seeking the protection of their interests or the resolution of grievances *within* the law, and indeed would have few reasons for taking much interest in the law at all (except perhaps for the narrow purposes of the 'bad man').[44]

These thoughts might lead us to feel some hesitation in embracing an official practice of recognition as a way out of the problems of fundamental disagreement. Officials, as much as the rest of us, think and function within the context of ordinary understandings and moral dilemmas, and the supposition of an 'official attitude' towards the interpretation of rules can be viewed as an attempt to identify conditions of convergence and harmony in the way that the law is discovered and applied. We are encouraged to think of such official practices as existing in detachment both from the rules (which do not specify the conditions of their own application) and from the background of social understandings (which continue to diverge and conflict).[45] But how, we may ask, does such a free-floating interpretative attitude establish itself, and how are participants in that practice to identify it?

Any systematic practice of interpretation is likely to generate its own rules and conventions: conventions that will differ in certain respects from the background understandings, and expectations that an ordinary person might possess. Yet (as we have seen) the interpretative activity needed for the application of general rules to particular situations does not consist merely of the application of static 'canons of interpretation' in each case, any more than it involves the imposition of rigid propositions or imperatives. In the absence of a means of specifying general conditions for the application of fixed rules to all conceivable situations (or at least dispositive conditions for so doing), each official or judge must at some stage resort to his own complex moral understandings of the main features of the case.

The 'top-down' image of legal officials making judgments about the application of law on the basis of settled *rules* of recognition, thus gives way to the idea of judges and officials deciding cases from the bottom-up: the traditional form of common law reasoning is a mode of moral reflection in which the decision is reached by the contemplation of the relatively fine distinctions that might be drawn between otherwise similar cases.[46] The

---

44 See O. Wendell Holmes, 'The Path of the Law', 10 *Harvard L Rev* (1897) 457.

45 H.L.A. Hart, *The Concept of Law*, 2nd edn (Oxford, Clarendon Press 1994). See my earlier discussion in Chapter 1.

46 See S. Coyle, 'Practices and the Rule of Recognition', 25 *Law and Philosophy* (2006) 417–452.

distinctions that count as morally *relevant* for these purposes are determined on the basis of fairly narrow doctrinal ideas and principles that are incapable of being fully articulated or understood outwith the immediate context of their application. A judge's deliberations are thus guided along paths that differ in various respects from those employed by the lay person, but the moral understandings the judge brings to bear are firmly rooted both in the shared background of attitudes and beliefs in which all thinkers reflect upon their moral experience, and in the rules and doctrines being applied.

(4) The recognition of the state as a distinct entity with the power to impose rules and alter entitlements naturally brings about a division of society into public and private realms. Legal rules for the regulation of private entitlements are then conceivable as a series of public interventions into the circumstances of private interests and choices. This is suggestive of an image of society in which the law is brought into conflict with the moral lives of individuals: an image that makes any attempt to resolve a shared sense of law's binding authority exceedingly difficult.

It is notoriously difficult to distinguish the public and private realms in an intellectually satisfactory way. Without collective recognition and control of private entitlements, individual rights, liberties and powers become illusory, and the private realm itself cannot exist apart from a general framework of regulation and governance that permeates the private lives of its citizens. At the same time, the modern view of the legal order is inclined to suggest the misleading notion of the individual as the locus of *private* rights and interests that are sharply distinguished from those of others, or from collective goals more generally. The legal order then exists to secure and balance those different kinds of interest.

This picture is misleading in various respects. When we speak of individuals having 'private' interests, we usually mean only to distinguish such interests from collective goals in the basic sense that the individual concerned is acting out of his own, privately formulated needs and desires rather than altruistically pursuing some public good. We do not (in other contexts at least) think of private interests as being *fully* distinct from collective or interpersonal concerns: insofar as a person's interests are developed and expressed only *within* a context of social interaction, those interests will be formulated against a background of joint understandings and possibilities for personal flourishing. Just as others' interests affect my life in certain ways, my interests have effects (sometimes very pronounced) on other people in my social circle. My interest in a contented family life (for example) pervasively shapes my interests in other areas of my life, just as my interest in amassing great wealth might give way to interests in being a charitable, or likeable, or even honourable person. We generally understand and accept such social and familial ties when formulating and pursuing interests.

The notion of each individual pursuing his or her own atomistic interests in myopic isolation from the lives of others is thus not an illuminating way of proceeding when contemplating the legal order of a modern society. The dichotomy of 'public' and 'private' is apt to suggest a particularly intractable problem for the legitimacy and binding authority of the law: against such a background, the legal order will appear as a monolithic system of impositions that interfere directly in each person's moral life and choices. By recognising that such an account may offer too simplistic a view of the competition between public goals and private interests, might we not come to view the questions of legitimacy raised by that picture as being unnecessarily stark?

Statist Impulses and Moral Visions

It is unclear whether these musings can blossom into a coherent understanding of the legal order. Indeed, we might view the statist conception of law as giving rise to a number of contradictory impulses that can only be jointly satisfied by imposing fixed theoretical frameworks for the understanding of law within the modern polity. If that is so, then a fully coherent theory of law will be achievable only at the expense of a detailed and genuine cultural understanding. The rigid analytical dogmas of legal positivism, on the one hand, and those of moral idealism, on the other, might be viewed as giving rise to divergent trajectories of thought concerning the way in which rational coherence in the law may be reintroduced. We can view the positivist as attempting to exhibit coherence and rationality at the level of policy, whilst maintaining a view of law as predominantly an affair of rules created by many different wills over time. Coherence is then the product of the deliberate pursuit of social goals, and of the existence of shared practices of recognition. The idealist, by contrast, is more likely to regard rational coherence as a matter of the scheme of justice or morality implicit within a body of law. Emphasis is thus placed not upon the humanly-created aspect of law, but upon standards of justice and rationality that underpin the ideal of legality independently of positive law-making authority.

The central question for modern jurisprudence might be seen as how to reconcile the formal, rule-based characteristics of the legal order with its systematic concern with values of justice and morality. These are, to a great extent, questions particular to a modern, liberal polity in which social welfare broadly depends upon complex and large-scale free market interaction. Within such a society, the procedural and structural formalities of governmental agencies will give the law a formal character that restricts its capacity for generating rich insights into the moral life. Yet the limitations associated with posited rules as a means of governance will lead jurists to view ideas of law and legality as reaching beyond those formal characteristics. The very formality exhibited by statism will thus stimulate the discovery of rich moral visions within the law, in abstraction from the black-letter content of posited rules.

The presence of such moral visions within the modern legal order may be regarded as a deeply puzzling phenomenon. Such visions seem to testify to the existence of rationally coherent ideas that underpin and form the interpretative background for the posited rules. Yet it is far from clear that a body of posited rules should inevitably form an internally coherent system. In a situation of prolonged political instability, for example, law may well be looked upon primarily as a body of authoritative commands: it may be felt that the most important feature of legal rules is their possession of the virtues of firmness and clarity, correspondingly little attention being devoted to the question of whether, taken together, those commands can be subsumed under more general principles. The values and motivations of the legislature might owe as much, if not more, to instrumental expedience and the maintenance of fragile political majorities as to rational coherence. The relative stability and peace of a market society is thus a significant feature in the explanation of coherence within the legal order.[47]

It is tempting to suppose that a statist conception of law is in some sense made inevitable by the circumstances of the modern state. Yet the possibility of a genuinely illuminating jurisprudence depends upon the ability to reach beyond the confines of a descending model of legal authority. Systematic forms of principled reasoning are intrinsically bound up with the ideals of justice and legality to the extent that the very possibility of law seems dependent on their existence. Our conception of the kind of coherence and rationality at work in law may vary according to shifting impressions of justice and legality; but of necessity the forms of legal reasoning exhibit more than a concern with formally derivable authority even in the face of a legal order predominantly understood as an array of posited provisions. One who altogether abandons the idea of principled or systematic reasoning thus rejects the ideal of governance through the rule of law.[48]

In the modern law, the systematic character of law continues to be understood in terms of the category of legal doctrine. Without a clear understanding of the relationship between legal doctrine and formally posited rules, little can be inferred about the moral nature of law within the modern polity. In the following chapters of this book I shall therefore be concerned with this relationship as it is manifested within the opposing currents of thought represented by positivism and idealism.

---

47 For further discussion of this point, see Chapter 7, below.

48 I thus assume that the form of systematic, principled reasoning is implied by Lon Fuller's eight 'desiderata' of legal order. In the later chapters of this book I shall go some way towards elucidating that claim. See Fuller, *The Morality of Law*, chapter 2.

Chapter 5

The Changing Face of Positivism: From Hobbes to Hart

The modern lawyer operates within a conception of law as a body of rules. To confront the law of contract, of torts, or of property, is to familiarise oneself with an intricate set of rules. Such familiarity is not yet legal scholarship, much less legal practice, for in order to use the rules as lawyers use them, the rules must be contemplated and considered, and the relationship between the different rules must be understood. Because the intellectual processes involved in handling the rules exhibit a high degree of sophistication, those intellectual processes may themselves become the subject matter of philosophical argument. Thus, we may regard jurisprudential theories as embodying differing understandings of the processes of handling legal rules; and we may conceive of legal theory as the attempt to grasp the moral significance of rules as a foundation for social order.

In Chapter 1, I suggested that theories of the nature of law are based on tacit assumptions concerning the human condition and of the place of law in securing a context for the realisation of human potentialities. The doctrinal legal science examined in Chapter 3 embodied a standpoint from which the law must be viewed as a systematic body of rights; for it was through the idea of a right that expression could be given to the fundamental juridical equality that was thought to define the moral condition of humanity. Legal positivism shared with classical doctrinal science an essentially Protestant view of the human condition, but here the law is not viewed as directly instantiating a moral ideal but rather a framework of rules that allow for the coordination and regulation of conduct in a context of disagreement about the nature of the human good. Such rules, it was thought, did not directly embody a specific conception of the good, but remained in some sense neutral as between conflicting conceptions of the good.

In the period between the writing of Hobbes's *Leviathan* and the publication of Hart's *Concept of Law*, the connection between the idea of a system of rules and assumptions about the nature of legality and the human condition became increasingly obscured. Partly this had to do with the notion that law did not exist to secure specific dimensions of the human good, but merely provides a neutral context for the pursuit and realisation of diverse goods and overarching social goals. Yet it is also the product of the decline and eventual suppression of metaphysics as an intellectual framework within which to develop juridical understanding. My aim in the present chapter will be to recover a tradition of moral reflection upon the nature and significance of law, understood as a body of rules. The form of legal science presupposed by this conception of law, although differing in numerous respects from that of classical doctrinal science, is (I shall suggest) nonetheless revelatory of important aspects of the human condition. This chapter will thus offer some thoughts about the relationship between rules and the rule of law, considered as embodying a moral ideal.

Legal Science in the Century after Hobbes

In the preceding chapter, I drew a distinction between the humanly-created aspect of legal order and its principled, systematic character. The statutory and doctrinal rules, definitions and distinctions with which the lawyer is required to gain familiarity can be considered as manifesting the human face of the law, for they are taken to be deliberate productions of the will. The processes of contemplation, on the other hand, embody most clearly the law's principled and systematic character. In a sense, one can only *distinguish* the humanly-created aspect from the systematic if one already associates the idea of legality with a descending conception of authority. For where law is viewed as a reasoning process, the rules, rights and doctrines of the legal order will be considered merely as offering concrete expression to established patterns of reasoning and recognised forms of pleading, which are themselves a product of artifice. Only where rules and doctrines are taken to be products of authoritative decision will they be viewed as elements of legal order distinct from contextual arguments and pleadings.

Legal writing in the century after Hobbes reflected a concern with the nature of black-letter law, and its relationship to 'equity'. The category of equity traditionally denoted an elusive but distinctive element of judicial authority, for it had long been recognised that no system of static rules could address all possible ends of justice in specific cases.[1] English law was peculiar amongst European legal systems in locating equity within a separate jurisdiction based on the specific authority of the Chancery courts. Thus, equity in English law came to describe a separate body of rules or 'maxims' capable of being identified with 'the whole of natural justice.'[2] The function of such rules was that of 'supplying that which is defective, and controlling that which is unintentionally harsh in the application of any general rule to a particular case.'[3] This ambiguity in the character of equity, as both a specific dimension of legal authority and the embodiment of the law's rational coherence, is reflected in Hobbes's attitude towards the interpretation of legal texts. The letter of the law, Hobbes remarked, can be pulled about in various ways to suit various ends, and is therefore not to be trusted as the unambiguous expression of sovereign will when used in legal argument. Only the 'Sentence' of the law, understood as expressive of the sovereign's intention, is to be trusted as authoritative, and this intention is synonymous with equity ('For it were a great contumely for a judge to think otherwise of the sovereign').[4] The bare texts of the positive law therefore stand

---

1   See for example M. Hale, 'Considerations Touching the Amendment or Alteration of Laws', in F. Hargrave (ed.) *A Collection of Tracts Relative to the Law of England* (London, 1787), 257; and H. Ballow, *A Treatise of Equity* (1793), 6.

2   Ballow (above, note 1), 6.

3   *Ibid.*, 9. (The remark is actually that of Ballow's editor, John Fonblanque.)

4   Hobbes, *Leviathan*, II.26, 326.

in need of a measure of interpretation 'so that the incommodity that follows the bare words of a written law, may lead [the judge] to the *intention* of the law, whereby to interpret the same the better.'

Just what measure of interpretation *is* required, Hobbes thought, will differ depending upon how one approaches the law. The civil law must be synonymous with equity (or reason), or else law becomes ineffective: because 'upon this ground any man, of any law whatsoever may say it is against reason, and thereupon make a pretence for his disobedience'.[5] For the interpretative practices that underpin the law's effectiveness to remain in place, individuals should thus refrain from disputing the merits of legal texts: such speculative inquiry is, thought Hobbes, a dangerous hobby. Only direct involvement in a genuine lawsuit legitimates speculation over the interpretation of the law in the light of equity and reason. In the *Dialogue ... of the Common Laws of England*, Hobbes reiterated his concern with the divisive construction of spurious arguments designed to ground opportunistic claims: 'For my part I believe that men at this day have better learnt the art of cavilling against the words of a statute, than heretofore they had, and thereby encourage themselves, and others, to undertake suits upon little reason.'[6]

Hobbes thus associated equity *both* with the powers of the court to make explicit the ideas of justice implicit within the positive law, *and* with the law's rationally coherent character (as a property of law distinct from its posited, rule-based character). Accordingly, '[t]he medieval doctrine of the Chancellor adjudicating disputes according to "Conscience" had to be conflated with the classical notion of any judge making equitable exceptions to general rules, and the common law forms which equity had historically modified had to be reduced to a body of positive rules.'[7] In Hobbes we can therefore find the beginnings of a formal conception of legal authority that demanded the recognition of a hierarchy amongst the sources of law. Juristic writers in the 18th century inherited such questions, and through them shaped the 'modern' outlook on legal authority, for the central issue of the legal significance of 'the principles of 1688' was exactly the issue of the relationship between the humanly-created aspects of the legal order, which depended upon a vertical conception of political authority, and the systematic and principled characteristics of law, which depend upon historical modes of authority.

Throughout its history, the rational nature of the common law had been associated with its historical pedigree. 'Law', wrote Lord Kames in his *Principles of Equity*, 'ripens gradually with the human faculties,'[8] and thus legal scholarship can only become a rational study when traced historically.[9] The rational character of the common law came to be associated with the characteristics of *Englishness* as a benign

---

5   Hobbes, *Dialogue Between a Philosopher and a Student, of the Laws of England*, p. 3. Hobbes uses the terms 'Equity', 'Reason' and 'Law of Nature' fairly interchangeably throughout the *Dialogue*.

6   *Ibid.*, 56.

7   D. Lieberman, *The Province of Legislation Determined: Legal Theory in Eighteenth Century Britain* (Cambridge, Cambridge University Press, 1989), 76.

8   H. Home (Lord Kames), *Principles of Equity*, 2nd edn (Edinburgh, 1767), 41.

9   Kames, *Historical Law Tracts* (Edinburgh, 1761), book 1.

and guiding spirit: the English law, as Matthew Hale argued, 'is not only a very just and excellent law in itself, but it is singularly accommodated to the frame of the English government, and to the disposition of the English nation, and such as by a long experience and use is as it were incorporated into their very temperament,' so as to become 'the complexion and constitution' of the English people.[10] The character of English liberties were thus not thought to be determined directly from abstract natural rights, but from the historic constitution. The constitution did of course embody natural law; but the liberties of the ordinary man were primarily conceived as historical products of the English character, reflecting dictates of natural law only secondarily.

Arguments centring on the existence of an 'ancient constitution' and, later, a 'Protestant constitution,'[11] embodied attempts to assert the traditional rights of the English people rooted in governance through *law*, headed by a constitutionally supreme monarch established by that law. Such arguments represented the effort to secure the middle-ground of English politics, distinguished at once from proponents of arbitrary or unlimited government, on the one hand, and the 'radical' natural rights theories (associated with Locke) on the other:

> The peculiar excellence of that admirable structure of society established in this country consists not, as we all know, in equality of rights and privileges; which, under the free and varied exertions of the human powers would be neither practicable nor desirable; but in that singular coherence and adaptation of its several parts, by which many classes and ranks of men, rising in orderly gradation, and melting as it were into each other, through the lightest shades of difference – united by a common interest and cemented by Christian charity – compose together into one solid, well-compacted and harmonious whole – presenting a scheme as beautiful in theory as it is valuable in practice, and productive of a far greater sum of utility and happiness than is attainable under any other form.[12]

Arguments of this kind effectively tied common law rationality to Anglican hegemony, thus allowing the rational and systematic character of English law to occupy a significant place in constitutional thought even as its proponents emphasised the constitutional superiority of monarchical authority. Eighteenth century political thought had ceased to centre upon the delineation of actual entitlements according to abstract natural rights, and instead concerned 'the possibility of demonstrating divine intervention and intention in human affairs as such.'[13] It was in the historic common law that the hand of Providence was most sought. William Paley, the leading voice in English utilitarianism in the 18th century, was thus not alone in seeking to present

---

10 M. Hale, *The History of the Common Law of England* [1713] (Chicago, University of Chicago Press, 1971), 30. On the notion of 'guiding spirit' or Geist, see Chapters 2 and 9 of the present book.

11 See J.G.A. Pocock, *The Ancient Constitution and the Feudal Law* (Cambridge, Cambridge University Press, 1987) and Clark, *English Society 1660–1832*, esp. 423–564.

12 W. Otter, *Reasons for Continuing the Education of the Poor at the Present Crisis: A Sermon Preached Before the Honourable Judges of Azzize on 16 March, 1820* (Shewsbury, 1820), 8–9; quoted in Clark (above, note 11), 186.

13 Clark (above, note 11), 259.

the essential characteristics of common law as a justification for established social forms and institutions.[14]

The need to explain the nature of English political society after 1688 resulted in the development, in the 18th century, of a juridical conception of politics. Yet the centrality of law to explanations of constitutional order created an obvious tension between the conception of law as a product of sovereign authority, and its nature as a reasoning process that grounds and embodies constitutional ideas. Appeal to the common law's historical pedigree was integral to the possibility of presenting the events of 1688 in terms that distinguished them from the radical impulses that led to the creation of Cromwell's commonwealth (and to the Revolution in France). At the same time, the historical character of the common law constitution could be viewed as forming the basis for the Convention parliament's actions, consistently with an understanding of the limited character of British monarchy, for in securing the Hanoverian dynasty, Parliament could be viewed, not as invoking a radical Lockean 'right of resistance', but as upholding the Protestant constitution by ensuring that the throne did not fall into the hands of a Catholic monarch. In this way, defenders of Hanoverian title sought to retain a degree of parliamentary control over the succession whilst avoiding the tincture of radicalism associated with a full-blown natural rights theory, such as that of Grotius or Locke. England's constitution was a government of law; but this meant *English* law, not the levelling perspectives of Lockean natural law.

A juridical conception of politics entails certain revisions to the notion of law as a reasoning process, for systematic doctrinal reasoning will cease to concern merely the expression of entitlements, and the refining of boundaries between competing interests, but will also concern the general political significance of entitlements and interests vis-à-vis the powers of the state. The moral character of doctrinal science thus gives way to a political vision in which legal writers attempt to discover within the law a general political theory from amid the more limited moral perspectives afforded by established doctrine. Where rights are connected with political theory in this way, the substance of legal doctrine as well as the form of law is relevant to political understandings. No longer is the legal treatise viewed as supplying an objective, apolitical view of the law, but is instead thought to concern the rational reconstruction of the legal order in terms of specific political ideologies.[15] This intellectual shift in legal science denotes the move from an ascending conception of legal authority, rooted in the moral understanding of the *phronimos*, to a descending, Ramist structure. This is because the discovery within the law of general principles and ideologies is naturally viewed as the outcome of systematic ordering and classification – the uncovering of systematic connections between the humanly-created rules and decisions, rather than the reflective articulation of moral understandings rooted in an experience that might fail to sustain the assumption of

---

14 See Chapter 4, above.

15 Kelsen's reduction of legal science to a 'method' or 'technique' is relevant here, insofar as he sought to outline a reasoning process independent of particular ideological orientations: see H. Kelsen, *General Theory of Law and State*, Wedberg trans. (New York, Russell & Russell, 1961), 21ff.

coherent order between fully articulated general principles. The systematic element of law, as a reasoning process, is thus distinguished from legal order, understood as a body of authoritative rules and decisions.

An understanding of doctrinal reasoning in Ramist terms (the definition of a categorical structure of deductive thought) naturally invites questions regarding legal authority, for the discovery of principled, moral perspectives within the law raises the issue of which amongst the various possible explanations of the significance of legal rules is *in fact* embodied by the settled law. If the 'sentence' of the law (in Hobbes's terms) must sometimes be understood in terms of the 'intention' of the law, in order to avoid injustice, then by what processes is that intention finally revealed? The rational coherence of the law is thus subsumed within the rule-based authority of judges to render decision. Judicial decisions then furnish the grounds of legal entitlement by supplying 'the principal and most authoritative evidence' of legally established entitlements and interests. Judges, in this way, become the 'living oracles of the law.'[16] This blending of rational coherence and juridical authority gave an increasingly central place to *stare decisis*, and the consequent hardening of justificationary arguments into 'rules of precedent': 'The doctrine of the law,' Blackstone said, 'is this: that precedents and rules must be followed, unless flatly absurd or unjust; for although their reason be not obvious at first view, yet we owe such a deference to former times as not to suppose they acted wholly without consideration.'[17]

These thoughts supply a formal context in which the intellectual processes of systematic contemplation operate; but they do not *explain* those processes, for how does precedent relate to legal doctrine, in which one may find the 'reason and spirit of [the laws]'? The structure of Blackstone's monumental *Commentaries* on the law reflects the gap between legal science, considered as a reasoning process, and legal order, considered as manifesting particular rules and decisions. The work consisted of a substantial Introduction, in which such processes are modelled in general terms on the basis of natural law doctrines, and four 'Books' in which the substance of the law is set out systematically and categorically, with none but a few passing references to the Introduction's intellectual scheme. Blackstone's text was thus to leave the connection between the law's rational coherence and its positive, rule-based order ultimately mysterious.

Any complex system of law is likely to require some form of systematic exposition: for we are liable to regard the conditions of intelligibility of law as depending upon the assumption that vast bodies of statutory laws and judicial decisions may be organised into more specific categories or doctrines according to underlying purpose. For example, the law relating to theft invites exposition in terms of concepts and ideas of property which also relate to the explanation of forms of ownership; and those ideas will in turn inform any attempt to make systematic sense of the law of trusts. Such explanations inevitably 'go beyond' the reporting of authoritative rules

---

16 Blackstone, I *Commentaries*, 69. 'Even in such cases,' Blackstone argues, 'the subsequent judges do not pretend to make a new law, but to vindicate the old one from misrepresentation.'

17 *Ibid.*, 70.

and decisions, and (because they seem inevitable) contribute to the sense of doctrinal science as occupying a mysterious place in the modern legal order. It matters little, in this respect, whether we view the coherence demanded by the legal scholar as a contingent consequence of the organised pursuit of social policy goals, or as the manifestation of the deeper rational properties of a body of rights.

The Nature of Positivistic Legal Science

It was the 'mysterious' place of doctrinal scholarship within the law that led Blackstone's former pupil, Jeremy Bentham, to launch a series of scathing attacks on the vision of law offered in the *Commentaries*. The opposing conceptions of legal authority that characterise their respective positions are in many ways reflected in the jurisprudential argument of English society (and by extension, that of common law society) to this day.[18] These notions of authority (as I argued earlier, in Chapter 4 above) may be distinguished from the legal thought of earlier ages in virtue of their assumption of a descending structure of political thought, for having isolated the systematic and coherent character of law from its status as an authoritative body of rules and decisions, it lay open to the juristic writers of the 18th century to offer an interpretation of the common law in two distinct ways. On the one hand, the common law might be presented as a fixed body of precedents that establish, by authority, a system of posited rules: the rational coherence of law being explicable as a function of the repeated resort to the rules, and convergent interpretations of their purported significance. 'Equity' would thus play a limited role in modulating the application of the rules to specific cases (treating like cases alike). On the other hand, the precedents may be viewed as mere evidence for rational principles that underpin and structure the positive rules; a view evident in Lord Mansfield's famous judgment in *Rust v Cooper*: 'Law does not consist in particular cases, but in general principles which run through the cases and govern the decision of them.'[19] Equity, then, plays a more significant role in the law; for it is:

> ... the soul and spirit of all law: *positive* law is construed, and *rational* law is made by it. In this, equity is synonymous to justice; in that, to the true sense and sound interpretation of the rule.[20]

The alternatives thus seemed to comprise an inaccessible idealism, based on increasingly abstract characterisations of justice, and a narrow positivism of formal, source-based rules. Bentham, in particular, had set about describing the common law as a series of particular decisions, rather than a body of general doctrinal rules:

---

18 A different, although closely related, set of arguments may be said to dominate the thought of civilian legal orders, centring upon the nature of interpretation and the status of constitutional convention and positive morality (so, at least, is my ill-informed understanding).

19 *Rust v Cooper* [1774], Cowper's Reports of Cases in the Court of King's Bench, 632.

20 Blackstone, III *Commentaries*, 429.

for 'to give [judicial decisions] any sort of connection with one another and with the rest of the matter of which law is made a set of general rules must be abstracted from them and worked up into the form of a treatise...'[21] Yet the treatise is not law, but the seamless blending of expository matter with the numerous justifying arguments which (in the author's mind) define the point or purpose of the rules. In this way, Bentham believed, we are led into the error of supposing the existence of rights, interests and obligations of which the authoritative rules and decisions are mere partial expressions. A rigorous separation of the expository matter from the censorial would thus reveal the law's imperatival character by dismissing the 'underlying principles' celebrated by Lord Mansfield, as mere phantoms.

Yet Bentham himself could hardly eliminate altogether the need for systematic exposition of the law; for as we have seen, systematic explanations of large bodies of particular rules and decisions is an intrinsic part of understanding the policies or purposes such rules are designed to serve. If the censor's role was to explain the utilitarian basis of legal propositions, the expositor was charged with organising the corpus of legal materials into a structure that reveals their rational and utilitarian character. The activity of doctrinal reasoning was, as Milsom observed, thus reduced to the 'business [of arranging] yesterday's results in whatever way will be most convenient for those working on today's problems.'[22] Law was thus not to be construed as a product of 'reason', but a body of discrete rules which, taken together, are capable of systematic expression in different ways for different purposes: in terms of the interests protected, or policies pursued.

It is clear that Bentham viewed the processes of legal contemplation as an intrinsic part of legal scholarship; but he was equally insistent that those processes were not *themselves* part of the law. The need for some form of systematic scholarship should not make us lose sight of the law's character as a body of imperatives and commands, rather than a body of general doctrinal rules. Bentham had responded to Blackstone's characterisation of these mental processes in ironic and uncompromising terms: 'Why did he not write in verse? It can certainly only be from an undue deference to modern prejudices that he consented to tread the career of humble prose. Verse is what his oracles, like those of the ancient sages, would have appeared in to best advantage.'[23] The point of these words was not merely to contrast the verse style with that of the ideal form of legal writing ('a science of which precision is the very life and soul'), but rather to suggest that the obvious metaphysical richness and fictional intent of poetic verse would put readers on guard against supposing that the entities of Blackstone's mental world (natural rights, principles of equity and justice etc.) were actual or real.

We may nevertheless question whether Bentham's own account of these intellectual processes is any more revealing of the nature of systematic scholarship. The activities of the expositor are *neither* those of the censor, *nor* those of a mere

---

21 J. Bentham, *Introduction to the Principles of Morals of Legislation* [1789], J.H. Burns and H.L.A. Hart (eds) (London, Athlone Press, 1982), 188.

22 S.F.C. Milsom, 'The Nature of Blackstone's Achievement', 1 *Oxford Journal of Legal Studies* (1981), 1.

23 See Bentham, *Of Laws in General*, 11.

reporter: to what status do the expositor's systematic reconstructions then aspire? This question reveals the problematic place given to doctrinal scholarship within a descending conception of legal authority – for suppose we were to take up Bentham's suggestion regarding the setting out of expository matter: what would legal science against the background of such a suggestion look like? The standard form of legal scholarship would likely favour the writing of explanatory textbooks, seeking to expound the technical content of the law in an orderly, functional way, over the production of general treatises in which the content of the law is 'derived' from reason or from abstract theories of justice. The purpose of such textbooks would be to facilitate learning of the law according to the various policy objectives that the technical content of law might be supposed to advance. In place of wide-ranging discussions of the purpose and aims of law, or the nature of entitlements, one might expect to find more limited attempts to set the rules and decisions in a particular area of law within the scope of policy objectives and pragmatic aims such as consistency, efficiency (and so on). The existence of more conceptual works of legal scholarship, especially those seeking some philosophical view of the legal order as a whole, would then be for the most part dismissed as of little relevance to the ordinary lawyer: works that might well exhibit qualities of 'cleverness' or theoretical 'richness' according to their own internal standards, but of interest only to other academic lawyers and philosophers.[24]

It is this mode of legal science that dominates at the present day. But the general lineaments of that form of scholarship testify to the problematic status of the doctrinal writer's propositions, rather than clarifying their place in legal thought, for much of the theoretical literature is concerned with the role and position of moral reasoning in law; and the obvious lack of consensus amongst legal philosophers on how to resolve that question underlines the unsatisfactory state of legal science on the model inherited from Bentham and his 19th century positivist heirs. Whether the doctrinal writer's propositions are regarded as 'unauthoritative' or not matters little to the issue of their theoretical importance in legal thought, as it is through such propositions that law is initially learned and understood; and it is through the same forms of argument that legal issues are debated in practical contexts as much as academic ones. In categorising the common law as a body of particular, unconnected decisions, Bentham sought to expel general doctrinal rules to the confines of the unauthoritative treatise, since 'to give [legal decisions] any connection with one another and with the rest of the matter of which the law is made, a set of general rules must be abstracted from them and worked up into the form of a treatise.'[25] But as such general rules and understandings are an integral part of legal understanding, what exactly does this definitional move accomplish? If legal understandings depend upon the systematic reconstruction of 'general rules' from the scattered particulars, to what does the adjective 'unauthoritative' serve to draw attention, if something other than the status of such rules as merely 'controversial' or 'defeasible'?

The jurisprudential scholarship of the present day can offer no very insightful answer to this question. I suggested in an earlier chapter that part of the reason behind

---

24 For further discussion, see S. Coyle, 'Two Concepts of Legal Analysis', 26–28.
25 Bentham, (above, note 21), 188.

this failure lies in the fact that legal philosophers have for a long time concerned themselves almost exclusively with the question of whether moral understandings lie within the law or outside it. Yet it should be obvious by this point that the *location* of such understandings does little to change their fundamental significance within legal thought and practice; for (to repeat) in order to use the positive rules as *lawyers* use them, the rules stand in need of considerably sophisticated forms of systematic contemplation, argument and evaluation.

Bentham's removal of general, systematic considerations to the subjective and barbarous treatise may be explained by his concern to present all aspects of legal understanding as products of the will. Once viewed as the outcome of scholarly deliberation *about* the law, general doctrine no longer represents an object of cognition, contemplated by the intellect, but is instead revealed as the subjective product of ideology. Legal scholarship is then seen to rest, not upon the discernment of entitlements, duties and interests lying behind the willed content of the law, but upon the clarification of technical rules in a way that facilitates their employment for chosen ends. We are then left with a problem, however. To accept this explanation of the relationship between the law's posited content and the needs of rational coherence, is to view law as a manifestation of power. What, then, justifies its existence? Merely agreeing with the predominant ideology enshrined within the law is insufficient to secure its moral legitimacy; for, as argued in the preceding chapter, human choices and preferences are to a significant degree shaped by the very social conditions brought about by law. We are forced, then, to return to the question of how the law can be simultaneously *reflective* and *constitutive* of social order.

Social Order and the Significance of 'Rules'

During the 18th century, Hume's analysis of English society as a 'government of law' increasingly came to be associated with the notion of government through *rules*. This intellectual shift is reflected both in the development of doctrinal legal science, and in the changing character of jurisprudential speculation as a series of questions *about* that doctrinal science. It was, more than anything else, the development of the modes and practices of market capitalism that brought this shift in attitudes about. The proliferation of new and innovative forms of dealing required not only substantial revision to the traditional conceptual categories of contract and property law, but the development of new forms of legal regulation operating within the sphere not of private law, but of public law.

The distinction between public and private law is both complex and contested. The emergence of public law is, however, of undeniable significance for legal thought. Private law, dealing predominantly with private transactions between individuals, can claim with some feasibility to represent a systematisation of ordinary shared understandings and intuitions about how people in society should relate to one another. The emphasis on remedies in private litigation reinforces this impression, for the law intervenes in private transactions only where established forms of dealing break down or reveal lacunae. The posited content of the law in this respect represents the attempt to refine and stabilise ordinary practices and intuitions, rather than a series of arbitrarily or ideologically selected impositions upon human behaviour. We may then think of private law as a framework for describing these '…horizontal relationships between citizens, in which private rights are conceived as having some absolute existence',[26] apart from the will of the legislator. Public law represents a different thought. Here,

> [t]he point was that the state should protect its notion of right and wrong by legislation … In these concerns, we can perceive a statist notion that the law was more than a system to redress wrongs alone, that it was rather a tool with which to shape society and govern by directives.[27]

Public law then represents a 'vertical system of social regulation and dependent benefits, in which the citizen can have only claims or expectations as against authority, rather than abstract rights.'[28] The judgments of Lord Mansfield's bench testify to the intense period of creativity within the common law during the expansion of mercantile capitalism, as well as the legislative activity. Yet the development of doctrinal responses to market enterprise, impressive though it was, served not to diminish but to enhance the idea that law was fundamentally an affair of rules, established by authority for the regulation of human conduct. Jurisprudence must then seek to explain how the moral basis of law (understood as governance through rules) relates to the idea of a shared practice, and hence how the political authority of a system of *posited* rules might nevertheless derive from shared assumptions and beliefs which reflect the law's intrinsically moral nature.

One prominent attempt to understand the legal order in terms of governance through rules is offered by H.L.A. Hart. Hart encourages us to think of the law as containing a rich tapestry of different kinds of normative standards to which we conventionally apply the word 'rule'. But this use of a single word to describe related social phenomena, Hart points out, should not blind us to an underlying diversity in function and normative effect: some rules lay down as compulsory a certain type of behaviour which ordinary individuals are expected to follow; others confer legal powers and permissions, and yet others set out procedures for when other rules are infringed. Finally, modern legal systems contain (often complex) rules that guide and govern the implementation and recognition of rules within the system. The latter can all be gathered under the convenient term 'secondary rules' whilst the former, behaviour-enjoining rules can be called 'primary rules'. Law is then the union of these two sets of rules.

Hart's understanding carries with it certain beliefs about the structure and operation of the common law which have sometimes been criticised as proposing a model of law inappropriately wedded to theories of statutory interpretation. Not surprisingly, the chief criticism of Hart's theory by a distinguished historian of the common law is that it is mistaken about the essential nature of common law scholarship and practice, for, if the law is identical with, and constituted by, a set of rules, we are led 'to conceive of the common law, somewhat perversely, as if it had

---

26 Milsom, 'The Nature of Blackstone's Achievement', 3.
27 Lobban, *The Common Law and English Jurisprudence 1760–1850*, 204.
28 Milsom (above, note 26), 3.

already been codified.'[29] By far the most contentious of the theory's insights in this context is the rule of recognition, according to which systemic rules are adjudged valid. The criteria of validity identify a legal rule by reference to its source – the fact that it was, at some point, laid down in a statute or decided case. But whilst we may be inclined to treat judicial decisions as sources of law in the relevant sense,[30] the common lawyer has good reason to resist the conclusion that such decisions are a source of identifiable rules, in Hart's sense.

Hart's conception of rules fails to fit common law patterns of reasoning for a number of distinct reasons. Typically, the *ratio decidendi* of a case will not contain anything that neatly qualifies as a 'rule', and the exact reasons even for important decisions are often the subject of intense lawyerly (and scholarly) debate. Moreover, the rather narrow class of cases in which common lawyers speak of 'rules', such as the rule in *Rylands* v. *Fletcher*, are seldom indicative of instances of deliberate judicial legislation: in such cases, the rule is not 'laid down' in the decision; the decision rather gives insightful or precise expression to ideas that have evolved in previous judgments only gradually and implicitly. Nor do such landmark rulings, important though they may be, give *definitive* expression to the rules formulated therein. Common law 'rules' are never frozen into an unalterable verbal form, and the best statement of authority for a particular rule is not necessarily the earliest case in which it explicitly appears: it is the continual refinement and ongoing reception of such rules that is significant for judicial practice, not any arguments about the formal authority of decided cases.[31]

The patterns of doctrinal argument embraced by common lawyers, and inherited from the 18th century, provide no clear dividing line between the authority of legal propositions and their substance as sound reasons for decision. The common lawyer thus moves within a conception of law in which the fact that judges often extensively reword, distinguish, widen or generally rework established rules appears entirely benign, for the 'rules' may embody complex ideas about the moral dimensions of specific situations to which differing expression must be given in each context of application. The fact that judges regard it as important to engage in lengthy explanations and analyses of a rule (even where they purport to agree upon the rule's general import and desirability) indicates the extent to which judges regard variant expressions of the rules as significant to their respective general understandings of the wider bodies of law from which the rules are drawn.[32] The common lawyer, then,

---

29 A.W.B. Simpson, 'The Common Law and Legal Theory', in *Oxford Essays in Jurisprudence* (Second Series, 1973) 77–99, at 81. See further 'The Survival of the Common Law System', in *Then and Now, 1799–1974*, (1974), 51–70 and 'The Analysis of Legal Concepts', 80 *LQR* (1964) 535–558.

30 I speak here of individual judgments as *sources*, rather than of judicial judgments overall as a *source* of legal rules and principles. Traditionally, common lawyers had spoken of 'sources' of legal principle without any belief in a formal doctrine of sources of law in terms of a closed list.

31 See Simpson, 'The Common Law and Legal Theory' (above n 29), section III.

32 The differences between this conception of doctrinal reasoning and that offered by the 18th century natural lawyers are discussed in Chapter 3 of Coyle and Morrow, *The Philosophical Foundations of Environmental Law – Property, Rights and Nature*.

operates within a conception of juristic thinking that renders doubtful the view that 'one could in principle both state the rules of the common law and count them like so many sheep...',[33] as one might enumerate statutory provisions.

Such criticisms appear to find some resonance in Hart's text. In a passage headed 'The open texture of law', Hart remarks that:

> Two principal devices, at first sight very different from each other, have been used for the communication of ... general standards of conduct in advance of the successive occasions on which they are to be applied. One of them makes a maximal and the other a minimal use of general classifying words. The first is typified by what we call legislation and the second by precedent. We can see the distinguishing features of these in the following simple non-legal cases. One father before going to church says to his son, 'Every man and boy must take off his hat on entering a church.' Another bearing his head as he enters the church says, 'Look, this is the right way to behave on such occasions.'[34]

In Hart's example, the first father in laying down an express general rule of conduct represents an analogy with legislation, whilst the second father (or rather his behaviour) provides a crude analogy with precedent – one that Hart goes on to refine. The interest in these examples lies not in their accuracy, however, but in Hart's suggestion that, although the models of legislation and precedent as devices for communicating general standards are 'at first sight' different, at a deeper level there is an underlying symmetry in the way these devices supply the conditions for application of the corresponding standards:

> Whichever device, precedent or legislation, is chosen for the communication of standards of behaviour, these, however smoothly they work over the great mass of ordinary cases, will, at some point where their application is in question, prove indeterminate; they will have what has been termed an *open texture*.[35]

This understanding of rules of the common law, playing as it does upon the vagueness which general classifying terms exhibit when applied to specific cases, presents an alternative explanation of the presence of 'general' doctrinal rules to that offered by Bentham. It is suggestive of a conception of judicial reasoning as involving disagreements about the existence and applicability of verbally fixed rules, the 'expository matter' identified by Bentham being an intrinsic feature of the explanation of such rules as grounds of decision. Yet we might well feel that differences in approach to questions of the interpretation of legal rules are rarely ascribable to disagreements over the wording in which the relevant ideas and principles are expressed.

Consider, for example, the rule in *Wheeldon v Burrows* that 'on the grant by the owner of a tenement of part of that tenement as it is then used and enjoyed, there will pass to the grantee all those continuous and apparent easements ... or, in other words, all those easements which are necessary to the reasonable enjoyment of the property

---

33 Simpson, (above note 29).

34 Hart, *The Concept of Law*, 124.

35 *Ibid.*, 127–8.

granted.'³⁶ Suppose it is argued that the rule in *Wheeldon v Burrows* lends support to the contention that rights under licence exercised continuously and openly will bloom into easements upon transfers of the servient land. It might be objected that the rule was never intended to apply to *all* openly and regularly exercised rights, but only to the narrower class of rights whose exercise is *necessary* for the enjoyment of the dominant tenement.

This disagreement might, on first appearance, seem to revolve around the proper construction to be placed on the phrase 'or, in other words': are these words meant to imply that the class of easements of necessity and the class of openly and regularly exercised rights are co-extensive, so that satisfaction of either criterion will be sufficient to imply the grant; or are we meant to conclude that satisfaction of *both* tests is required? Yet few, if any, of the main lines of argument bearing upon the nature of easements of necessity centre upon the correct meaning to be given to Thesiger LJ's use of the word 'or'. Rather, the argument turns upon the identification of the justifications and principles in the context of which the rule must be explained.³⁷ Are implied grants, for example, referable to long-established principles of non-derogation from grant; or are they to be understood by reference to a wider doctrine of necessity, ultimately underpinned by principles of fairness or reasonableness?

Such questions cannot be answered within the confines of Thesiger LJ's remarks in *Wheeldon v Burrows*. Instead, participants in the debate are required to orientate their viewpoints within a framework of legal principles and decided cases whose significance is capable of being understood in different ways. These alternative understandings might be considered (at least loosely) as responding to different moral and political visions, implicit within common law patterns of thought, and hence as having little to do with verbal disputes centred upon fixed rules.

Given the manifest difficulties afflicting the view of the common law as a system of posited rules, it is worth reflecting on the reasons why the early positivists placed such emphasis on black-letter rules as the primary means by which the polity should structure and regulate human life and social interaction. The positivists' commitment to determinate rules stems from a concern that, if rules are as pliable as the common lawyers suggest, then it is hard to speak of judges being bound by rules at all: where points of law are decided according to standards which evolve and mutate with successive applications, according to shifting conceptions of reasonableness and justice, it seems more accurate to speak of cases being decided according to those underlying values rather than by reference to fixed rules.

Such doubts about judicial reasoning should perhaps not be lightly dismissed. As long as rational coherence in the law is viewed as a product of an underlying

---

36 (1879) 12 Ch D 31 at 49, *per* Thesiger LJ.

37 See Simmonds, *The Decline of Juridical Reason*, 18. It is worth noting in passing that such interpretative disputes, even where they do bear directly on the issue, do not have all that much in common with 'open texture' disputes in Hart's sense. Open texture problems relate to the application of general predicates and noun-phrases in concrete situations, whereas in the present context the imagined dispute more properly concerns the *rationale* behind various, quite specific, rival interpretations.

conception of reason, jurists need not be troubled by the fact that legal rules lack an authoritative verbal form: for alternative formulations of the rules will merely reflect the various ways in which the underlying conceptions can be fleshed out in particular contexts of judgment. Such a view of law is, however, likely to retain its attractiveness and plausibility only as long as the caste of lawyers and juristic scholars involved in the determination of legal principle remain homogeneous in their interpretations and outlooks, for if the high level of cohesion and consensus in outlooks breaks down, a central argument for law's political authority is removed. On the one hand, law can no longer claim to represent a society's shared morality, because individuals will disagree about the standards of rightness and the good applicable in legal judgments. On the other hand, the law's claim to embody transcendent conceptions of moral rightness will give way to sustained disagreement about how the transcendent principles are to be given concrete expression.[38]

The legal philosophies of Hobbes and Bentham are designed to address a world in which the assumptions of the medieval jurists no longer hold. Rather than deriving from rational contemplation, law is instead viewed as the product of powerful authority, in the form of willed prescriptions. Legal rules do not *reflect* shared expectations or standpoints, but rather *create* expectations by imposing order on an otherwise formless social world. The discussion in Chapter 4 served to highlight various problems with this approach, for it was observed that the presence of explicit prescriptions alone cannot provide adequate foundations for stable social order: legal rules inevitably address *forms* of behaviour rather than individual actions, and thus (to return to my earlier assumption) require contemplation before they can be applied in each case. Litigation, however, arises out of disagreement about the existence or applicability of legal duties. Suppose we accept that legal rights and duties are defined by explicitly formulated rules. Litigants might then be expected to appeal to the rules in support of their opposing arguments and claims. The presence of extensive divergence in social understandings of morality and right would not be brought to an end by such rules; rather, the rules would simply act as a focus for diverging arguments and points of view.[39] Thus, both social order *and* authority intimately depend upon the interpretative consensus and harmony in outlooks that the posited rules were meant to supply.

Now, suppose we regard Hart's theory as responding to these issues by effectively rejecting the view of legal doctrine held by classical positivists such as Hobbes and

---

38 Blackstone, in particular, emphasised the importance of a traditional and rigorous common law scholarship as a means of avoiding the creation of a caste of lawyers whose inability to reason would lead to corruption and incoherence in the law (see Blackstone's Introduction to the *Commentaries*, vol I).

39 It might be observed that a ruling by the court effectively brings such disagreement to an end. This is true, but only within the limited context of the case itself, for the existence of disparities between any two cases will reintroduce disagreement about the intended scope of the ruling. Bentham, of course, embraced the view of common law as a body of particular, unrelated decisions. But as my arguments in the preceding section were designed to show, the obvious need for legal understanding to proceed by constructing general rules from the scattered and detached particulars, offers Bentham no early release from this set of problems.

Bentham. Hart may be seen as exploring the sense in which legal rules are not *posits*, but *practices*.

Hart initially delineates the idea of a practice by distinguishing practices from 'habits'. Contrast the statement that people go to the cinema every week with the statement that one should remove one's hat when entering a church: the former is best described as a habit, while the latter indicates a genuine normative practice. (We might in fact be uneasy with Hart's use of the word 'habit' in this context as presupposing certain psychological or physiological factors which we would not normally associate with a mere regularity in one's behaviour. I will therefore speak instead of an 'accidental convergence in behaviour'.)[40] Why should we be tempted to speak of the latter, but not the former, as a genuine normative practice? The answer, Hart suggests, is that it is only in relation to genuine normative practices that we typically employ the terminology of 'ought', 'must', 'can' and so forth. Thus, the distinguishing mark of normative practices is that they essentially involve the use and understanding of a reflective vocabulary.[41]

It appears, both from Hart's initial and cursory discussion of 'social rules', and from his later, more considered, discussion, that our general justification for asserting the existence of a rule will be that we can (even if we do not) frame it in a *proposition* that essentially employs this normative terminology: 'A valid will must be signed by two witnesses'; 'Contracts for sale of land must be constituted in writing,' and so on. *These*, it will seem, are *laws*. Thus, we might be tempted to conclude, the existence of a rule depends upon the presence or availability of such a form of words. Hart at several places seems to endorse this conception of rules: rules are at various points in the text equated with 'statements;'[42] rule-scepticism is diagnosed as the feeling that rules 'and the corresponding use of words like 'must,' 'ought,' and 'should,' is fraught with confusion.'[43] Legal rules are said to have 'a central core of undisputed meaning,' and legal reasoning may involve a choice 'between alternative meanings.'[44] But despite Hart's discussion of examples in which verbally formulated propositions are evident,[45] it is not clear that rules *must* possess a unique verbal form. The selection of these examples, perhaps, owes more to their straightforwardness and simplicity as a means of conveying complex ideas, than to any suggestions that rules *must* boil down to canonical instructions.

---

40 In Hart's initial discussion of the distinction he does in fact employ the term 'mere convergence in behaviour', though he goes on to refer to 'habitual behaviour', and later simply 'group habits'. See Hart (above, note 34), 9–11. By the more involved discussion on p. 55, Hart's use of the word 'habit' as the main descriptor for regular convergent behaviour has become entrenched.

41 *Ibid.*, 9–10. See also 57.

42 *Ibid.*, 11. (Hart's discussion here denies that rules are merely predictions as distinct from guides; he does not deny that rules are statements.)

43 *Ibid.*

44 *Ibid.*, 12–13.

45 Hart variously discusses s.9 of the Wills Act 1837 (pp. 12–13), the Fifth and Fourteenth Amendments to the Constitution of the United States (13), the rules of chess (56–57), among others.

Hart's suggestions offer an illuminating account of a rule as a *practice* lying behind the form of words (if any) used to describe it. The form of words is simply an attempt to articulate and distil the critical and reflective attitude that participants in the practice have towards that practice. Because our reflective attitudes might be highly complex, it is not inevitable that we should be able neatly to capture our views about what the practice requires in a particular form of words.

Take a simple example: suppose that I teach kung fu twice a week to a small group of people. Since this is something I do every week, it certainly constitutes a regularity in my behaviour; but it is more than a mere regularity: insofar as my behaviour forms a basis for certain legitimate expectations on the part of the students (including my spoken or implied promises to offer an ongoing course of instruction) it constitutes a normative practice, or rule, in Hart's sense. But even though we might agree on the existence of basic features of the obligation, it is highly doubtful whether I, or my students, could offer any simple statement that could be regarded as a definitive explanation of what the 'rule' *is*. I may of course, if pressed, offer examples of circumstances that I would view as bringing my obligation to an end: if I broke my leg, say, or if I inadvertently caused serious injury to one of my students, or if I subsequently found out that members of the class were using lethal techniques to attack and rob pensioners, I may feel unable to continue and thus released from further obligation. But even if I were to work out an ever-lengthening catalogue of such examples, the infinite scope for further, unseen possibilities guarantees that I will never succeed in framing a definitive proposition that exactly captures the extent of my obligation. Even if I were to do so, it is possible that my students and I may disagree about *which* examples constitute the limits of my obligation.[46] Now, if we cannot do this in the context of a simple practice such as this one, so much less will it be true that widespread social practices necessarily reduce to simple canonical instructions on which we can all agree. Much more likely, different participants in the practice will vary in their understandings of exactly what the practice entails.

Hart speaks of a reflective attitude as involving the treatment of a rule as a standard of criticism. But just as individuals may differ in their attitudes to the rule, so they may possess variant conceptions of the conditions under which such criticism is warranted for breaches of the rule, for although the existence of a social rule requires some level of agreement in judgments about what the rule demands, such agreement is likely to consist not in convergent understandings, but in a series of overlapping understandings based on potentially conflicting rationales.[47] Most complex social practices are thus unlikely to reduce to forms of words on which there is general agreement. They will tend, instead, to depend upon sophisticated

---

46 The obligation in question is thus non-canonical in at least two senses: first because there will in general be no single proposition that is capable of representing the exact content of the obligation (given the pro tanto nature of many obligations) and secondly because those involved with a given normative practice will seldom fully concur on the limits of, or indeed reasons for, the obligation even where there is substantial convergence in judgments.

47 'Each [person] ... not only [follows the rule] *in a certain way* himself but 'has views' about the propriety of all [following the rule] *in that way.*' *Ibid.*, 57.

and elusive considerations that are not capable of comprehensive articulation in abstraction from the circumstances to which they obtain.

Hart's argument might therefore be seen restoring the place of legal doctrine, in the form of 'general rules', from the exile to which Bentham had confined it. The notion of a 'rule' can be viewed, in this way, as shading off into broader normative considerations, rather than existing in rigid distinction from them. Whether we refer to something as a 'rule' or a 'principle' or a 'maxim' largely depends upon the role we perceive it as playing in our normative deliberations: whether, for example, we want to emphasise its status as a moral value, or as a normative constraint upon our behaviour which is to some extent independent of its moral value.[48]

The Limits of Legal Positivism

For Hobbes, as for Bentham, the ability to represent the common law as a set of particular verbal rules seemed central to the possibility of the rule of law, as doctrinal exposition encouraged belief in the presence of objective, general rules underpinning the particular decisions of the court, where in fact there existed only 'unauthoritative' ideologies. The need for systematic contemplation of the authoritative legal rules thus represented to such writers a deeply disturbing feature of judicial practice: if such ideological constructions essentially presented as objective that which is, in reality, the product of subjective understanding, is not the 'government of law' heralded by Hume revealed as an illusory achievement, a mere distorted projection of a 'government of will'?

The more sophisticated understanding of rules encountered in the writings of Hart reveals this dichotomy as a false, or harmless, one. Consider again the examples Hart offers as loose analogies with the modes of reasoning involved in following statutory rules and precedents. In the first example, a father says to his son 'Every man and boy must take his hat off upon entering a church,' In the second example, the father bears his head upon entering a church and says 'Look, this is the right way to behave on such occasions.'[49] Hart's example is designed to draw out the differences between 'rules' of precedent and promulgated rules or orders. Clearly, in the second example, the father's actions can be construed in a number of different ways: does the father intend his son to remove his hat upon entering any kind of building, or only a church? Should hats be removed only on Sundays (if that is the day upon which the action is performed), or at any time one enters a church? Is the action of smoothing back the hair a part of the behaviour the son is supposed to copy, and is the fact that the left hand is used rather than the right important? Suppose the

---

48 In various passages, Hart notes that the doctrinal principles of the common law are 'not brought into being by *anything analogous* to explicit prescription' and therefore that 'there is no authoritative or uniquely correct formulation of any rule to be extracted from cases.' Hart (above, note 34), 79 and 134.

49 *Ibid.*, 124. (Hart goes on to say that the second example would more closely resemble precedent if the father gave no verbal instruction to his son, but simply expected the son to regard the father's activities as indications of the appropriate standards with which to comply.)

father's face bears a complicit grin at the time the hat is removed: does that indicate mere embarrassment at the performance of a 'superstitious' ritual, or the implication that, to be polite, one ought *not* to remove one's hat? (One could go on.)

It initially seems as if the son, in Hart's example, is left without any clear guidance as to the desired outcome, and must therefore invent a rationale by imputing purposes to the father's actions according to his own ideological presuppositions. Yet the son is not *completely* without an understanding of what is being required; for the context of action narrows down the possible interpretations of the father's behaviour to *plausible* ones. The father's action occurs not in a social vacuum, in which nothing can be safely inferred about others' likely beliefs and attitudes, but against a rich background of textured social understandings and shared values within which father and son both move. It is in virtue of such understandings that others' words and actions are intelligible to us at all. But although shared understandings reduce the number of possible interpretations, they do not eliminate variant interpretations altogether; nor do they provide an unambiguous insight into the *moral* grounds of the father's action; after all, we cannot immediately infer whether the father is a religious man showing respect before his God, or whether he is an atheist exhibiting respect for the beliefs of other church-goers (or, lacking such respect, performing the action merely to avoid criticism).

In view of this, much is left up to the son in deciding how and when to perform the demonstrated behaviour on future occasions, much as a judge follows precedents without thereby exhibiting robotic submission to 'mechanical jurisprudence', for it is only through coming to understand the *point* of the rule that a general rationale can be discovered from the particular examples of its use. Ought one to remove one's hat on entering a mosque? Is such an action expected when entering the house of a friend who has suffered the loss of a close relative? The presence of a verbal rule (as in Hart's first example) does little to change the reasoning processes involved, for such examples can only be grasped by virtue of the notion of *respect*, and some understanding of the occasions on which it is appropriate to mark one's respect. It is of course true that the rules could be expanded to include such examples; but no set of rules can hope to give comprehensive coverage to human actions at the level of concrete particulars. Eventually, we are forced back on more general considerations. In such cases, Hart said, the interpretation of a form of words 'no longer characterises the nerve of reasoning involved in determining what is the right thing to do.'[50]

We might initially believe that the presence of an authoritatively formulated rule constrains the available choices more than does an unwritten rule, since it can act as an agreed focus for rival interpretations. But the open-texture of language, by virtue of which such rules operate as general standards, ensures that a written rule will in principle provide no greater level of agreement than does any other kind of shared standard. The vision of the rule of law associated with classical forms of positivism (that law must consist of clear, precise, *imposed* rules) is therefore incapable of providing the kind of foundation needed for long-term order and stability.

A society that aims to achieve long-term peace and stability must ensure a degree of harmony between its laws and background understandings and shared values.

---

50 *Ibid.*, 127.

The powerful form of legal authority advocated by Hobbes will be acceptable only to prudentially reasonable individuals who realise that their attempts to impose subjective interpretations of virtue are likely to be unsuccessful and destructive. I may have a violent objection to bikes in parks, or a strong desire to ride my bicycle where I like; but if I believe that asserting this right may lead to uncontrolled outbursts of violence or anarchy then I may instead accede to (what is in my opinion) an unjust law. Even if I felt that I might prevail through violence on this issue, I might consider that a more general application of a might-makes-right attitude would lead to my defeat on issues I cared more about (property ownership or the security of my family life, say). But I will only make this calculation if I feel that the values promoted by the legal system *as a whole* are values worth maintaining in the face of doubts or disputes about the merit of particular rules.

What matters for the rule of law is *not* that rules impose rigid and clear standards over a society divided by conflicting moral, political and religious views, but that the rules simultaneously reflect the evaluative underpinnings of our form of social life *and* provide foci around which our ordinary, intuitive interpretations of moral right and collective good can cluster. The mistake of earlier positivists was, according to Hart, their belief that the rule of law must be founded on the assumption that all law '[owes] its status as law to a deliberate law-creating act'.[51] On the contrary, the law can make a direct contribution to social order only if it closely describes *and* refines a society's shared values. That, it seems to me, is the fundamental insight in legal positivism.

---

51 *Ibid.*, 44.

Chapter 6

The Limits of Legal Positivism

In Chapter 5, I argued that the notion of legal rules present in Hart's theory allows for some understanding of the relationship between the posited, or humanly-created aspects of the legal order, and its principled, systematic character. The idea of a 'rule' or 'convention' does not inevitably point to the existence of fully realised or articulated standards, as social conventions may denote more elusive and complex considerations in which meaning is grasped only incompletely, and at a relatively low level of abstraction from concrete situations. Within such situations, the forms of reflection involved in determining 'the right thing to do' may be characterised as a matter for the intellect as much as for the will, without in any way detracting from the conventional character of obligations, or of a view of law as consisting in deliberately formulated rules.

In the present chapter, I shall argue that it is possible to maintain these insights only if we give up a central idea of Hart's theory: that legal rules depend for their 'validity' upon formal processes of 'recognition'.

Validity and Recognition

In an important passage in *The Concept of Law*, Hart states:

> We only need the word 'validity', and commonly only use it, to answer questions which arise *within* a system of rules where the status of a rule as a member of the system depends upon its satisfying certain criteria provided by the rule of recognition. No such question can arise as to the validity of the very rule of recognition which provides the criteria; it can neither be valid nor invalid but is simply accepted as appropriate for use in this way.[1]

This statement is drawn from a discussion in which Hart seeks to clarify the characteristics of the rule of recognition in relation to the claim that its validity cannot be *demonstrated* but merely *assumed*. Clearly, Hart believes, any application of the predicates 'valid' or 'invalid' to the rule of recognition results in circularity, since that rule embodies criteria of validity applicable to legal rules generally. Hence, any attempt to account for the existence of the rule in terms of its 'validity' will depend upon an antecedent practice of recognition that itself requires explanation. (Suppose that we attempt to enshrine the rule of recognition in a statute: then we would require some explanation of the legal status of such an enactment by reference to a practice of recognition that exists antecedent to, and independently of, the enactment.) The rule of recognition, therefore, plays no part in the conventional categories used in

---

1   Hart, *The Concept of Law*, 109.

the description of the status of legal rules. It is not a proposition *of* law in the usual sense, but a proposition *about* law.

It is worth reflecting on the reasons for which Hart says we need a concept of 'legal validity'. We need such a concept, he argues, in order to answer questions that arise *within* a legal system concerning the status of rules. Terms such as 'validity,' 'invalidity' and so forth are deployed in order to allow us to voice particular conclusions and claims about the existence of legal rules without engaging in arguments relating to the desirability or value the rules might be said to possess.[2] The proposition that a particular legal rule is 'valid' thus need not involve any appraisal of the rule's moral standing, nor need it involve assessments of the policy or purpose that the rule serves. Whether or not such evaluative considerations do play a part in claims regarding the existence of rules will depend upon the precise criteria provided by the rule of recognition (whether, in particular, the criteria of recognition include criteria relating to moral worthiness).

These views seem to involve Hart in a rigid distinction between legal validity and evaluative assessments of the substance of legal rules, and thus imply a model of rules characterised by quite stark and implausible divisions between law and morality: the criteria of validity (it may be argued) identify a notional set of propositions (the 'valid' rules) which, taken together, constitute the totality of rules, principles and standards that comprise the law at any given time.[3] On this view, legal reasoning consists of the 'interpretation' of fixed rules in the light of alternative conceptions of their underlying purpose. Since interpretation, of necessity, takes us beyond the bare wording of the rule, 'hard' cases in which rival conceptions of the rule compete with one another come to be portrayed as disagreements about the morality of particular approaches to questions of social order and justice.

In Chapter 5, I offered various reasons for *contrasting* Hart's notion of rules with a theory in which legal rules exist in distinction from the processes of systematic contemplation wherein the rational and coherent nature of law is manifested. Thus, the discussion above cannot represent Hart's final understanding of the processes of recognition. Within that discussion, it was assumed that the purpose of a rule of recognition is to articulate a conception of 'legal validity' in which the giving of good reasons does not establish the validity of legal propositions, for only if the ultimate criteria of validity rest *simply* upon 'official acceptance', and not upon the possibly complex reasons officials may have for describing certain rules as 'valid', are the official practices of recognition capable of description without reference to complex moral justifications.

The claim I wish to make is very simple: in order for Hart to retain the valuable elements of his theory of legal rules, the notion of 'official acceptance' must be taken to refer to a complex set of reflective attitudes in which the giving of reasons is indistinguishable from the process of 'recognising' the existence of valid rules.

---

2   Hart's discussion of the rule of recognition is prefaced by a contrast between a 'statement of legal validity' and a 'statement of value': see Hart (above, note 1), 108.

3   See A.W.B. Simpson, 'The Common Law and Legal Theory', in Simpson (ed.) *Oxford Essays in Jurisprudence*, Second Series (Oxford, Clarendon, 1973), 77–99 at 81.

But if this is the case, the idea of a 'rule of recognition' plays no interesting part in establishing valid legal propositions.

It is far from clear that a description of a widespread social practice can entirely avoid consideration of the participants' critical and reflective attitudes toward the practice. If we regard a reflective attitude as a participant's self-understanding of what the practice demands, in given situations, and if we regard an individual's ability to arrive at such an understanding as being dependent upon his ability to form some conception of the *reason* for the practice, then it seems we cannot escape involvement in moral questions that go well beyond a 'simple' description of external facts about what participants 'accept'.

Suppose we make sense of the initial understanding of recognition, above, as the suggestion that officials might have good reasons for endorsing and complying with criteria of validity even where such commitment is driven largely or exclusively by prudential considerations. It might be thought that those reasons are then irrelevant to the understanding (and 'acceptance') of those criteria. Such understanding, however, would require the adoption by prudential officials of the internal point of view (the point of view of one who wholeheartedly accepts those criteria). Such understanding thus also requires prudential officials to justify, or reflectively endorse, their standpoints as to what exactly the internal point of view requires in specific terms. I thus return to my claim, in Chapter 5 above, that in order for legal rules to be employed as lawyers use them, the rules must be subject to sophisticated processes of contemplation. This applies to legal 'officials' as much as to anyone else, as prudential alignment with the criteria of recognition, as much as genuine moral commitment, requires a fine-grained understanding of the way in which the criteria are to be expressed and applied. At this very specific level of law-ascertainment, did Hart genuinely believe the criteria on the basis of which particular judgments are made are reducible to a notional set of requirements, a grasp of which is independent of officials' beliefs about justice, right and so on?

It is not difficult to find passages in Hart's writings that support such a view. At several points Hart emphasises that, unlike systemic legal rules, the existence of the rule of recognition is an external matter of fact. In a complex legal order, Hart states,

> The statement that a rule exists may now no longer be what it was in the simple case of customary rules – an external statement of the *fact* that a certain mode of behaviour was generally accepted as a standard in practice. It may now be an internal statement applying an accepted but unstated rule of recognition ... In this respect, however, as in others a rule of recognition is unlike other rules of the system. The assertion that it exists can only be an external statement of fact.[4]

Hart's reliance on the internal/external distinction in this context is potentially misleading. The distinction is deployed in order to highlight the different sense in which we speak of the existence of patterns of recognition by which we identify systemic rules, when compared with statements that particular systemic rules 'exist'. In the case of the latter, the existence of a particular rule is not determined (in a

---

4   Hart (above, note 1), 110. And again: 'Its existence is a matter of fact.' (*Ibid.*)

complex society) by the fact that it is to be found in the actual practice of a social group, but because it satisfies that society's criteria of validity. Hence, the claim that such a rule 'exists' comes to the same thing as the statement that it is 'valid'.

As we have already noted, the notion of validity in such contexts is intended to provide a measure of certainty about what the legal rules are, without the need for difficult inquiries into the extent to which the values promoted by the rule are actually endorsed in society generally, or are worth endorsing, and so on. It is precisely for this reason that, according to the positivist, law is capable of making a decisive contribution to social order in a world of doubt over moral values. Suppose we grant that argument: then the patterns of recognition that allow us to escape involvement in those difficult questions cannot *themselves* require recognition in that sense, in order to exist; either they are widely followed, or they are not. If they are not, then no settled practices of recognition exist by reference to which systemic rules can emerge; but where a practice of recognition is widely employed, it is the fact of the acceptance of the practice that alone matters rather than any spurious attempt to suggest the practice is 'valid' in terms of other, widely accepted practices.

Having deployed the internal/external distinction as a means of demonstrating the special significance of the rule of recognition vis-à-vis systemic rules, Hart should not be thought to be committed to the conclusion that the practices that comprise the portmanteau term 'rule of recognition' lack an internal aspect. In demonstrating that a social practice can exist due to the fact that it is widely accepted and exhibited in the behaviour of its participants (rather than emerging from assessments of validity relative to other accepted social practices), we may yet resist the obviously false conclusion that participants in the practice lack any reflective idea of what they are doing: that they act out of mere habit, rather than purposively and deliberately. Although its *existence* is a matter of fact, the rule of recognition cannot be fully described in purely factual terms:

> The case for calling the rule of recognition 'law' is that the rule providing the criteria for the identification of other rules of the system may well be thought a defining feature of a legal system, and so itself worth calling 'law'; the case for calling it 'fact' is that to assert that such a rule exists is indeed to make an external statement of actual fact concerning the manner in which the rules of an efficacious legal system are identified. Both these aspects claim attention but we cannot do justice to them both by choosing one of the labels 'law' or 'fact'. Instead, we need to remember that the ultimate rule of recognition may be regarded from two points of view: one is expressed in the external statement of fact that the rule exists in the actual practice of the system; the other is expressed in the internal statements of validity made by those who use it in identifying the law.[5]

It is, of course, the latter (internal) statements that are of most importance in determining what the rule of recognition actually demands. Whether or not an official's actions (in pronouncing certain rules 'valid') fall within accepted practices of recognition will depend upon the extent to which that official's judgments of validity coincide with collective judgments about how and when primary rules are 'valid'. Where there are widely accepted practices of recognition establishing fairly

---

5   *Ibid.*, 111–112.

precise criteria of validity, we might expect a high degree of agreement in judgments among officials as to what the 'valid' rules are. But even against the background of a stable practice of recognition, there may yet be considerable disagreement not only about which particular rules qualify as 'valid', but also concerning the very basis for determinations of validity in the first place: such disagreements are capable of articulation even within an established practice of recognition that enjoys wide acceptance.

Consider, for example, the controversy about whether English law of contract contains a rule to the effect that a contract is void if entered into on the basis of a fundamental mistake of fact shared by both parties. Some support for such a doctrine can be gleaned from some widely known and important cases on contract; yet there is a persistent view among contract lawyers that those cases can equally be understood as applying established principles relating to failure of consideration. Here, disagreement about the 'validity' of a legal rule of common mistake (if we are right so to characterise the disagreement) does not revolve around the question of whether a particular proposition satisfies established criteria of validity. It rather points to a more fundamental disagreement as to what those criteria actually demand. Each lawyer's perceived warrant for construing the case-law in a particular way (the way that supports his argument for the existence, or inexistence, of the rule) will reflect differing conceptions of the basis upon which rules of the common law are identified, or recognised as being valid. Conversely, consider the (established) rule that parole contracts require consideration. No contract lawyer would argue that such a rule is not a 'valid' rule of English contract law. Yet if several contract lawyers were questioned as to what exactly grounds the shared judgment of the rule's validity it is highly doubtful that each lawyer would produce an identical argument for the rule's pedigree. Writing in a slightly different context, A.W.B. Simpson noted that:

> if six pundits of the profession ... are asked to write down what they conceive to be the rule or rules governing the doctrine of *res ipsa loquitur*, the definition of murder or manslaughter, the principles governing frustration of contract or mistake as to the person, it is in the highest degree unlikely that they will fail to write down six different rules or sets of rules. And if by some happy chance they all write down (for example) 'killing with malice aforethought' an invitation to explain what *that* means will inevitably produce *tot jurisprudentes quot leges*.[6]

Patterns of recognition even within areas of law that enjoy a high level of determinacy may thus reveal, if probed, a number of competing conceptions of what makes legal rules 'valid'. These conceptions, in turn, will rest upon variant beliefs about the nature of law held by participants in the legal order, based upon differing levels of insight, reflection and articulation.[7] The 'rule' of recognition, therefore, is likely to amount to a complex (and far from wholly coherent and consistent) practice in which individual judgments of validity ('internal statements') made by officials in the course of their overall practice, will derive their shape from sophisticated and highly refined attitudes towards the legal order generally.

---

6 Simpson (above, note 3), 88.
7 See my more general discussion in Chapter 1.

Hart must accept some such view of the processes of 'recognition' in order to preserve his understanding of legal rules as being closely tied to forms of systematic contemplation. For the idea that participants' acceptance of a rule of recognition and their reasons for accepting (what they believe to be) that rule can be in any way separated, is to suggest a disparity between form and content that is wholly unsustainable: each participant's beliefs about the rule of recognition (as reflected in their actions and judgments) are inevitably shaped by their perceived warrant for preferring particular understandings of the requirements of that rule over other, variant understandings. Hence, each participant's beliefs about what the practice demands will not be capable of articulation in isolation from beliefs concerning the reasons for understanding the practice *in that particular way*. Rather, his ability to express his beliefs will intimately depend upon his reasons for believing the practice as possessing a certain point or purpose, and as requiring articulation according to its underlying purpose.

Recognition and its Limits

Simpson's argument is drawn from a wider discussion, which seeks to challenge Hart's notion of 'valid rules' as failing to take account of the subtleties of doctrinal reasoning in the common law. In order to meet this challenge, I have argued, Hart must view the processes of recognition as involving complex and sophisticated patterns of reasoning and critical reflection on the part of participants within the legal system, rather than simple conformity to canonically accepted propositions. As Hart observed, '[n]o doubt the practice of judges, officials, and others, in which the actual existence of the rule of recognition consists, is a complex matter. As we shall see later, there are certainly situations in which the questions as to the precise content and scope of this kind of rule, and even as to its existence, *may not admit of a clear or determinate answer*.'[8] One page on, Hart emphasised that the 'range of fascinating and important questions' which confront the attempt to pin down exact criteria of validity '[require], for a full answer, on the one hand a grasp of some fundamental issues of constitutional law and on the other an appreciation of the characteristic manner in which legal forms may silently shift and change.'

Participants, Hart suggests, 'must, in general, be *critically* concerned with [deviations from accepted standards of recognition] as lapses from standards which are essentially common or public.'[9] But what is to form the critical basis of such judgments except highly refined conceptions of what the standards require, based on reasoned reflection of the purpose and rationale of those standards? Comparisons of rival points of view relating to matters of legal validity are unlikely to identify black-and-white divisions that can be tested against the 'simple' fact of common acceptance. We might bring to mind the numerous controversies which surrounded the judicial interpretation of s.70(1)(g) of the Land Registration Act 1925, or the significance of the words 'continuous and apparent' in the classic case of *Wheeldon* v.

---

8 Hart (above, note 1), 109. Emphasis added.
9 *Ibid.*, 116. Emphasis added.

Burrows.[10] Debates such as these are not resolvable on the basis of identifiable lapses from accepted standards. It is instead complex (and not easily expressible) variations in approach to those very standards that provide the grounds of disagreement: variations that are themselves incapable of straightforward separation from more substantive disagreements relating to the content of particular rules.

If such views establish the possibility of a 'rule of recognition', however, they also demonstrate its irrelevance, for, as argued above, the point of such a rule was that it articulated a form of legal scholarship in which the 'validity' of legal propositions is separable from arguments concerning their desirability. Yet as we have seen, even a settled practice of recognition may leave open many troubling questions that preclude any hard-and-fast formulation of a legal system's criteria of recognition. Such questions will come to the fore of legal debate when fundamental disagreements of legal doctrine are probed to their fullest extent. Where such disputes occur, I have argued, we are forced to concede that the judgments of individual participants as to the requirements of the practice in particular contexts merge with any justifying arguments those participants have for construing the practice in that way. This, I have further suggested, entails the lack of any clear boundaries between 'established' criteria of validity and the moral beliefs of those who employ them.

My arguments (if accepted) demonstrate that the processes of contemplation involved in the application of legal rules are intrinsically moral rather than formal. Legal thought in this way resembles a process of Aristotelian *phronesis*, for it involves a moral understanding that is apprehended only in conjunction with particular cases and which cannot without distortion be given definite form as a body of fixed principles. The judicial application of law in concrete cases therefore does not unfold in a straightforwardly logical way from broad understandings of 'validity'. Specific moral determinations are rarely detachable from the wider moral context within which an individual describes his views about a practice, as an individual's *in situ* moral judgments themselves form part of the individual's self-understanding of the broader significance of the practice. Because these judgments are not determined in a purely logical way by the broader moral outlook, the attempt to ground them in wider principles will seldom be genuinely independent of the terms in which those principles are described: for the ordinary thinker, those principles will come into focus just to the extent to which that thinker can formulate and give expression to specific judgments *in situ*.

This does not mean, however, that the doctrinal writer or judge must *accept* the moral perspective enshrined in the rules, for, as Hart observed, participation in such forms of moral reasoning may stem from purely professional or prudential concerns, or from 'disinterested interest in others.' Although it is not an ideal example, consider an agnostic who cynically adheres to Christian values out of a concern with avoiding an eternal punishment in which he does not fully believe.[11] The agnostic's

---

10 (1879) 12 Ch D 31. See my discussion in Chapter 5, above.

11 The Pascalian individual would more likely be motivated by avoidance of punishment than by securing a supposed everlasting reward. My remarks about this person (if they are correct) apply *mutatis mutandis* to the atheist who wishes to become a cardinal out of a desire for nothing more than the trappings of wealth and power that come with such an office.

endorsement of Christianity may be accurately identified as prudential rather than devout; but this is not true of any attempt to articulate the specific implications of Christian doctrine for issues such as transubstantiation, the nature of the soul or the idea of a just war. The agnostic's participation in the full range of moral and theological debates is unaffected by his prudential or disinterested standpoint: his views about *what to do* (or how to live) according to a set of abstract precepts continues to demand difficult moral judgments on his part about what is the *best* way to live, even if the ultimate reason for the investigation is instrumental rather than wholeheartedly supportive.

In the same way, official participation in the administration of justice may not stem directly from any moral attitude on the part of any official participant toward that practice; but any specific determination of the demands of that practice in concrete instances will require officials to take up standpoints on what we should take the correct standards involved to *be*. These specific questions require participation in moral debates and understandings even if the ultimate motivation for participating *at all* is one of cynical self-interest or disinterested concern: delineations of the specific demands of justice are seldom a matter of identifying the exact content of official attitudes and outlooks, but of putting forward suggestive understandings of a law's purpose within the context of wider moral and political intuitions and beliefs. If the notion of a 'rule of recognition' is simply a shorthand expression for referring to such processes of contemplation, then it offers no independent basis for reflection upon the nature of law or legal argument.

Recognition and Construction

The argument of this chapter has been concerned with the notion of a rule of recognition and that of a practice or convention. Efforts to overcome 'legal positivism' in modern jurisprudential thought have often, similarly, focused on a rejection of the idea of a rule of recognition. Where such efforts have not sought to eliminate law altogether as a category distinct from the exercise of political power, they have tended to evolve into forms of idealism.

We might understand the situation in the following way. Law requires the possibility of regulating complex patterns of conduct by reference to shared rules even in circumstances of widespread doubt or disagreement about what the appropriate standards should be. The relationship between law and society therefore seems to involve the notion that legal rules might 'exist' or possess formal authority even when they are not fully reflected in the general patterns of conduct of the persons to whom they apply. At the same time, no rule is likely to possess effective authority unless the legal system as a whole is observed and accepted in ordinary social practice. How, then, does one establish the content of authoritative legal rules? Moral considerations cannot supply the appropriate criteria, for the function of law is to establish publicly ascertainable rules in the absence of firm moral consensus; yet neither can legal authority be inferred from empirical facts about the use of political power without legal authority becoming indistinguishable from political authority generally. In the latter case, legality would have become grounded once again in the uncertainties of a 'habit of obedience'. A rule of recognition seeks instead to ground legality in the patterns of recognition and acceptance among a body of officials.

In dismissing the concept of a rule of recognition the temptation is therefore to suppose that law requires some other, more elusive ideological basis if it is to avoid eventual exposure as the unadorned exercise of power by the body of officials, for if official patterns of behaviour do not involve *recognition* of validity, then law becomes exposed instead as a direct product of will. The form of positivism found in Hart would thus have ceased to concern the nature of the power being exercised, and has instead come to centre only upon the distinctive manner in which it is exercised. To view legality in this way is to view legal propositions as being sustained and underpinned by a complex set of conventions. We might then challenge the idea of a convention as possessing no intrinsic normative import, and thus as being incapable of grounding legal authority. The authority of law, therefore, would seem to depend not merely on the form in which power is exercised, but upon the purposes and goals *for* which it is exercised. Legal authority will accordingly appear to require the subsumption of individual rules and decisions under more general principles forming part of an ideology of justice.

The presence of moral disagreement in society means that any such ideology of justice will be most naturally regarded as inherently a Protestant one: living in a society that requires the presence of stable conventions upon which to base its social intercourse and economic activity, the individual is required to 'interpret' shared rules and practices in the light of his or her own moral convictions. 'Interpretation' of this sort is suggestive of a split between cognition and construction, as, if legality cannot be founded upon the recognition of certain empirical facts, it will seem that the required starting points must issue from intellectual acts that construct them. I traced earlier the philosophical origins of this essentially voluntaristic picture of juridical thought;[12] and in the remaining chapters of this book my principal aim will be to explore the errors of thought upon which such a view of legality and cognition is based. Here, I wish to examine one specific dimension of the question that connects closely with the concerns of the present chapter. The particular issue I have in mind relates to the dynamic tension that exists between recognition and construction, when the former is abandoned in favour of the latter as an explanatory device.

Hart's concept of 'recognition', it is worth underlining, is itself essentially a voluntarist one. That is because a rule of recognition only succeeds in establishing legal validity by reference to empirical facts (thereby achieving the separation of law from morality) when considered from the 'external' standpoint: the distinctive nature and function of rules, and of notions of 'validity', obligation and so on, can only be grasped fully, however, by adopting the 'internal' standpoint of one who adopts the rule as a standard for governing and evaluating conduct. From the internal standpoint, a rule exists not simply by virtue of the existence of an observable pattern of official conduct; rather its existence derives from official *acceptance* (that is to say, from an act of will).

---

12 See especially Chapter 2 above.

Suppose we focus on the 'external' point of view. A shallow critique of Hart might accuse him of seeking eventually to base the notions of law and legal authority upon empirical facts about official behaviour and use of power. But what is it that supplies the relevant understanding of 'official' (if not the law itself)? Should our convergence in identifying the appropriate 'officials' or the shared acceptance of their behaviour as furnishing a basic rule of recognition be explained as a convergent *ideological* outlook, or is it underpinned by empirical factors that are at once external to belief and determining, in some sense, of the correct beliefs that one may have? Hart may initially seem to have a way out here, for he famously suggests that the social functions fulfilled by law are not simply a matter of the *form* in which power is exercised but are in part understood by reference to basic features of human nature and of the human social condition. These include the basic goal of survival, and certain basic necessities vis-à-vis social order (such as rules restricting the use of violence, recognition of property and so on).[13] Such necessities are not definitive of an ideological position (Hart claims), as they embody the fundamental basis for all humane ideologies not aiming simply at the destruction of humane civilisation (and thus of law). Yet at the same time, recognition of these basic elements involves recognition not of brute facts, but of fundamental values: a 'minimum content' of natural law.[14]

As Kolakowski pointed out, however, attempts of this kind to identify the basic presuppositions of one's own civilisation are unrealisable, '[b]oth the general morphology of civilisations and the descriptions of their constitutive characteristics [being] notoriously controversial and heavily loaded with ideological biases…'[15] Hart too, in the form of his 'minimum content' theory, has his own myth of modernity, replete with ideological biases. Idealist critiques of positivism might then be construed as seeking to transcend those biases by purging the individual thinker of such historical legacies and embracing the possibilities of purified rational autonomy. The agent, in seeking an 'interpretation' of his own cultural situation, effectively seeks knowledge of the will; convergence in interpretations being guaranteed by the fact that all Protestant agents operate, in this way, within shared external conditions which serve to anchor their constructive ratiocinations to the here and now. History is thus transformed from a rich potential source of self-understanding into a mere set of constraints of 'fit' that limit the sphere in which autonomous reflection is possible. A cultural milieu being itself, in these terms, an object of the will, such external constraints themselves become capable of revision or transformation in the light of the very intellectual processes they serve to ground. Cultural observations, as well as the derivation of social scientific laws, are revealed as 'theory' and are 'not to be

---

13 Hart (above, note 1), 199. See also my earlier discussion of Hart's treatment of 'survival' in Chapter 1 above.

14 It is indeed at this point that Hart comes closest to adopting an intellectualist, rather than voluntarist, picture of legality. See my earlier discussion in Chapters 1 and 2.

15 L. Kolakowski, *Modernity on Endless Trial* (London, University of Chicago Press, 1990), 3.

conceived as a report from experience but rather as an elaboration of abstract models never to be perfectly embodied in experimental conditions.'[16]

That this view of the status of 'theory' lies at the root of idealism may be revealed by recalling to mind the basic features of the Kantian philosophy on ethics. Suppose we wished to contemplate a certain range of ethical objects such as rights. Unlike the classical ethical writers who sought such knowledge in a substantive theory of the human good, according to Kant this would involve an understanding of the formal properties of equality and of the moral autonomy of rational human beings. Human rationality itself (as a defining characteristic of morally autonomy) is that which supplies ethical knowledge, for the categorical imperative (to act only in accordance with those principles that one can will to become a universal law) is at the same time an expression of the very condition of formal equality between morally autonomous agents.[17] Being purely formal, such an idea of human reason is in fact (at the same time) a pure construction of the will, for there is no cognition of an object that is external to 'reason' itself in the contemplation of ethical objects. Famously, the Kantian philosophy of right ran aground precisely because the search for substantive moral truths on the basis of purely formal features of rationality and equality propels the theory into complete abstraction. Yet we may equally ask how each agent's autonomous, Protestant acts of willing can lead to eventual convergence on a set of universal laws? Pursuing this question (which I raised in Chapter 2) a short way allows for some light to be shed on the idealist's general approach to legality.

One way in which Protestant agents might be brought into rough convergence in their ethical judgments is through the presence of shared elements of language and culture. It is, after all, only by participating in a shared 'form of life', and by possessing broadly similar interests and convictions, that genuine disagreement of the kind envisaged by the idealist can arise: for otherwise such disagreements could not be given rational expression (or, if they could, would not stem from autonomous contemplation of *the same* objects). We might then take the presence of linguistic or cultural forms through which the meanings and intentions of others are rendered intelligible to us as marking the baseline or starting point for explanation of why autonomous agents should achieve a reasonable convergence in their judgments. A shared vehicle for the expression of thought implies, in this sense, a set of shared concepts and possible means of combining them to form arguments. Hence (it might be thought) the possibility of convergence is implied by the very circumstances (those of rational intelligibility) that give rise to disagreement and autonomous agency. This view is manifested, with fluctuating levels of explicitness, in various forms in modern philosophical thought. One can see it, for example, reflected in Rawls's idea of the 'original position': here, individuals are deprived of all knowledge of what makes one person distinct from another, of their own personal capacities and features, and of their own preferences and conceptions of excellence and the good life. They must then agree upon a set of principles and institutions that will govern their society, the result of that agreement being both rational and just insofar as

---

16 *Ibid.*, 7.

17 Kant, *The Moral Law: Groundwork of the Metaphysics of Morals*, H.J. Paton trans. (London, Hutchinson 1948), 84.

it is free of the taint of personal interests. In this way, the presence of a common language, and perhaps also a shared conception of basic needs, provides a starting point from which fully autonomous agents might converge upon a set of ideals.[18]

Explanations of this kind are, in the end, of doubtful value in supplying the grounds upon which rational convergence is possible among autonomously reflecting agents for they overlook the obvious truth that a shared language and shared cultural conceptions and preoccupations are not definitive of a rough and provisional starting point for explanation, still less a neutral bedrock upon which to build: their existence is instead the very thing that needs to *be* explained. Language is essentially a creature of society, and linguistic practices tend to require and give expression to incredibly complex patterns of coincidence in understandings. Being the very means through which our interests and conceptions are given self-expression, language is far from constituting a detached and independent instrument for conducting civilised arguments but rather itself depends upon a long history of civilised and rational interaction. The possibility of convergent interpretations of legality, therefore, might be viewed as depending not upon ideologies constructed by reason, but upon the existence of intelligible relationships of sociability and power that might be 'recognised' as the general conditions in which rule through law is realised.

The idealist is thus left with the same dilemma as the positivist. Avoidance of the extreme abstractionism of the Kantian jurisprudence requires recognition of external constraints of 'fit' (such as language, culture, shared values etc.) as the general conditions or anchor-points around which introspective interpretations can cluster and converge. Yet the involvement of those same conditions in the activity of constructive interpretation demands treatment of such constraints as finally 'human creations or abstractions that are useful in ordering and summarising our experiences, but which exist only as constructs.'[19] Unless rooted in 'recognition', theories of legality cannot avoid being propelled into abstraction; but blindness to the 'constructive' dimension of such theories entails attachment to a moribund and unsatisfactory empiricism.

It is not my present concern to suggest a way out of this dilemma, although my discussion in Chapter 9 will suggest that it is the implication of a stark intellectual division between the processes of cognition and those of construction that is to blame, and which must be overcome if progress in jurisprudence is to be made. My aim in this present section has been rather to demonstrate that a dynamic tension exists between the notions of recognition and construction, for there can be no possibility of treating legality as an object of 'pure' recognition or 'pure' construction. Thus, the intellectual difficulties faced by legal positivism, as outlined in this chapter, are in fact shared by idealism in virtue of the embeddedness within both traditions of certain epistemological assumptions. This can be seen perhaps most clearly when idealism is viewed as a form of legal writing.

---

18 The reader might reflect upon analogous strategies of explanation in Hobbes, Grotius, Kant and others discussed in earlier chapters of this book. For discussion of the deeper philosophical presuppositions of Rawls's theory see especially Chapter 9 below.

19 A. Perreau-Saussine, 'Bentham and the Boot-strappers of Jurisprudence: The Moral Commitments of a Rationalist Legal Positivist', 63 *Cambridge LJ* (2004) 346–83, at 367.

Considered as a form of legal writing, idealism is profoundly anti-canonical in that legal texts are represented as attempting to give expression to underlying principles and ideas. As such, no especial significance can attach to the specific wording used in the most important form of written law-text (within the context of adjudication): the legal judgment.[20] The preceding discussion of legal positivism ought to serve as a reminder of the inadequacies of attempts to derive formalistic rules or authoritative meanings from cases, even where some particular technical term or phrase (such as 'malice aforethought') is in question. Yet the anti-canonical tenor of common law rules must not lead us to lose sight of the important fact that such rules exist within an intellectual milieu in which an unusually exacting level of effort and attention is expended in the construction of statutory texts and of judicial formulations of such ideas as reasonable foreseeability or the neighbour principle. Ignoring this important fact, the existence of alternative formulations of certain rules or ideas may incline us, by a too hasty intellectual step, to the conclusion that no special weight attaches to particular verbal forms used in judgments or to conventional forms of expression at all.

The gap opened up by this step is best explained as follows. The idealist may claim that the lack of a unique verbal form attaching to common law 'rules' reveals that the common law in fact operates at the level of 'principles'. Lacking a distinctive form, principles cannot be validated by authoritative *recognition*, for such recognition could perforce attach only to a specific form of words through which the principle is given current authoritative expression. The 'validity' of principles must then relate to their broader interpretation, which might be 'constructed' in various opposing ways. This represents an elusive, but significant shift from an observation about the fluidity of expression to a claim about fluidity of substance. The shift is elusive because it addresses an intersection of philosophical standpoints that are not easy to differentiate with precision. A rough attempt might nevertheless involve, on the one hand, the proposition that law represents a body of technical knowledge that is capable of bearing a potentially infinite variety of possible descriptions; on the other, the thought that the particular terms in which competing conceptions are advanced are constitutive of a shared object, which represents an object *of cognition* only in a reduced and attenuated sense.

Lawyers tend to think of the law as being found and stated (with varying degrees of accuracy and specificity) in judicial judgments. Suppose we were to move from the abandonment of the idea of authoritative 'recognition' to one of interpretative construction. How would the relationship between a body of law and a reported judicial judgment then be conceived? We might begin by observing that bodies of law in general serve a combination of more-or-less visible goals: tort law (for example) is concerned with the compensation of certain types of harm, property law with the regulation and fairness of transfers, etc. These aims, embodying moral projects, might be given expression in various ways. But if we treat the description of such projects as one of interpretative construction, we will be inclined to understand those projects not

---

20 The presence of complicated rules and practices of statutory interpretation invites many practical complexities here (though not, I believe, many additional theoretical factors). On that ground I will focus here upon the written judgment and reported case as the prime examples in question. My remarks, again, are directed to English common law specifically.

by immersing ourselves in the contemplation of the numerous specific circumstances in which (for example) the forms of tortious harm are considered, but by freeing our understanding of the terms in which any specific judgments are made. In doing so, we might hope to identify principles that transcend the varying contexts addressed by the specific judgments. Thus, it will come to appear, nothing can be 'recognised' in the wording of a written judgment except the elusive and shadowy reflection of a principle to which no definitive expression can be given. As principles outstrip the capacity for expression, in this way, the written judgment (being 'frozen' or static) can then represent a mere instance of application, not a genuine part of the understanding of an object of cognition. Whilst affirming it in one sense, this view effectively obliterates the distinction between *obiter dicta* and *ratio decidendi* as lawyers typically understand it: for the interest in each case will be directed towards the reasons for decision considered (ultimately) as deriving from 'the general part of adjudication', and in establishing the former as the specific conclusions of the latter.[21]

The implications of this direction of thought will be more fully explored in the remaining chapters of this book. However, it has been the immediate purpose of the present discussion to highlight the essentially similar metaphysical and epistemological assumptions (that of a radical split between cognition and construction) underlying *both* idealism *and* legal positivism. Sharing such philosophical concerns, I wish to suggest, we find in idealism not a useful alternative to the positivist's vision of legality, but rather an opposing treatment of common starting points resulting in a transformed reflection of an essentially positivistic intellectual milieu.

From Positivism to Idealism

I have suggested that the legal and political discourse of the modern polity can be understood as a running battle between two contrasting understandings of legality. Both of these understandings, I have argued, are in a general sense concerned with the relationship between the posited, rule-based characteristics of law and its systematic and rationally coherent properties. Positivists accordingly tend to conceive of legal order as a form of social convention, and thus as an instrument for the pursuit of loosely related social goals. Idealists, by contrast, regard the law as an expression of fundamental equality, legal thinking centring not upon conventional rules but upon interests and entitlements that may transcend the limits of conventionally adopted goals. I describe these general understandings as 'intellectual traditions' in order to highlight their centrality and adaptability within modern legal thought:

---

21 See R. Dworkin, *Law's Empire*, 90: 'Jurisprudence is the general part of adjudication, silent prologue to any decision at law.' No doubt an interpretation of this passage could be made that avoids this charge (perhaps by differentiating between immediate reasons for decision and the more generalised and unstated grounds ultimately underpinning them). But then a central theme of Dworkin's theory, that of the overriding need for consistency at the level of principle, derives much of its force from the suggestion that the force of specific decisions (whether recognised to be of generalised application or confined to given facts) derives from their supposed relationship to considerations of a highly general nature at the level of jurisprudential reflection.

it is to be hoped that the reader may perceive in these rough characterisations the general forms of juridical consciousness that receive endlessly variable expression in the numerous theories of the nature of law with which the modern jurisprudential scholar is familiar.

Insofar as one may point to such general characterisations, there exists a dynamic tension between positivism and idealism, for the form of positivism described in the preceding two chapters leads readily to idealism. The central insight of Hart's legal philosophy, I argued, lies in its understanding of the way in which verbally constituted rules are construed in terms of their perceived point or purpose. Once our attention is shifted from the form in which law is presented to us (i.e. as a system of black-letter rules), and we direct our concentration more directly to the values and principles the rules serve, we will begin to develop an idealised concern with those values and principles as being worthy of sustained exposition in their own right. Since the contribution of law to social order depends upon the embodiment by the black-letter rules of a system of values that adequately protect individual interests, our concern naturally shifts towards a principled identification and articulation of those interests, and an insistence that the values that define and underpin those interests are given prominence in legal determinations of right. Rational coherence within the law will then be viewed not as a mere surface feature brought about through the pursuit of mutually reinforcing policy goals, but as a deep and necessary expression of the very idea of legality.

Within a community that develops this general outlook, however, the exact delineation of the boundaries between competing rights and interests will come to be regarded as a pressing question. A reliance on precisely formulated rules and articulated standards will seem inevitable, and it will then seem that social order is guaranteed as much by a system of specific rules and decisions as it is by enlightened values. Hence a sustained idealistic concern with rights and interests will tend to gravitate legal thought back towards positivistic concerns with formal, ascertainable rules.

An understanding of our modern legal practices might require us to abandon the assumption that those practices, taken as a whole, ultimately offer any coherent political expression of the role of law in modern society. We might instead view the legal order as a composite product of rival conceptions of the nature of our social and political life, and of law's role in structuring and regulating that life. Positivism and idealism represent not only competing political visions, but also powerful centrifugal forces in legal thought. The legal thinking of any particular time-period in modern history will be characterised by the centrality it gives (usually unconsciously) to one of these perspectives at the expense of the other. Because *both* perspectives derive from assumptions about social order and rights which have been central in shaping modern political thought, it is highly unlikely that forms of positivism or idealism could emerge that would successfully eliminate the possibility of commitment to the rival standpoint.[22] Instead, it is more likely that one approach to law rather than the other will come to dominate legal thinking in the light of prevailing political

22 One might distinguish, in this respect, extreme forms of positivism and idealism (such as the theories of Bentham and Kant), which will be significantly unstable, from more modest formulations (such as Hartian positivism and 'liberal' idealism of the kind I suggest is at

ideas and attitudes: a sustained commitment to free enterprise and laissez-faire economic liberalism, for instance, will tend to encourage a view of law as a body of conventional rules and standards that leave as much scope to individual freedom as possible; whereas a strong political concern with issues of social justice will foster a view of law as a body of rules and principles concerned with the systematic protection of rights and interests.

It is possible to view this dynamic tension as an intrinsic property of legal doctrinal scholarship. A society that has achieved doctrinal legal science is likely therefore to oscillate between positivism and idealism in the light of prevailing political conditions, as long as the notions of individual right and the rule of law form a central part of the canon of concepts through which we reflect on the form of our political life.

work in Dworkin's writings) which are, in consequence, both more stable and less easily distinguished.

Chapter 7

Beyond Positivism and Idealism

For the great majority of legal philosophers writing since the mid 20th century, jurisprudence takes the form of an inquiry into the truth of 'legal positivism', understood as a theory about the nature and functioning of legal institutions. The central question in this debate has concerned the possibility of offering 'neutral' descriptions of these institutions, aside from arguments pertaining to their moral desirability. One who embraces the possibility of descriptive analysis, arrived at in isolation from more overtly deliberative processes, exhibits a concern for the general features of social institutions over the particular, for the application of institutional rules and procedures to specific cases is thought to consist of bringing to bear criteria that exclude a great many of the contextual considerations that might otherwise apply to our understanding of what is desirable or right in the circumstances: it is after all the function of rules, and thus also of the institutions of which they form part, to guide decisions in just this way. It comes as no surprise, therefore, that legal positivists should find it difficult to accommodate within their general picture of the functioning of such institutions, the form of legal thought found in common law, for common law reasoning emphasises just that sensitive exploration of the moral dimensions of specific situations that resists wholesale transformation into general rules.

It might have been expected that critics of legal positivism would challenge that position by seeking to rehabilitate the forms of deliberation that characterise the common law's concern with the moral dynamics of particular situations. Yet the concern with general explanations has spread beyond positivism, enjoying wide acceptance within jurisprudence even where such explanations are thought to depend upon grounds other than descriptive neutrality.[1] Thus, for instance, a view of the process of legal reasoning as involving the application of general principles of justice to particular cases by a process of 'constructive interpretation' is one that itself reflects a belief in the presence of two distinctive sets of intuitions: one set of intuitions hinging on a familiarity with the facts, our comprehension of which is guided by another set of intuitions comprising insights into justice, right, etc. Within such a vision, the abstract and general features of legal institutions are linked with more specific deliberative processes by an 'interpretative attitude' which exists in detachment from both sets of intuitions.[2]

This view shares with positivism an understanding of the process of normative reasoning that is grounded in moral voluntarism, for the belief that values derive

---

1   See S. Coyle, 'Two Concepts of Legal Analysis', 15–17.

2   For further remarks on this conception of 'reflective equilibrium', see Chapter 2 above.

from a source other than 'mere convention', like all manifestations of the fact/value dichotomy, is the belief that the source of morality lies in the will. Careful reflection upon historical practices cannot *reveal* insights into the nature of the good; rather, an exercise of will is required in order to *impose* an evaluative interpretation upon the mute facts of experience. Life prior to the emergence of such an attitude (were such an existence imaginable) is thus dominated by unconscious attitudes of 'runic traditionalism' and the existence of 'static' and 'mechanical' visions.[3]

Voluntarism is particularly seductive in relation to legal thought, for it is hard to resist the suggestion that our very notion of legality depends upon the linking of discrete facts by association with general rules. As one eminent figure observed, 'Particular decisions become the foundation for general rules, which are afterwards limited by particular exceptions, and these exceptions being also generalised and reduced into different classes, are again subjected to future limitations.'[4] The notion of 'general rules' readily implies the sort of symbiotic relationship between inductive and deductive processes characteristic of interpretative forms of reasoning. Indeed, the gradual transformation of English common law and equity into a system of case-law might be said to reflect the belief that the presence of deductive elements in legal thought is a key tenet of the administration of justice. Within such a structure, the certainty associated with governance and adjudication through rules will seem opposable to areas of discretion, memorably characterised by Lord Camden as 'the law of tyrants.'[5] The reflective processes traditionally associated with the 'spirit of the laws' (*mens legum*) or 'equity' thus came to signify a body of precedents operating with the same regularity and certainty as the positive law, constraining the Chancellor 'not to act arbitrarily according to men's wills and private affections, so the discretion which is exercised here is to be governed by *rules* of law and equity...'[6]

Where the law is viewed as consisting of general rules constructed from interpretations of scattered particulars, it will seem as if such rules are expressions of the outcome of a collective choice between competing political values and interests. Legal practices are forced to play a reduced role in juristic thought by supplying

---

3   See R. Dworkin, *Law's Empire*, 49. In occasional passages, Dworkin appears to share a sense of the difficulty: 'I enclose "preinterpretive" in quotes because some kind of interpretation is necessary even at this stage. Social rules do not carry identifying labels' (*ibid.*, 66). But how can social practices be classified or sustained except by some purposive sense of their value? My discussion in Chapter 1 was intended to reveal the inexorable connection between purposes and general moral visions in the context of such classificatory exercises. Thus, Dworkin's vague suggestion that 'perhaps ... we may therefore abstract from this stage in our analysis [i.e. the 'preinterpretive' stage] by presupposing that the classifications it yields are treated as given in day-to-day reflection and argument', appears overly dismissive of some complex and highly important, yet elusive considerations.

4   J. Millar, *An Historical View of English Government*, 4 vols, 3rd edn (London, 1803 and 1812), vol. 4, 280.

5   See J. Parkes, *A History of the Court of Chancery* (London, 1828), 461, and the excellent discussion in Lieberman, *The Province of Legislation Determined*, Chapter 3.

6   *Cowper v. Cowper* (1734) 2 P Williams, 753, per Sir Joseph Jekyll MR (quoted in Lieberman, above, note 5, 80, emphasis added).

the necessary interpretative context against which such constructions are worked out. The scattered and sometimes contradictory nature of the particular rules and decisions might then be thought to explain how the processes of interpretation can be *constrained* by the facts of experience which are the object of explanation, whilst at the same time capable of offering diverse and conflicting insights into that experience. Each interpretation, then, discovers coherence in the law by giving emphasis to certain facets of legal practice whilst downplaying or dismissing others. Law is, in this view, a process of gradual self-transformation into its own ideal aspiration.[7] However, although the implication that legal and social practices may be ambiguous or less than fully comprehensible even to participants is surely correct, the suggestion that what must be clarified is the *will* in relation to confused particulars, has had a lasting and damaging impact upon jurisprudential thought, for the joint pursuit of coherence and certainty amid the conflicting facts of legal experience is apt to propel juridical thought into a dense matrix of abstract rules and exceptions, running in a direction counter to a genuinely textured and detailed knowledge of moral life.

To reject this conception of legal reasoning is often thought to be to abandon oneself to an intellectual sin known as 'particularism'. Some degree of generality in moral thinking is, of course, an inescapable feature of moral wisdom. Yet the character of that generalisation ought not to be lightly confused. Millar's words, quoted above, lend themselves to an interpretation along the lines lately set out, in which the relevant intellectual processes involve endeavours of 'constructive interpretation' or reflective equilibrium. But they may also be suggestive of a quite different set of intellectual processes, in which emphasis lies not upon the guiding of particular decisions by general rules or hypotheses, but instead upon the sensitive exploration of the particular through careful attention to the moral features of individual situations. Particulars can be apprehended by the intellect only when viewed in combination, as part of a structured whole; but they are never understood through abstract rules or principles. The moral knowledge sought by Millar, then, would represent a body of ideas incapable of being fully grasped or articulated in abstraction from particular judgments and decisions which are perceived more clearly and immediately by the moral understanding: a mode of thought in which particulars are related to a general framework in which, rather than *by* which, they are understood. Such a conception prompted Matthew Hale's observation, in his preface to Rolle's *Abridgment*, that the common law is 'more particular than other Laws, [and thus] more numerous and less methodical' and so possessed of 'greater advantages: namely, it prevents arbitrariness in the judge, and makes the law more certain.'

The need for sensitive and careful reflection upon particulars as a condition for moral understanding ought to have alerted us to the fact that experience itself (when understood as a conjunction of such particulars) is an object of the understanding, rather than a set of 'givens' which are simply perceived. As such, the established features of legal and social practices constitute a source of moral understanding, and cannot operate merely as 'constraints' upon an otherwise freely floating interpretative

---

7   See Dworkin (above, note 3), 400.

will.[8] A view that takes seriously the sense that moral understandings are discovered and clarified through reflection upon experience is one that reveals the idioms of freedom and constraint, in this context, as overly simplistic.

Legal theories do not merely offer static representations or depictions of legal practice, however. Inasmuch as legal theorists belong to an identifiable caste of lawyers, jurisprudential understandings at least partly constitute their object of inquiry. This observation is not meant to incline us towards the dismissive conclusion that all available theoretical positions share in some more complex and yet-to-be-discovered truth; but it should serve to remind us that the influence of such positions may be darkly reflected to varying degrees in the legal consciousness of the modern lawyer. For legal practice is, in the end, a body of intellectual traditions, and juridical understandings such as idealism and legal positivism both sustain and are sustained by, the intellectual traditions of which they form part. In tracing these influences, my aim, it scarcely need be said, has not been to *defend* legal positivism, or its rivals. It has rather been to demonstrate the centrality and importance of some key theoretical ideas to the juridical consciousness of the modern lawyer, and to suggest that other aspects of modern legal practice and scholarship can coexist with such ideas only discordantly and in tension. In the present chapter I wish to bring into focus those dimensions of legal practice that diverge most strongly from the theoretical assumptions implicit in both positivism and idealism, and which are, as a necessary consequence, largely ignored in modern legal theory. By so doing, it is hoped that legal theory may progress beyond the narrow intellectual categories in which it is currently enmeshed.

The Character of Legal Reflection

Law represents both an aspirational moral ideal, and a set of variable, human arrangements. The variability of those arrangements, and their tendency to embody divergent or ambivalent ideas, has led to the suggestion that legal practices may be represented in different ways, as expressing differing ideals: the law of tort may be viewed as embodying ideals of economic efficiency *or* corrective justice precisely because the practice of tort lawyers variously reflects concerns with *both* sets of ideals. Instead of seeking to uncover the sources of tension or fragmentation within shared practices, modern legal philosophers have adopted the voluntarist belief that human practices are therefore 'morally neutral' or mute phenomena, awaiting an 'interpretation' with which to invest them with moral significance.[9] Legal

---

8   As Nigel Simmonds has observed, 'Shared understandings may be eroded, but they never become "constraints" within which the interpreter may move freely. Precisely in being understandings, they inform and guide interpretation at every point.' See Simmonds, 'Between Positivism and Idealism', 50 *Cambridge LJ* (1991), 326.

9   It matters little whether interpretation is held to be necessary to an understanding of such practices: a view of practices as 'mere conventions' is expressed with particular strength in Dworkin's earlier writings, for example: see Dworkin, 'The Model of Rules II', in *Taking Rights Seriously* (London, Duckworth, 1978), esp. 54ff. Dworkin's later writings suggest a

reasoning, at an abstract level, involves at root an evaluative choice between rival interpretations.

Such a view is perhaps an inevitable consequence of an increasingly widespread conception of law as a technical instrument grounded in formal rules and doctrines. Legal actions in contract, for example, having shed their traditional association with limitations upon usury, are viewed as formal instruments for the facilitation of exchange and voluntary dealing. A general interpretation of the law of contract will then be naturally viewed as the attempt to identify the general interests that are served by the existence of such economic forms, and to state general limitations upon those forms of dealing by reference to moral or political principles of a necessarily more abstract character than the mundane and technical reality addressed by the formal rules and decisions. In this way, the reflective processes involved in the administration of justice become steadily more detached from the ordinary context of action, addressing instead broad moral and political visions.

Interpretative understandings of this kind do not easily manifest the sensitive exploration and dissection of factual situations that are the bread and butter of legal argument, for the reflective understandings sought (in distinguishing one situation from another, or in judging similar cases as demanding the same treatment) are not incidents of 'interpretation', at all. My point is not intended simply as a criticism of views that lazily treat practices as 'texts' to be studied, for the intellectual processes involved may be quite similar, as Hart observed. Rather, (as Hart again correctly said) in either case interpretation 'no longer characterises the nerve of reasoning involved in determining ... the right thing to do.'[10] One who exhibits the virtues of sound legal scholarship thus tends to be praised for his insight, sound judgment and analytical skill, rather than a mere facility with interpretation.

These facts about legal scholarship should be obvious. Yet the prevalence of interpretative theories has tended to mask the reflective nature of legal thought by *contrasting* the lawyerly processes of rule-application with the moral and political vision of the jurisprudential theorist. Lawyerly virtues of argument and scholarship are thus obscured by the thought that such intellectual operations are sustained by an implicit background of moral and political thought which lawyers do not consciously address in their arguments. Such background theories are then the stuff of 'normative jurisprudence', a pursuit of legal philosophers to be carefully distinguished from the technical practices of lawyers; or they form the basis for idealistic visions in which moral and political values constitute 'the general part of adjudication' and (where not raised explicitly in legal judgment) the 'silent prologue to any decision at law.'[11] The legality of the vision is preserved through the thought that lawyers (or legal

more measured view, though essentially the same attitude is present: see my discussion in note 3 above.

10 Hart, *The Concept of Law*, 127.

11 Dworkin (above note 3), 90. Legal positivists would, of course, deny these last two claims. But they would not, I think, dissent from the basic idea involved, that (having described the 'valid' rules of a legal order) normative jurisprudence consists of the application to law of specific moral or political theories: see for example J. Raz, 'Interpretation Without Retrieval', in A. Marmor (ed.) *Law and Interpretation* (Oxford, Clarendon Press, 1995), 155; also the essays in L. Alexander (ed.) *Constitutionalism: Philosophical Foundations* (Cambridge,

philosophers) address a distinctive dimension of moral or political concern: that of legal *rights*. Legal thought, on this view, consists not in a distinctive process of moral reflection, concerned with the moral features of particular situations, but in a principled understanding of the general moral and political significance of a system of rights.

It is no accident that the idea of a 'right' in modern jurisprudence plays a central role in connecting the notion of law as a moral and political ideal to the lawyerly perspective that views law as a set of mundane arrangements for the administration of human affairs, for in comprising both a legal instrument *and* an important political idea, rights provide the intellectual fulcrum about which it is possible to link abstract theorising with the more limited technical horizons of legal practice. Rights are 'hard' as well as 'soft': they are *both* precise forms of legal relationship *and* bearers of a wide and deep political significance. In this way, general political theories can be offered as interpretations or 'reconstructions' of a body of laws, for lawyers can be viewed as discovering and articulating internally coherent interpretations of systems of rights. The distortive impact of these ideas upon our understanding of legal reasoning tends to go unnoticed in part because of the suggestion of a gap between the 'surface' level of mundane rule-application and the 'deep' structure of moral and political values that underpin them. Legal reasoning then resembles less a sustained tradition of theoretical reflection, and more an intellectual tug-of-war between the specific forms of rule-application and the more abstract flights of political theory.

These combinatory forces in legal thought are most seductive, but also most difficult to contain, where the aspirational ideal at work in the law is thought to embody a deep commitment to liberal conceptions of justice. One potent version of the argument centres on liberalism's elevation of the right to a status higher than that of the good. From this point of view, modern political culture is the inheritor of fragmented interests and a partial breakdown in the structure of the shared practices and institutions that sustain the liberal polity. This fragmentation is *both* the central problem *and* the central feature of a system of politics that creates a space in which dissenting voices may be exercised. Such spaces amount to interstices of freedom within a system of imposed rules designed to place limitations upon autonomous words and actions which, if left unchecked, would ultimately destabilise and undermine the social structures they inhabit. The domain of private law may be represented as that area of life in which fundamental conflicts of interest are addressed through the orderly processes of litigation. Private law cannot *dissolve* such tensions, for areas of freedom within a pluralistic society are inherently unstable.[12] Thus, private rights come to be associated with aggregative forms of reasoning that attempt to impose some reasonable ordering upon the competing interests.

A society that focuses on rights in this way inevitably perceives the law as an instrument for securing 'the good' in a reduced and attenuated sense. This is because

---

Cambridge University Press, 1998). The activities of Bentham's 'Censor' also constitute a good example.

12 See I. Berlin, 'The Pursuit of the Ideal' in *The Crooked Timber of Humanity* (London, Fontana, 1991), 13: 'Some among the great goods cannot live together ... We are doomed to choose and every choice may entail an irreparable loss.'

lawyerly interpretations of a system of rights will be seen as expressing, not a specific conception of the good, but particular dimensions of liberal autonomy and equal concern. Such strategies pose inherent problems for an account of legal doctrine, however, for the preservation of law's perceived liberal neutrality (as between specific conceptions of the human *telos*) can be achieved only through the development of legal theories that attempt to divorce juridical concepts and arguments from matters of wider moral and political concern. The possibility of individual rights will then be thought to hinge upon the existence of detailed practices involving doctrinal rules and principles that possess sophisticated meanings in isolation from broader forms of collective political introspection. Yet the association of private rights with aggregative forms of reasoning means that the realm of private entitlements could never be *fully* insulated from the aspirations and goals of the public sphere. The traditional lawyerly virtues of impartiality and dispassionate analysis would thus come to be looked upon as intellectual mirages concealing and sustaining complex inequalities within the fabric of existing social institutions.

An attempt of this kind to unite the mundane and aspirational aspects of law in the ideal of liberal neutrality is thus vulnerable to the criticism that it is ultimately self-refuting. Liberal rights require a context of stable institutions and shared practices which nurture the social freedoms on which they are based. Maintenance of social institutions and practices cannot be achieved on the basis of *neutral* interventions in the political controversies which would otherwise undermine the basis of social order, however. The strategy of placing the right before the good may thus invite rejection as the formalistic orphan of a narrow and demanding positivism. Yet the concern with neutrality has proved remarkably resilient in recent political thought, partly because it is readily transformable into a rich concern with human equality and democratic respect. A liberal polity may then itself mutate into an idealistic politics of principles in which law represents, not an instrument of policy, but the articulate search for an elevated moral perspective through which rights may be related to or derived from fundamental principles of justice.

The elevation of mundane argumentative practices and institutions to the level of philosophical principle inevitably reduces the opportunity for the recognition of pluralism and diversity of values and perspectives within established practices. Theoretical 'interpretations' of inherited social arrangements may thus erode liberal understandings by replacing them with imperial visions: the integrity of rights ceases to be a matter of the comparative stability and immunity of private entitlements from revision in the light of principles of general political concern, and instead becomes a question of the integrity and consistency of a body of principles inherently and pervasively shaped by publicly determined standards of justice. The 'liberal' nature of society, then, is reflected in the view that questions of individual interest are a matter for joint interpretation and concern. From the midst of a theory of rights an overriding conception of the good thus makes a pale and shadowy re-emergence.

Both the positivist and the idealistic varieties of legal theory obscure the significance of the reflective dimension of legal thought. Yet, given the obvious ability of idealism to resonate with prevalent political attitudes and aspirations, it is not, perhaps, the legal positivist's vision that presents the greatest potential for the distortion and erosion of liberal understandings, but the starry-eyed idealist's. We should resist the tendency to view the law's transformative capacities as consisting of deliberate efforts to adapt an inherited set of principles to the problems raised by a constantly changing social world. The effect of social changes (as well as changes in philosophical perspective) on the intellectual landscape tend to be understood only gradually and in retrospect. 'The mistake,' as Milsom observed, 'is one of scale. The changes the historian can see were too large to be seen by the lawyers he is thinking about; and the problems the lawyers were thinking about were too small for the historian to see ... What the large change does is to concentrate demand, raising small daily problems in a particular area; and small and marginal solutions accumulate into central changes.'[13] There are, Milsom concluded, 'no great ideas.'

The characteristic form of common law reasoning is one in which *rationes decidendi* create fairly specific precedents rather than wide and general commitments to a particular set of values that form the interpretative background for concrete situations. To recognise a form of moral reasoning in which the ethical is understood through engagement with the variable particular, is to embrace a moral vision that is distinct in important ways from the idealistic elevation of law to the level of moral principle. Morality addresses a context of shared practices that contain within themselves the potential for fragmentation and division. Rather than seeking to connect instances of fragmentation within practices to the experience of a shared existence, the idealist relates abstract theories of value to aspects of that experience: instead of a deep and significant cultural knowledge, we then have opposing 'conceptual schemes' anchored in idealised versions of that experience. Recent moral philosophy has embraced this view: 'What we have shown is that it is absurd to look for a justifying ground for the totality of beliefs, something outside this totality which we can use to test or compare our beliefs.'[14]

By diminishing experience from a rich source of moral insight into an arena of contingencies to which more permanent moral insights are applied, idealism embodies an ethical vision only tenuously anchored in the mundane realities that supply the ordinary context of motive and action. This is because those mundane realities are produced and sustained by human practices that reflect diversity and pluralism, but also tolerance. In transforming social practices and institutions into an ideal embodiment of public virtues, the pursuit of consistency will encourage the development of overriding perspectives that inevitably treat certain aspects of a fragmented vision as having more centrality or importance than others, reducing the capacity for the expression of liberal tolerance. Such imperialistic visions might thus hope to sustain themselves by feeding off those aspects of social life that nurture

---

13 Milsom, 'The Nature of Blackstone's Achievement', 1.

14 D. Davidson, 'A Coherence Theory of Truth and Knowledge', in E. de Pore (ed.) *Truth and Interpretation: Perspectives on the Philosophy of Donald Davidson* (Oxford, Blackwell, 1986), 312. Raymond Plant, who also cites this passage, argues as follows: 'There is no Archimedean point from which we can see the world or "the given" from outside a particular set of beliefs, and thus there cannot be a justified claim to absolute knowledge if this means depicting the "given" more adequately than any other conceptual scheme...' R. Plant, *Politics, Theology and History* (Cambridge, Cambridge University Press, 2001), 96.

the beliefs that gave rise to them.[15] Liberalism is best thought of not as a particular body of beliefs, however, but as a tradition: as such it may be expected to contain within itself the numerous contradictory impulses felt by the diverse participants who think of themselves as 'liberals'. A liberal understanding of the rule of law is thus revealed not by 'fitting' abstract theories to partially described practices, but through the sensitive exploration of overlapping modes of thought that might coexist within a body of practices only in complex patterns of tension.

The difference in approaches I am suggesting bears some similarity to that identified by Michael Walzer, in the following passage:

> One way to begin the philosophical enterprise – perhaps the original way – is to walk out of the cave, leave the city, climb the mountain, to fashion for oneself ... an objective and universal standpoint. Then one describes the terrain of everyday life from far away, so that it loses its particular contours and takes on a general shape. But I mean to stand in the cave, in the city, on the ground. Another way of doing philosophy is to interpret to one's fellow citizens the world of meanings that we share. Justice and equality can be conceivably worked out as philosophical artefacts, but a just or egalitarian society cannot be. If such a society isn't already here – hidden, as it were, in our concepts and categories – we shall never know it concretely or realise it in fact.[16]

The idealist may be motivated by the desire to reconcile the existence of pluralism with the need for unconditional standpoints from which to engage in moral contemplation. Yet morality is universal, not in the sense that particulars must be related to detached and unconditioned universals, but in that particulars contain the universal, as part of their intelligibility: for, in this way, particulars are a prism in which aspects of the human condition are reflected (sometimes obscurely). Morality may thus be said to concern universal ideas without issuing in standpoints that avoid immersion in 'conditions'.

Idealism, by nature, tends to underestimate the importance of the mundane forms of rule-application with which the ordinary lawyer is familiar. Because the idealist views rules as 'mere conventions', in themselves devoid of moral significance, it must then seem as if ordinary rule-applying processes hide or suppress a more fundamental dimension to legal thought of which the practising lawyer is largely unaware. Operating at the 'surface' level of adjudication, lawyers are inevitably portrayed by the idealist as a pretty unreflective bunch, operating within a complex structure of deeply principled ideas of which they may catch no more than the odd fleeting glimpse.[17] This view has obvious comforts for the legal philosopher, whose job is then to enlighten his legal brothers to the existence of that elevated moral perspective. It is the obvious fact that specifically legal modes of argument

---

15 See for example J.L. Austin, 'Three Ways of Spilling Ink', in *Philosophical Papers* (Oxford, Clarendon, 1969), 285, which talks of the 'freedom in the "structuring" of history ... by means of words'.

16 M. Walzer, *Spheres of Justice* (Oxford, Blackwell, 1983), xvi. See also Walzer, *On Toleration* (New York, Yale University Press, 1997), Chapter 1, esp. 1–5; Plant (above, note 14), 116.

17 Cf. Dworkin's suggestion that jurisprudence is the '*silent* prologue to any decision at law': *Law's Empire*, 90.

and conflict-resolution exclude moral or political reasons that may otherwise have a bearing on decision that makes idealism such a splendidly adaptable thesis: for any attempt to 'go beyond' or restate the settled rules and established doctrines will appear to embody underdeveloped forms of philosophical idealism, awaiting a deeper and more general justification by the philosopher. Employing the distinction between 'surface' conventions and 'deep' or underpinning principles, the philosopher may point with relative ease to the common law's 'inadequately theorised' and 'insufficiently systematised' state as the product of a lawyerly failure to 'think in terms of overarching principles' or develop a fully reflective 'rights consciousness'.[18]

The common law mode of reasoning is one in which judges modify existing doctrines and standards as they apply them. It takes no great familiarity with case-law, moreover, to comprehend the fact that there is, in the context of juridical thought and judgment, no clear distinction between those two intellectual processes: the lack of a fixed verbal form indicates the operation of ideas that depend for their form upon the precise manner of their articulation in each case. Because such meanings may be formulated with greater or lesser degrees of reflective insight, it becomes impossible to separate a 'surface' meaning for rules and doctrines from a deeper, philosophical level of meaning. Legal thought is thus more closely depicted as involving the gradual deepening of a reflective understanding, rather than the application of abstract theoretical insights to floating sets of 'givens'.

Juridical argument thus constitutes a form of thought that becomes increasingly distorted as it is systematised, for the pursuit of theoretical coherence demands the isolation of a manageably small set of considerations (conceptions of justice or fairness, etc.) through which currently diverse particulars are to be classified. Yet the complex concerns that make up the law of contract, of tort, property, etc., are identifiable with no finite set of considerations running through every case, or informing decision at every point. Common law precedents can be developed along various differing trajectories, and often contain many possible lines of development. Doctrinal rules thus tend to be subject to complex exceptions, distinctions and rationalisations both general and highly specific. Being shot through with competing concerns and overlaid by regulatory regimes, legal rules represent complex jurisprudential ideas reflecting a heady mixture of ends and purposes. Such richness is not easily reflected where legal thought is alleged to serve a limited number of interpretative ideals, for to impose a framework of abstract ideals upon legal thought is to solidify the form and possible meanings to be given to doctrinal ideas: we must see them as (perhaps unconsciously or unreflectively) serving *these* ends, at a suitable level of abstraction. General interpretative principles would doubtless necessitate the creation of complex exceptions to mitigate potential injustices in particular cases; yet any attempt at formulating a principled basis for such departures would either itself embody abstract ideals subject to open-ended exceptions and modifications, or lead to massive injustices and distortions in its application to specific cases that may, although similar, be viewed as morally unalike.

Lofty principled reasoning of this sort runs counter to the actual tradition of common law scholarship and adjudication. To a large extent, the wisdom or justice

---

18 J. Wright, *Tort Law and Human Rights* (Oxford, Hart Publications, 2001), 5–7.

of a legal judgment is a function of the terms in which the case is conceived: this is because legal disputes do not come before the court as untheorised phenomena requiring *ab initio* resolution, but, to a considerable extent, as situations whose moral features are classified and demarcated in the light of established doctrines and definitions. Not all features of a dispute are relevant for the legal treatment of a case, but only those that are significant when viewed through the prism of legal doctrine. The issue of moral significance is seldom, in law, a question of general political standpoints or moral ideals, but more often conformity to relatively narrow, technical concepts such as duty-of-care, bona fide purchaser, intangible interference, etc. The understanding and application of these concepts does, of course, imply broader moral or political points of view, but the degree of concreteness and precision with which doctrinal principles are typically formulated as reasons for decision allows juridical reasoning to remain relatively insulated against wider currents of political thought, and the terms in which individual cases are understood do not ordinarily presuppose a commitment to a quite general set of political ideals according to which clashing interests can be ordered or reconciled. The traditional form of common law reasoning is thus one in which shifts in general moral values and principles come to our attention only gradually and retrospectively: a line of decisions is seen as promoting or implying certain values, and over time a particular understanding of those values, or a few rival understandings, will come to dominate, until they give way to doubt and are ultimately supplanted by newer, alternative conceptions. The general point I am making may become clearer by consideration of the following examples.[19]

1. *St Smeltings v Niffing*: The plaintiff bought property in an area containing a good deal of heavy industry, but there were no factories in the immediate vicinity of his estate. Nevertheless, the plaintiff complained of noise and pollution from a processing plant situated one mile away from the property. On appeal, the court held that whilst there was clear interference with the plaintiff's property rights, it is not open to everyone to raise an action in these circumstances: that which would constitute nuisance in a rural environment does not necessarily amount to nuisance in an urban context of well-established industry.

2. *Slack v Sharkey*: The facts broadly resemble *St Smeltings*, except that a new rendering plant, operating round the clock, was established on a plot adjacent to that belonging to the plaintiff. The court distinguishes *St Smeltings* because it is impossible to avoid liability by pointing to the urban and industrial character of the area if the new user constitutes a notable increase in noise or pollution: one cannot override long-recognised and fundamental property rights in this way.

---

19 For an extended discussion of the 19th-century tort cases on which these examples are based, see S. Coyle and K. Morrow, *The Philosophical Foundations of Environmental Law* (Oxford, Hart Publications, 2004) Chapter 4. My reliance on fictional adaptations here is intended as a means of simplifying the lines of authority and reducing the complexity of and number of issues involved in their real-world counterparts.

3. *Sneak v Whiffland*: Residents sought an injunction where an abattoir is built to the rear of a housing estate. The court reaffirms the principle in *St Smeltings*, but grants the injunction. A major factor in the court's deliberations is that much of the detritus is shipped in from outside the immediate area: 'Pollution from Birmingham should not be visited upon the blameless residents of Newcastle.'

4. *Trollop v Fester*: Sewage from a local water treatment plant under local authority control enters and contaminates the plaintiff's watercourse. The court held that although the Authority has a statutory duty to make adequate sanitary provision to local residences, this duty is to the whole district, not to specific individuals. The plaintiff cannot be given standing to enforce, since the recognition of distinct claims under the Act would undermine the provision of an important public service. In such cases, private interests must be balanced and traded off against the public interest.

5. *Leaky v Fishy*: Run-off from a local authority sewage treatment works enters the plaintiff's land. The court held that there is nothing in previous law to protect statutory authorities from liability where a private individual or company would be so liable. However, sensitive consideration must be given in each case as to whether an injunction or damages is the most appropriate remedy. Given that statutory duties operate in most cases, there is a presumption that damages are appropriate in the absence of significant indications to the contrary.

6. *Tarr v McAdam*: Emissions from a gas works damaged crops on the plaintiff's farm. The court reaffirmed the *Trollop* ruling, but noted that it is important to distinguish infrastructure-based enterprises from commercial concerns. The common law cannot have had in mind to extend immunity to private concerns operating in the public interest. The existence of duties of care to community residents does not override liability if nuisance is caused by their discharge. The presumption in *Leaky* only holds if the injury to the plaintiff's rights is small and can be evaluated in monetary terms. Since in the present case the nuisance threatens the plaintiff's livelihood, an injunction is appropriate.

7. *Bruise v Shiner*: Discharge from a sewage outlet destroyed crops on the plaintiff's farm. The court awarded damages but not an injunction: the defendant had a statutory duty to treat sewage, and the discharge was an unavoidable consequence of that process. Whilst defendants cannot have carte blanche to pollute simply in virtue of being a statutory provider, an injunction is unavailable if the costs of imposing one to the defendant are far greater than the damage done to the plaintiff. This is surely about balance in respect of public and private interests, not the absolute and narrow-minded protection of property rights.

8. *Sloane v Ranger*: A power station caused unusual amounts of atmospheric static electricity, which interfered with radio and television reception in the local area. The immediate decision concerned a group action by residents. It was held that the residents could not succeed: a tort against land cannot be converted into a tort against the person. Such actions may only succeed if property rights are directly affected.

The court emphasised the property basis of liability in nuisance, stating that it is not a simple matter of balancing public v private interests.

These examples are no more than vaguely suggestive of the range and complexity of the considerations involved in common law adjudication. In those examples, no clear distinction exists between a surface level of rule-ascertainment and a deeper process of modification and systematisation. No set of general principles, capable of articulation in abstraction from the facts, is being 'fitted' to a floating set of particulars; and the justice or soundness of the judgments would not be improved even if it were. The contexts of judgment are too kaleidoscopic and varied to admit of an informative set of principles of justice from which the particular decisions may be regarded as fragmented instances. Doctrinal integrity is not, therefore, a matter of discovering unifying perspectives within the law at the level of abstract principle, but the refinement and clarification of a body of ideas in relation to particular cases. By focusing on 'interpretation', idealism overlooks an important dimension of legal thought.

Legal Reason

In this and the preceding chapter, I have suggested that many of the intellectual disagreements on which modern jurisprudence is centred are in fact merely differing embodiments of an overarching set of ideas that constitute a taken-for-granted background to modern philosophical thought. These ideas hover around notions of liberalism, equality and the centrality of ideas of justice and right to political thought. One is frequently reminded, when approaching these debates, of Fukuyama's claim that the final form of human society is marked by the liberal democratic state with a commitment to market capitalism and basic human rights, and that the emergence of such social forms represents, in some sense, 'the end of history'.[20] To view the liberal democratic state in this way (as the ultimate refinement of political order) is to regard liberalism as a coherent historical process, and to view the present form of that process as the teleological endpoint in which that process culminates. Such a view is uneasily reconciled with modern liberal thought, for in attributing to liberalism a historical essence and a teleological trajectory, the position exhibits a metaphysical richness at odds with the general suppression of metaphysical standpoints within modern moral and political philosophy.

The view of liberal democratic governance structured around capitalism and rights as a high watermark in the history of political thought is deeply problematic, aside from philosophical doubt about 'essentialism'. The idealistic conjunction of a liberal form of government with the recognition of fundamental rights is one that exhibits considerable dynamic tension. Modern understandings of 'right' are (as I argued in Chapter 3) the product of a Protestant conception of the political realm. Such understandings are an essential part of a Protestant world-view for they give structure to the idea of conflict between distinct forms of the good. Liberal politics is

---

20 See F. Fukuyama, *The End of History and the Last Man*, revised edn (Harmondsworth, Penguin, 1993).

not an immediate consequence of Protestantism, as the existence of plural conceptions of the good does not entail any belief in the possibility of their coexistence within the unified state, nor of the virtue of toleration in facilitating private project-pursuit.[21] The intellectual and social context within which Protestant beliefs emerged serves to highlight the obviously illiberal character of the juridical framework of 'subjective' rights that underpin Protestant thought: Grotius, Hobbes, Pufendorf, Locke and Wolff were not members of a fledgling liberal tradition. Those who may be described as 'early liberals' – Constant, Mill, Tocqueville – wrote upon central themes not of right or justice, but of toleration, individualism and freedom.[22] As Geuss observed, 'no particular saliency had been attributed to justice' in liberal political thought prior to Rawls. Justice played no great part in the writings of the early liberals, for they recognised in a perhaps more clear-sighted way than their modern successors, the tendency of a theory of justice to create centralising or unified perspectives within politics that operate to suppress or threaten individualism. Thus, for such writers, '"being just" is the appropriate defining character trait of the administrator, functionary or bureaucrat rather than that of the politician or citizen.'[23]

The tendency within modern jurisprudence to celebrate liberal social forms has frequently led to an obscuring of the dynamic tension between liberalism and Protestant political thought, for although both Protestantism and liberalism concern individual freedom, the underlying conceptions of freedom are somewhat different. The nature of the distinction can be discovered by examining the idealistic understanding of the adjudicative context. By construing rights as central to legal thought, the liberal idealist connects questions of social and political justice much more firmly and directly with the adjudicative process. Unlike the wider political process, in which each person's voice is drowned out by an ocean of similar voices, the adjudicative process is one in which each person's claims can be heard and evaluated specifically and directly. But the same conditions that make idealism an attractive philosophy of law also undermine the value and purpose of rights as the principal means through which individuals can assert and defend their interests. By threatening the integrity of private law as a body of principles distinct from general political debate, idealism casts into doubt the reality of blocks of private life marked off from public scrutiny and regulation.

The traditional conception of adjudication is one in which parties to a dispute submit pleas to the court and present reasoned arguments and proofs for a decision in their favour.[24] It is this dimension of adjudication that lies at the centre of idealistic assumptions about the judicial process as a special and essential form of participation in legal decision-making through which individuals can directly articulate and

---

21 For the notion of private project pursuit, see Simmonds, 'The Possibility of Private Law', in J. Tasioulas (ed.) *Law, Values and Social Practices* (Aldershot, Dartmouth, 1997).

22 Even so, liberal tolerance was thought to concern, not a positive virtue of the celebration of pluralism, but an acceptance of the essentially private nature of faith and the impossibility of its coercion by external forces: see R. Geuss, *History and Illusion in Politics* (Cambridge, Cambridge University Press, 2001), 73–84.

23 Geuss, *Outside Ethics* (Oxford, Princeton University Press, 2005), 15.

24 L. Fuller, 'The Forms and Limits of Adjudication', 92 *Harvard L Rev* (1978) 353, at 364. See also O. Fiss, 'The Forms of Justice', 93 *Harvard L Rev* (1979) 1.

protect their fundamental interests. In his impressive article 'On the Form and Limits of Adjudication', Lon Fuller presents an argument that we can see as constituting a devastating problem for legal idealism of this kind. Fuller develops the idea of a 'polycentric' problem: a problem in which the solution depends upon the resolution of tensions within a complex web of relationships where '[a] pull on one strand will distribute tensions after a complicated pattern throughout the web as a whole'.[25] Problems of this kind bear certain similarities to the behaviour of a spider web:

> Doubling the original pull will, in all likelihood, not simply double each of the resulting tensions but will rather create a different complicated pattern of tensions. This would certainly occur, for example, if the doubled pull caused one or more of the weaker strands to snap. This is a 'polycentric' situation because it is 'many-centred' – each crossing of strands is a distinct centre for distributing tensions.[26]

Where rights serve to connect legal thought with lofty philosophical ideals, such problems are brought to the fore, for the parties to a case are regarded as asserting claims that depend not just upon the history and circumstances of the dispute between them, but upon broad and general principles that apply to all. An individual's rights thus appear in the guise of interests wielded and asserted in the context of complex patterns of similar and competing interests, delineated not simply by reference to established rules but according to broad conceptions of equality and the good. The 'legal' dimension to adjudication is then preserved by the representation of such overtly political concerns as elements in the construction of 'juridical equality'. Yet the presence of such political elements in juridical reasoning comprehensively undermines the driving insight that the judicial process offers individuals a direct means of defending their interests against outside intrusion. By requiring rights to be delineated in a broader context of competing political assumptions, rights function effectively only insofar as they conform to collective notions of what each individual's legitimate interests are. In such circumstances, the idea that adjudication furnishes individual litigants with meaningful control over their own interests is an empty form indeed.

Fuller believed that polycentric problems constitute the limits of effective adjudication,[27] for in the context of clashing political values and ideals, the ability of the litigant to offer reasoned arguments and proofs is fatally undermined: the plaintiff cannot *prove* the existence of an entitlement, because such proofs presuppose the existence of a stable structure of rules and doctrines against which competing claims can be evaluated and tested. The possibility of offering reasoned arguments in favour of a given standpoint is similarly undercut, as the process of reasoning is one no longer rooted in a context of stable assumptions and accepted starting-points upon which the litigants' 'reasons' can focus. Rather than offering reasoned interpretations of established doctrines and principles, the party wishing to assert that a right has

---

25 Fuller (above, note 24), 395.

26 *Ibid.*

27 Fuller's reasons differ rather considerably from mine, but his arguments might be seen as addressing parallel and perhaps wider concerns. There is a great deal in Fuller's careful treatment of polycentric problems that merits consideration. See Fuller, *ibid.*, 394.

been infringed must orientate his claims within a context of political and moral thought where disagreement attaches not just to the interpretation of rules, but also to the question of what are the permissible starting-points of the reasoning process. Potentially intractable political and ethical dilemmas would then have been converted into legal questions that lie at the very heart of doctrinal understandings.[28]

Such trends are difficult to resist in modern legal thought, for juridical argument increasingly centres upon the grammar of rights. The beguiling effects of legal instruments such as the Human Rights Act 1998 encourage the belief amongst jurists and legal philosophers that they are witnessing the creation of a new form of social order, in which justice and rights are given a central place in political decision. It is perhaps the extreme versatility of the language of rights that allows jurisprudential and political writers to present rights as uncontroversial starting-points for reflection, for the absorption of the notion of a 'right' into the general political consciousness is such as to suggest the grammar of rights as a free-standing framework for politics, as well as a familiar and well-understood legal instrument. Legal thought can then slide easily between these two senses of 'right', giving rise to the suggestion that in focusing directly upon individual rights, the legal process reveals its own deep structure as the refined articulation of social values. This intellectual shift therefore represents both the juridification of moral discourse, and the politicisation of law.

In one sense, rights *are* a central feature of the adjudicative process. It is an obvious fact that courts have the power to impose certain conditions upon litigants who submit complaints before the law. Such powers are not restricted to the imposition of damages or injunctions, but include a diverse range of remedies such as the giving of effect to contractual or testamentary provisions, distraining of goods, orders for the transfer or restitution of property, the restriction of specific actions (e.g. restraining orders) etc. Insofar as the grant of any of these remedies can be described as imposing an obligation upon the defendant, the plaintiff can be said to possess a right to its performance. Thus, in an equally obvious way, the behaviour that led to the plaintiff's raising of the legal action can be viewed as a violation of the plaintiff's rights: the operation of noisy industrial machinery next to heavily populated areas, and the production of noxious emissions may both be said to violate the rights of those affected by them; yet the issues raised in the examples explored in the preceding section hinged upon considerations that were both broader and more complex than questions of individual right. Issues of public health, public nuisance or developmental land use are matters that concern dimensions of justice and legality beyond that of entitlement, and cannot be reasonably reduced to a consideration of the rights of those who happen so far to have been affected.[29] It is thus a distortive and misleading error to explore such questions from a starting point in the legal rights of those involved.

---

28 One recent advocate of human rights-inspired idealism is openly circumspect about the possibility of proving rights claims: see F. Klug, *Values For a Godless Age: The Story of the United Kingdom's New Bill of Rights* (London, Penguin 2000), 18. Such claims take place in the context of a 'debate without end' where understandings of rights shift in the light of changing moral, philosophical and political ideals.

29 Finnis, *Natural Law and Natural Rights*, 218.

The centrality of rights within adjudication is thus a function not of their general significance in political argumentation, but of the fundamentality of rights to the expression of jural relations. Adjudication naturally concerns specific dimensions of the legal relationship between plaintiff and defendant, and rights form the protective instrumentalities through which the law operates to remedy breakdowns in such relationships. Insofar as litigation concerns the relative standing of litigants, therefore, rights form an intrinsic part of the administration of justice. The significance of rights lies in their close association with legal remedies, in this way. It is possible to exaggerate and distort this important insight, however, by pursuing it within the following, seductive line of reasoning: 'Remedies' (we may say) 'are the outcome of legal decision. The process of legal argument is thus in some sense an attempt to reach a conclusion as to what, in each case, is the appropriate remedy to impose. Since a remedy is imposed to correct the infringement of the plaintiff's right, adjudication can be regarded as a series of opposing arguments about the existence or substance of legal rights. Because judicial decisions are expected to exhibit as far as possible the property of justice, arguments about legal rights go to the very heart of theories concerning the nature and demands of justice.'

Idealistic trajectories of this sort ought to be resisted. Legal argument is not an ungrounded exercise in the identification of entitlements, but a reflective engagement with doctrinal concepts and principles through their endless specification in particular decisions. Whilst some doctrinal principles serve to specify forms of entitlement (such as the rules governing testate succession), others address matters of policy or technical aspects of the law's operation or coherence of purpose that are unrelated to the existence or exercise of rights: rules regarding the court's powers of interpretation in relation to inchoate negotiable instruments, or the assignment of evidential burdens, considerations of public order, or desirable limits upon private behaviour, or of the conditions in which inferences about intention can be deduced from past action, and so on. Such ideas are explored and refined in the context of litigation, and thus have certain effects upon the litigants' jural relations; but they are not *themselves* addressed to relational ideas, and are thus not greatly illuminated by being regarded as elements in a calculus concerned with spelling out the relative boundaries of such relationships. The legal order is not simply a horizontal system of private entitlements and interests intersected by a vertical system of social regulation,[30] but the creation of a complex framework of social practices and forms of governance (such as a civil bureaucracy, the economy, welfare and emergency services, 'the state', etc.) which sustain the polity in which such rights and policies interact.

The interpretation of such diverse aspects of the legal order as factors in the determination of 'rights' or dimensions of justice is both easy and seductive. But we must also keep in mind the importance of the social framework in which such phenomena exist and function, and of the law's role in maintaining that framework. (Indeed, it may be more apposite to speak of a number of distinct yet overlapping frameworks of social order and governance, and of the centrality of the legal order in securing the smooth interaction of the various frameworks.) Notions of justice

---

30 Milsom (above, note 13), 3.

may play a significant part in relation to some areas of this framework, but they are unlikely to be omnipresent within it, for much of social life consists of sporadic interaction between strangers of whom we know relatively little, on the basis of informal social rules rather than well-understood conventions that are capable of being fully articulated by the relevant participants. Governance often consists not in the deliberate redistribution of powers or resources in relation to such modes of interaction, but in the provision of an orderly basis on which the interaction can continue. In this way, a major project of governance (and of law) might be seen as attempting to give transparency and structure to otherwise shifting and ambiguous aspects of everyday life.

The factors that guide decision in a large number of cases are not deliberately chosen elements of a theory of justice, but doctrinal considerations of a broadly conventional nature that seek to give greater definition to the content of informal understandings on which the majority of social relationships are based. The rules of contract, or the definition of a gift, say, are of this kind in that much of their understanding finds its root in somewhat amorphous social conventions, whilst at the same time seeking to restructure such conventions by assigning clear meanings to doubtful aspects of established practice and resolving ambiguities that hinder their operation. In such cases, the process is one of gradual refinement and adjustment, not the selection or evaluation of distributive or aggregative policies, for in administering the general framework of social interaction, central aspects of the legal order may not be directly focused on the reconciliation of conflicting sets of interests, at all. Rights indeed feature in the end-points of adjudication, but they do not represent the heart of doctrinal systems of law.[31]

The Withering of Ideals

Raymond Geuss has drawn attention to a liberal society's capacity for self-delusion: as society swings to the right economically and politically, it increasingly seeks solace in theories of social justice as a kind of 'compensatory fantasy', much as Feuerbach suggested the image of God as the necessary personification of those strengths and virtues of which humans, lacking them, must construct as ideals.[32] Such theories provide the comforting vision that utopia resembles the basic structure and features of the society of the present, only slight changes in direction or attitude being needed to advance towards the ideal. The effect of such intellectual tendencies is to elevate the social and political forms of the day to the status of historical inevitabilities: the conjunction of liberalism, democracy, human rights and the free-market being celebrated as the final form of enlightened human society. We may thereby effectively disguise, even from ourselves, the obvious truth that *every* political system has its ideal form: communism, aristocracy, anarchy, as much as liberalism. Yet it is not the ideal forms (which do not emerge as genuine possibilities in the real world), but the

---

31 I discuss this point in more detail in Chapter 8.

32 See R. Geuss, *Outside Ethics*, 34–35; L. Feuerbach, *The Essence of Christianity* (New York, Harper & Row, 1957). I borrow the ideas in the rest of this paragraph from Geuss, *Outside Ethics*, Chapter 2.

historical record of the real political movements in the world that carry the name of such systems, that reveal most clearly the 'essence' of the political philosophies they claim to instantiate.

The relationship between opposing packages of ideals and the social objects theorised by them, is never likely to be straightforward. This is particularly so in the case of highly articulate objects such as the law, which are in part constituted by those ideals. We may expect such objects to act as a prism through which the constituent ideals and other, mundane and pragmatic realities may be confusingly and distortingly refracted. The legal order of the British polity is a complex historical object created in part by the divergent traditions of positivism and idealism. Yet its central processes of moral reflection belong to a tradition of ethical thought lying wholly outside the philosophical world which those major traditions inhabit. It thus reflects an aspect of human social nature that is both enormously complex, fragmented and possibly incoherent. The moral nature of law lies ultimately neither in a positivist-inspired liberal 'neutrality', nor in idealistic reflections upon encompassing systems of rights, but rather in an intellectual world beyond both sets of ideals.

Chapter 8

Liberal Politics and Private Law

The legal philosophies I have been considering in the body of this book, those of positivism and idealism, are in an important sense philosophies of public law. Where law is viewed as a body of rules which in some way depend upon official practices of recognition or judgment, the distinction between deliberately enacted public systems of regulation and the existence of a horizontal system of private entitlements will seem of no great importance to an understanding of law: the horizontal relationships will be seen as serving a social purpose, and as being therefore sustained and regulated by the exercise of public powers. Autonomous transactions serve useful economic or redistributive goals and are *therefore* legally permitted. Such permissions are then considered to be defined as much by the absence of direct regulatory measures, as by the matrix of social institutions maintained by legislative power. Similarly, where law is perceived to consist of civic conceptions of justice rather than state-enacted rules, then the principles governing private transactions will be fully understandable only in the light of general interpretations of the legal order which take centrally into account its aggregative and distributive goals.

The form of moral reasoning exhibited within the structures of the common law, by contrast, depends upon an intellectual underpinning grounded in private law as a body of thought intellectually distinct from public law. The notions of justice and entitlement that inform the processes of judgment in the common law are to be distinguished from the notions of justice that operate in the sphere of public law, for they are structured by ethical values remote from that of the common good. Private law concepts address the value of private transactional behaviour as a distinct dimension of the social to that of collective action. Transactions of that kind are not simply allocative or redistributive mechanisms, but possess an ethical importance that must be pursued outside the confines of a regulatory framework. In order to operate in this way, the system of horizontal entitlements must be distinguished from the public law rules that concern the administration of general social interests.

It is the purpose of this chapter to explore the position of rights within the liberal conception of social order. A society pervaded by well-defined social roles (regarding the family, labour, religion, etc.) would have no need for a doctrine of rights; for people would belong to identifiable social groups with established privileges and responsibilities. Moral and social intercourse in such a society would operate according to entrenched considerations of rank and status rather than precisely defined entitlement. Suppose, however, that notions of social rank are slowly eroded, and the boundaries between social groupings become more relaxed, or in some cases eliminated. The notions of privilege and responsibility would then gradually recede from public thought, to be replaced by the general idea of a society of *opportunities*. Increased social mobility would then lead to a certain degree of fragmentation within social life, with the result that previously settled social understandings become oppressive or contentious. The need would thus arise for the replacement of informal understandings with a body of rules designed to structure competition by clarifying the conditions in which opportunities may be legitimately pursued. Social expectations will, finally, have ceased to revolve around the particular characteristics and position of the person, and will instead have come to be structured by a system of rights and duties applying to indistinguishable units or bearers of entitlement.

The central question of political theory in the modern world is to a large extent the question of how the obviously disparate and competing nature of concrete individual desires and needs relate to the fundamental equality of each individual as an autonomous bearer of rights and duties. Like all genuine philosophical problems, the existence of diversity and competition within a notionally more inclusive equality may be reflected upon in a variety of overlapping ways. One obvious dimension to the problem concerns the uneasy relationship between rights and the legal framework of regulatory instruments within which the rights are recognised and enforced. For it is rights, rather than the specific attributes and capacities that constitute the personality, that identify the juridical individual. But if rights are the product of a framework of *collectively constituted* norms and values, what significance attaches to the notion of the individual as a locus of impulses and autonomous decisions? If rights are necessary to sustain a genuine realm of private autonomy in which private ends are distinct from public goals, then what are we to make of the fact that such rights derive from legal rules designed to prevent *illegitimate* interference with the interests of others? Rights, it will then seem, concern both the self-directive pursuit of private goals *and* the protection of aspects of the personality from interference in a way that undermines the belief in genuine autonomy. In our theoretical understanding of the nature of legal rights, the value of self-directive autonomy confronts the value of passive benefit-receipt.

Rights, Interests and Legal Doctrine

Jurisprudential theories of rights have traditionally hinged upon two rival understandings of the nature of rights. One such theory, the Interest theory, holds that legal rights serve to protect or embody important interests of the right-holder. The other theory (the Will theory) claims that rights protect certain choices of the right-holder. My discussion in this book has so far avoided the Will/Interest debate in order to focus attention upon the difficulties attendant on the idealistic view that rights occupy a central place in legal thought. Implicit in my discussion was a suggestion that idealist philosophers tend to regard rights as serving interests rather than the will.[1] Idealism is not *logically* committed to the Interest theory; yet, by a suggestive

---

1   I do not believe anything in my preceding discussion is blunted by that suggestion, for the centrality of rights would have the same damaging features if aligned with the protection of choices rather than interests. My implication that idealists favour the 'Interest' view nevertheless captures faithfully, I believe, the sympathies of most idealists of whom I am aware, for the centrality of theories of justice to idealistic conceptions of liberalism naturally

conjunction of intellectual tendencies, idealism serves to connect the central role of rights with the notion that rights serve interests rather than choices.

Liberal idealism has a strong affinity with an 'Interest theory' of rights, for in placing rights at the centre of a theory of justice, legal doctrinal understandings are naturally viewed by the idealist as concerning the identification of 'interests' that require vindication through the processes of adjudication. Autonomous decision, on this view, is but one interest of human actors to be weighed and balanced against others with which it may conflict. The conception of interests at work in such thinking is one in which an actor's own prioritising of his interests is 'hardly dispositive' in relation to the legal enforcement or relaxation of the legal duties that protect those interests.[2] Rights must then be viewed not simply as legal instruments associated with the operation of remedies, but instead as important political ideas within a general theory of justice through which interests are evaluated. Since individuals disagree about their rights and interests, and since those disagreements arise from a social context of scarcity, competition, cooperation, economic variability and ever-changing desires, rights come to be seen as a matter for collective decision as part of a political process in which other social goods are at stake. Interests become a matter of what individuals *would* recognise if they were free of the imperfections and inequalities (both advantageous and disadvantageous) that pervade their lives.

According to liberal idealism, then, rights mark out important interests in which every individual has a stake, and which result from collective reflection into the nature and characteristics of individual wellbeing as a source of interests. One might well wonder to what extent such a conception of political liberalism remains moored in values of liberal pluralism,[3] as it is by no means clear that a liberal philosophy of society can be structured around a central theory of justice. Traditional forms of liberal thought combine a Protestant focus on the individual with a generalised suspicion of the state's ability to enact totalitarian restrictions upon freedom. By contrast, the view of rights as interests defined in the light of some general notion of 'liberal equality' seems far removed from the Protestant concern with the autonomous decisions of individuals who make choices in the light of their own conceptions of their interests. Now, liberalism denotes a historical tradition comprising conflicting-yet-overlapping strands in the real world of politics, rather than a set of ideas with a fixed intellectual essence. Lacking fixed historical limits, 'liberalism' can function as the inspirational core of social philosophies with otherwise little to unite them to the 'classic' historical paradigms of liberal thought. Neither, however, are such historical forms wholly irrelevant to an understanding of the liberal ethos.[4] Hence it is that philosophies that derive their animating spirit from one or more of these historical bases may eventually transform liberalism into its opposite.

---

promotes the value of passive benefit-receipt over that of self-directive autonomy. I discuss this point further below.

  2   M.H. Kramer, 'On the Nature of Legal Rights', 59 *Cambridge LJ* (2000) 473–508, at 497.

  3   See N. Simmonds, 'Rights at the Cutting Edge', in M. Kramer, N. Simmonds and H. Steiner, *A Debate Over Rights: Philosophical Inquiries* (Oxford, Clarendon, 1998), 129.

  4   R. Geuss, *History and Illusion in Politics*, 71.

The 'liberal equality' approach compels us to look upon the law as a coherent expression of justice governed by categorical principles. The possibility of presenting legal rules and decisions as instances of more general principles and categories appears as no accidental consequence of academic scholarship, but (it is thought) as the result of a coherent moral vision running throughout the law. Law can then be represented as a form of moral association precisely *because* it gives expression to a substantive moral ideal. A now familiar argument is set in motion in an attempt to present such lofty ideals as elements of a *liberal* understanding of law and society. The liberal character of the theory is preserved through the notion that the 'substance' of these moral ideas must be connected with jurisprudential understandings of the established rules and doctrines of the legal order, and that each person may 'fit' those substantive ideas to the rules and decisions in different ways. Yet the reality of such connections, as we have seen, is open to doubt: the idea of equality signifies nothing unless it is connected with specific situations that may be compared as equal or unequal in relevant respects. However, the concept of equality itself can do very little to clarify which peculiar features of a case are 'relevant', so that there are potentially limitless ways in which various cases can be presented as embodying specific equalities or inequalities. Any theory that locates the law's moral nature in substantive moral ideals is thus forced to justify general and inevitably contentious understandings of the nature of equality.

The derivation of a hierarchy of 'interests' from a general theory of justice has tended to be somewhat illiberal in both conception and execution. The liberal ideal is one in which each person has a separate voice in the determination of social good. Liberals have thus tended to regard ideas of virtue as being rooted in the experiences and understandings of individual actors who possess the ability to reflect critically upon their experience. Even if we can correctly assume that individuals in general possess the intellectual wherewithal to transcend their sectional interests in coming to an understanding of social good, the presence of uncontentious standpoints on matters such as equality and justified entitlement could only emerge as a contingent feature of moral experience. A morality of ideals, finding its source in an intellectual realm divorced from daily life, will then seem to embody an elusive and difficult body of knowledge requiring patient analysis by the educated philosopher, rather than the shambolic and untutored reflections of the layman. If such ideals reveal aspects of human wellbeing, then it is finally a society's intellectual leaders who must articulate and explain the substance of human interests, rather than its confused and misguided citizens.

The idea of wellbeing in Protestant political thought comes to us not as some generalised idea that can be contemplated independently of individual wills and desires, but as something that can only be defined by each person in the light of their own experiences and needs. It is perhaps the fact that individuals may develop openly distasteful, odd or destructive preferences which prompts the search for 'external' standards, anchored not in the circumstances of individual lives and choices but in some abstract realm of moral value. It is then tempting to regard a person's interests as a matter of what that person *would* recognise as being good for herself if placed in appropriate conditions or blessed with certain insights into the rational or the reasonable:[5] might we not seek to explain the differences in the way each person values things by the presence of bias and ignorance brought about by purely environmental factors?

Liberal thinking is a form of thinking 'that needed to be embedded in a more encompassing form of reflection',[6] as liberalism is sustained by a Protestant ethic which views moral experience as fundamentally variegated and uneven. We can then perceive idealism as attempting to flatten out our moral life into a level perspective for the application of moral ideas to all, and as therefore constituting a shift away from a form of reflection in which liberalism can survive as a meaningful ideal. Judgments about what is in a person's interests become *counterfactual* judgments,[7] which lead us to a reformulation of the central question of political theory: we ask not, 'how can each person's interests be reconciled with those of others?', but 'under what conditions is an individual's own assessment of his situation definitive?' A person's entitlements will come to be regarded increasingly as a matter for collective determination and enforcement, rather than that person's control over aspects of their moral life.

Such a view of rights maintains a sense of their fundamental importance only by eroding the freedom and autonomy which it is the function of rights, in a liberal theory, to preserve. Liberalism stands in some tension to forms of reflection that seek the resolution of conflicting moral standpoints in sweeping theories of the good, for we can view perpetual disagreements concerning the good not as problems to be ironed out by some more encompassing moral theory, but as features that define the human condition. Human societies can then be looked upon as evolved responses to the problem of disagreement, and as thus constituting a source of moral insight into human nature. Now, if there are no natural or predetermined social roles and hierarchies, but simply a set of problems up for collective determination, then no aspect of individual lives is in principle off limits to public scrutiny and regulation. It follows that a meaningful doctrine of individual rights must be capable of shielding individuals from the intrusive gaze of the state (as well as intrusions by other people) by establishing and preserving blocks of private life over which those individuals exercise a measure of normative control. Without the presence of legal claims against interference, liberties, immunities and so forth, the notion of individuals having interests distinct from those of the collectivity would have become a comforting fiction.

The notion of a 'right' is connected in liberal thought to the idea that individuals possess certain abilities and characteristics that do not belong to society, and over which society cannot make unlimited claims. As long as individuals retain a sphere of personal autonomy in which they can resist injunctions to act to their detriment in favour of the common good, they remain free to formulate and pursue courses of action whether or not such actions conform to broadly conceived collective interests. It is this notion of self-directive autonomy that underpins the liberal ideal of the individual as a thinking being with a level of self-control, rather than a mere drone

---

5   See the excellent discussion in R. Geuss, *History and Illusion in Politics*, Chapter 2.
6   *Ibid.*, 104.
7   *Ibid.*, 101.

labouring for the benefit of the hive. Rights, in liberal thought, are therefore not things that each person has insofar as society grants them out of its aggregative and distributive projects, but something a person owns.[8] Now, the recognition of such rights is, of course, underpinned by mechanisms of collective enforcement, and thus the boundary between the public and private realms cannot be drawn with any rigidity. The integrity of rights is then not a matter of the supposed moral 'neutrality' of legal rules, nor of the creation of idealistic visions within legal order; it is preserved rather by the law's embodiment of a specific form of moral reasoning, based upon the development of a body of richly defined doctrines and rules that are contemplated and applied in relative isolation from more general investigations into the political good. Such reasoning represents a concern, not with the aggregative and distributive aims of public law, but with the value of private achievement and endeavour.

Private Law, Powers and the Will

Private law may be viewed as a form of political association underpinned by an idea of the moral life of the polity as an unstable and deeply irregular landscape in which no level horizons for moral reflection are possible. Such an underpinning is essentially an inherited product of the 19th century. The characteristic feature of such a body of law is its *adaptability*: because each case to come before the courts is different (as no two cases arise in exactly the same way, or in exactly the same circumstances), each case demands precise and careful deliberation rather than a tailor-made judgment fashioned from stock rules and principles. The rules of precedent and *stare decisis* were thus designed to set each case within specific limits, to render their peculiar features intelligible to judges who could then bring their amassed experience to bear on the particular facts of the case. Legal decisions create precedents, in general, not by laying down formal rules to be followed in the future, but instead by sharpening judicial awareness of dimensions to a problem. The rationality of private law adjudication thus consists in the thought that the distinctive features of each case demand close and separate attention, and may be brought within the scope of broad and categorical principles only at the risk of distortion.

The legal thought of the 19th century resembles a framework of ideas structured around the pursuit of private interests. Within this structure of thought and practice, a 'right' is conceived as a claim for the redress of a wrong, lying effectively in private hands. The law provides mechanisms for redress, through the establishment of complex forms of action, and it is up to each litigant to pursue a claim by selecting the relevant form. The rise of statist conceptions of the legal order created a context in which law was no longer viewed as simply *facilitating* private pursuits, by resolving ambiguities and instabilities within the informal social rules on which social concourse is based; but rather as *regulating* such pursuits with regard to the complex public and private interests involved. The realisation had begun to dawn

---

8   See C.B. Macpherson, *The Political Theory of Possessive Individualism: Hobbes to Locke* (Oxford, Clarendon, 1962).

on lawyers that the law had become more than a system for redressing wrongs, but could also be seen in more general terms as an instrument of social engineering and rule-based governance. Rights featured importantly within this bifurcated notion of law as private instruments through which individuals could exercise control over aspects of their lives, by making decisions in relation to the doctrinal rules as they affected their interpersonal relationships: by waiving or asserting claims, exercising powers and waiving immunities, and by ordering their affairs within areas of liberty between the rules and obligations. Private law thus operated in a context in which rights were not identified with, but opposed to, collective measures for the protection of individual interests.

Modern branches of private law are characterised by a fusion of traditional bodies of doctrinal rules with deliberately imposed regulatory regimes designed to pursue more broadly defined social goals. The modern lawyer thus inhabits an intellectual world in which it is increasingly difficult to represent the legal order as a system of imposed rules and sanctions constituting public and general standards of conduct, and a distinct system of doctrinal ideas and principles through which individuals could organise and structure their private lives. Within this complex world, the categorical divisions adopted or presupposed by the practitioners of the 19th century seem inevitably contrived and increasingly out of step with reality: for we are used to moving within a legal world in which complicated statutory regimes fuse with developed systems of doctrine to regulate private and commercial contracts, compensation for personal accidents, the use of property and the like, and we accept such amalgamated approaches as an unproblematic aspect of legal life. The idea of the law as embodying two distinctive but interconnecting realms, one system of imposed rules establishing public standards of conduct, and a separate system of evolved doctrinal rules for the regulation of private life, comes across as artificial when measured against today's complex realities; whereas the view of law as a single, coherent and integrated system of principles addressed at once to the large concerns of state and the small detail of private lives, strikes the mind as a plausible and powerful insight.

Fuller was one of many jurisprudential writers who were aware of this general shift in legal thinking, and who sought either to understand it or to contain it.[9] Fuller had attempted to separate those cases in which a litigant has some meaningful control over the way in which her interests and claims are represented, from those in which polycentric features of the case make the litigant's participation in legal argument meaningless. Yet Fuller was also aware that '[t]here are polycentric elements in almost all problems submitted to adjudication...' and that the distinction between polycentric questions and 'straightforward' doctrinal problems 'is often a matter of degree'.[10] Since adjudication operates in a context wherein doctrinal rules are

---

9   See for example M. Cohen, 'The Basis of Contract', 46 *Harvard L Rev* (1933) 553; R. Pound, 'The End of Law as Developed in Legal Rules and Doctrines',27 *Harvard L Rev* (1914) 795; more recently Milsom, 'The Nature of Blackstone's Achievement', and D. Kennedy, 'From the Will Theory to the Principle of Private Autonomy: Lon Fuller's "Consideration and Form"', 100 *Columbia L Rev* (2000) 94.

10   Fuller, 'The Forms and Limits of Adjudication', 397.

increasingly underpinned and supplemented by black-letter provisions (and where those black-letter provisions are fleshed out and interpreted against the background of established doctrinal ideas or general conceptions of 'right'), it becomes difficult to point to cases in which a ruling as to the rights and duties of the parties will have no wider, unforeseen impacts upon the treatment of future cases. Indeed, as Fuller noted, *any* system of laws containing a reasonably robust doctrine of precedent will render the separation of public and private spheres in this way largely artificial.[11] Fuller nevertheless believed that the point of such a separation was intelligible: 'It is a question,' he said, 'of knowing when the polycentric elements have become so significant and predominant that the proper limits of adjudication have been reached.'[12]

A 'Will' theory of rights may be distinguished from the Interest theory in the view taken of the boundary of private law, for where rights are viewed as consisting of protected choices of the right-holder (to waive or enforce duties, transfer property etc.), adjudicative reasoning will tend to retain its traditional focus upon the actual dealings of the parties to a case, thus excluding from deliberation a great many of the polycentric issues directly confronted where rights are regarded as defining interests in terms of some broader notion of the common good. Justice in the field of private law reflects a concern with the way in which relations between the parties came about, and it is therefore within the context of fairly focused doctrinal and circumstantial concerns, rather than in a spirit of wide-ranging political and social inquiry, that questions of legal right are typically addressed. The Will theorist thus regards rights as instruments of private law, to be distinguished from public law rules operating to protect interests in line with general social goals and policies. Perceiving no essential distinction between the two kinds of instrument, Interest theorists have tended to view the dichotomy between public and private law as relatively permeable and arbitrary: public law being the area of law in which various benefits are established or created, and private law concerning the way in which such benefits are applied. The Will theorist, on the other hand, sees in that dichotomy an important distinction between divergent modes of reasoning and argument: one focused upon public goods and collective policies; the other upon the establishment of a framework of rules by which the individual is left to order and prioritise his own affairs in ways that may conflict with the public good or the private aims of others.

If that argument is valid, then it is not the presence or absence of legal protections that is central to the notion of a legal right, but rather the ability of the right-holder to exercise autonomous judgments about how such protections are brought into the service of his interests. It was Hart who first clearly traced the way in which rights

---

11 See also Cohen (above, note 9). Any system of private rights depends, of course, on collective recognition and enforcement. It is therefore difficult to imagine a form of legal order in which there would be no public interest in the content of private law rules. The issue for the Will and Interest theories, however, concerns the peculiar form in which such interest is (or should be) manifested.

12 Fuller (above, note 10), 398.

serve the private pursuit of interests.[13] Hart observed that the unifying feature of the four Hohfeldian entitlements, the reason we are tempted to refer to such distinct ideas as 'rights', is that '…in all four cases, the law specifically recognises the choice of an individual either negatively by not impeding or obstructing it (liberty and immunity) or affirmatively by giving legal effect to it (claim and power).'[14] Hart's insight serves as an important reminder of the connection between rights and remedies: by focusing on a person's ability to make normative determinations about his situation, or to pursue his projects unimpeded by the choices of others where he lacks the ability to make positive determinations, rights operate within the established and stable boundaries of relatively precise doctrinal rules designed to sustain and reinforce widely observed social norms of promising, transacting, and so on.

An interest theory of rights obscures the essential role that rights play in separating the autonomous pursuit of private interests from aggregative forms of reasoning which may be *directed* at individuals. We might pursue this issue by means of a distinction between rights and regulation. Suppose one were to treat the distinction between the variable entitlements of private law and those general benefits bestowed by public law as effecting a division of *waivable* and *unwaivable* rights. Certain rights (especially those created by public law, or criminal law) might then seem to trade autonomy for wellbeing in line with broad social policies. A society will engage in such trade-offs where there is a strong reason to believe that individual or collective welfare would be threatened if certain choices were left to the uncoordinated wills of individuals. The withholding of benefits or the application of penalties on grounds of race is one of a number of issues recognised as being too important to both individual wellbeing and to the society's collective self-image to be left to private decision. There is an obvious sense in which such protections count among a person's *rights*. Minimum wage laws, for example, undoubtedly confer complex entitlements on workers (including claim-rights to be remunerated above a certain level), but simultaneously restrict the aggregate of choices open to a person to act within the law:[15] certain otherwise valid contracts of employment can no longer count as legally enforceable bargains.

Such regulatory regimes vary the extent of individual entitlements in many ways, both positive and negative. By altering our perspective, we can examine those effects in different ways: a focus on each person's claim-rights to levels of remuneration from within a given range are naturally presented as affording positive recognition to choices which each person might make to accept offers and make legal bargains within that range. Viewed from the perspective of the consequent reduction in opportunities for legitimate employment, however, the lack of legal

---

13 H.L.A. Hart, 'Definition and Theory in Jurisprudence', in *Essays in Jurisprudence and Philosophy* (Oxford, Clarendon, 1983) 21–48, 35–36. See also Hart, 'Legal Rights', in *Essays on Bentham* (Oxford, Clarendon, 1982) 162–93. Hart's suggestions have been taken up and further explored and refined by later writers. See for example Simmonds (above, note 3), 218–229.

14 Hart, 'Definition and Theory in Jurisprudence', (above, note 13), 35.

15 In restricting the scope of legal action, such laws effectively reduce a person's freedom overall: see M. Kramer, *The Quality of Freedom* (Oxford, Oxford University Press, 2003).

recognition accorded to a person's choice to accept an employment offer in violation of such protective and regulatory norms does not sit as easily with ordinary notions of a 'right'. We will rather look upon those norms as having conferred extensive disabilities and liabilities along with liberties and claim-rights.

A concern with individual wellbeing does not invariably take the form of a concern with the recognition of rights. The project of effecting some overall shift in the distribution of benefits across society (such as the institution of a minimum wage) is not *the same* project as balancing the rights of every person to secure and pursue a worthwhile life: it constitutes instead the desire to modify the extent of each person's legal entitlements in order to secure some other social advantage (aside from the protection of rights), such as the workability of a system of protections that would collapse if left to the play of market forces. Rights conferred by statute as part of some wider strategy or social goal are rarely considerable in isolation from the complex regulatory mechanisms that guarantee the effectiveness of those rights as demanded by the strategy. It is perhaps the idealistic tendency to look upon such regimes holistically which explains the Interest theory's treatment of regulatory provisions as aspects of questions of right. Regulatory provisions are then capable of being seen as directly defining the boundary between competing rights, rather than as higher-level norms defining the operative bounds within which rights compete. In such cases, it is the failure to see that there are in fact *two* distinct sets of questions involved (questions about how individuals' lives are to be regulated in their own and the general interest, and questions about the effects such regulations will have on the complex web of entitlements that obtain between those individuals) which may lead to the supposition that questions of choice are to be disposed of *within* the language of rights (by drawing a distinction between waivable and unwaivable rights) rather than a context in which rights compete with other values and interests.

Now consider the example of statutory employment rights that protect workers from unfair dismissal on grounds of race, religion, disability etc. If such rights are to operate successfully, it is clear that employees must possess legal disabilities preventing them from alienating their legal protections as part of the normal bargaining process between employer and employee. We can therefore view such protections as helping to define the *kind* of agreement that can exist between the parties to a contract of employment: such agreements will include duties owed by the employer towards the employee, which the latter cannot give up or trade for some other proposed benefit. The inalienability of the rights to which such duties are attached is, however, connected with the issue of waiver only through quite complex chains of reasoning, for although the right-holder lacks the legal power to bring such duties to an end, she can clearly control the application of the duty by deciding whether to sue or not to sue.[16] The choice of the right-holder thus remains

---

16 The right-holder may, of course, possess some residual powers to bring the duties to an end: for example by serving notice on the contract as a whole, or perhaps by electing not to raise an action upon the duty within the scope of prescribed time-limits. We might think of the alienating/not-exercising distinction as pointing to different ways in which a right can be waived.

central in determining when the right will be brought into play in the service of her interests.[17]

Now, the notion of 'waiver' cannot be wholly confined to a decision over whether to sue: the distinction between alienability and enforcement might prove important in some respects, but it is not absolute. Where officials of the state retain the power to waive or compel performance of duties on their own initiative, or where statutory duties can be modified or eliminated only through further acts of amending legislation, the gap between alienability and enforcement becomes somewhat tenuous and unreal. The boundary between right and non-right is a matter of evaluative judgment, however, rather than analytical stipulation. Rights can be associated with powers of waiver in numerous possible ways, each with its distinctive effects upon the right-holder's choices. In some of these cases, the right-holder's vestigial control over some legal advantage may incline us to regard that advantage as a 'right'; in other cases we might view the holder as having insufficient power to decide the application of advantageous legal rules to her own situation, and thus regard his position as regulated rather than entitled. Such judgments are not typically governed by strict semantic criteria, or by values that apply evenly to every case. They are rather guided by a rationale.

In order to see why that rationale ought to be construed in terms of the right-holder's self-directive autonomy rather than the coarser notion of 'passive benefit-receipt', consider the notion of an unwaivable right. Unwaivable rights presumably refer to situations where the right-holder enjoys the benefit of some advantage (a claim-right or immunity, say) unadorned by any power to determine the way in which that advantage applies to her situation. In such cases, we might then look upon the person concerned as having a right, coupled with a *disability* to deflect the benefit of the right. This can be illustrated by the position of a free-thinking member of a caste-system, who may have extensive claim-rights against all physical contact by members judged to be 'inferior' within the social hierarchy, but who objects to the system of rules and regulations that perpetuate such class distinctions. Such a person could, of course, condone or even encourage infractions of his own claim-rights, but he would be incapable of waiving the duties of the underclass towards him, whom the state may continue to punish mercilessly. Could we really speak of measures that establish categories of unlawful interference in this way as conferring *rights*?[18] (Suppose the man wished to marry a woman from within the underclass, but was prevented from doing so by the presence of such 'rights'?)

In the vast majority of situations, the subjects of legal advantages do not possess such extensive disabilities, but continue to exercise vestigial control over the application of their entitlements as they see fit. The right-holder, in most cases, can

---

17 There will be occasions, however, on which this is not the case. For a much longer discussion, see S. Coyle, '"Protestant" Political Theory and the Significance of Rights', 56 *Northern Ireland LQ* (2005), 551–584, at 576–577.

18 We are particularly likely to answer in the negative if the person encouraged the infractions as part of his efforts to instigate a change in the regime – by encouraging inter-class contact, say, and in initiating such contact as a means of garnering signatures on a petition or for the purposes of organising a pressure group.

decisively shape the legal response to her situation by electing to raise an action, or in some cases merely by reporting infractions. Only in cases where the recipient of some advantage has no possibility of shaping the outcome (where, for example, the failure to receive some benefit, or to report the infraction of a duty, is *itself* an actionable wrong) is that recipient wholly devoid of legal powers to determine the application of entitlements to her life. Regulatory systems will, in general, therefore invest the right-holder with interstitial powers to enforce or waive correlative duties. Hart drew attention to the propensity for claim-rights, powers and immunities to establish a perimeter of indirect protection for legal liberties whose exercise might otherwise be rendered worthless: since liberties consist merely of the absence of duties to refrain from performing the permitted action, liberty-holders are quite unprotected from interference by others, in pursuit of their own liberties, which can frustrate and render nugatory such attempted exercises of liberty. The liberty to carry on a business in a hostile marketplace, for example, enjoys considerable protection from established claim-rights against libel, theft, restrictive practices, insider dealing and the like. In the same way, a person's established rights can protect and define interstices of *power*, for each person typically possesses an array of immunities against prosecution for failing to raise or pursue actions established as possibilities by statute, coupled with general immunities against alteration of one's existing legal entitlements by the action of officials seeking to raise or abandon legal actions on one's behalf. The law also confers myriad bilateral liberties that make possible appropriate choices about how each person will manipulate their other entitlements in the world of social interaction, by asserting and pressing claims, threatening legal action, or securing alternative benefits by agreeing to waive an action at a particular point in time. The state's regulatory mandates will thus almost inevitably confer significant and important interstices of power.

The notion of a right, like the question of control, is an evaluative one that can change within a context of varying degrees and kinds of vestigial power. The notion of a 'right' is not one that derives its shape from the drawing of convenient analytical boundaries, but from judgments whose conceptual associations are inseparable from the *point* of reflecting on the standing of individuals vis-à-vis their fellow men and the state. If the point of making such judgments reflects a concern with delineating those areas in which a person's life is free of collective control, it becomes clear that not every conferral of a legal advantage will amount to a 'right'. Certain immunities, for example, will qualify as rights even where the holder retains very little vestigial power over their application, since they provide important forms of negative protection to personal autonomy. (We can view immunities against wrongful arrest and prosecution as being of this kind.) Other readily imaginable unwaivable forms of immunity, on the other hand, do not by ordinary standards count among a person's rights. Suppose the rules of a respected scholarship programme, for instance, provide that applications from scholars over the age of 30 will not be considered. If I am above that age, I am legally immune from having my existing entitlements enriched by the exercise of any power of the awarding body in deciding to whom the scholarship should go. The relevant difference between these two immunities lies in the point for which they were conferred: my immunity from arbitrary arrest exists to protect me from intrusive, autonomy-reducing powers of state officials, whereas the point of the immunity conferred by the scholarship rule is not to protect me, but to establish parameters within which others can compete on a level playing-field. Whereas the first is focused on *my* choices, the latter is the consequence of the choices and actions of others.[19] Only by keeping such distinctions carefully in mind can we avoid the idealistic fallacy of regarding formal and doctrinal rules of widely differing sorts as elements in a general interpretation of a system of rights.

Our perception of the public law/private law distinction to a great extent depends on our underlying notion of private entitlement. The preceding discussion has therefore attempted to identify the distinctive importance of private law rules by reference to an understanding of private entitlements. A sense of this importance, I have suggested, can be gained only through the recognition that private rights serve the value of self-directive autonomy rather than the goal of passive benefit-receipt. The animating spirit of those ideals is not difficult to discern. Public law, structured around the notion of benefit-receipt, reflects a body of ethical thought in which the good is realised through the organised pursuit of collectively determined goals. Private law represents instead a form of thought in which the good is realised through private transactions, where redistributions occur not on the basis of a centralised and coherent plan, but through the operation of a framework of rules which enable autonomous and self-directive activity. Private entitlements function within this structure not as markers of politically contentious interests, to be endlessly debated in legal thought, but rather as the instruments through which a relatively settled framework of rules are applied to individual action.

A jurisprudence of 'interests' necessarily bases its demarcations upon notions of equality. But a satisfactory theory of justice cannot place a doctrine of equality at its heart, for different people will inevitably *value* specific dimensions of equality differently. It is thus easier to accommodate pluralism within a theory of justice by subordinating the goal of benefit-receipt as far as possible to that of self-directive autonomy. Yet the legal thought of the modern day exhibits all too often the opposite trend. The law of contract, to give but one example, is no longer viewed as giving legal recognition to antecedently understood practices of bargaining, in which emphasis is placed upon giving effect to the will of the parties. Instead, the law is viewed as effecting the realisation of specific dimensions of fairness or equality thought to be inherent in the notion of the individual-in-society. The emphasis is then placed not upon the will of the parties, but upon the fairness of practices of dealing, considered according to a broader theory of justice which exists in detachment from the contextual concerns of those involved. Such an intellectual shift can be

---

19 The same holds true of the other Hohfeldian relations. A power to waive or enforce contractual rights is naturally spoken of as a right since it allows me to make significant determinations about my legal relationship with others. But if I crash my car into another's, I also exercise a legal power since I thereby alter my legal relationship vis-à-vis that person (and anyone who is injured as a result of the crash, and presumably his and my insurance companies). It would be ludicrous to speak here of a *right* to crash my car, since crashes are generally *accidents* rather than the outcome of a deliberate choice: the power here exists as a mere consequence of unintended action, not as a legal protection for an authoritatively recognised choice.

accommodated within liberal individualism only by a philosophically dubious and morally unacceptable notion of an 'individual'.

Individualism and Autonomy

Liberal society is structured by the notion that it is the 'individual' that lies at the heart of moral understanding. Yet individualism, precisely in seeking a *systematic* understanding of individual wants and deeds, becomes a theory concerned with faceless units rather than the full-blooded person. This contrast is marked by a changing conception of the point of moral thought: no longer is morality conceived as being concerned with fostering virtuous dispositions required for the excellent and worthwhile life (and as thus expressing concern with personal wellbeing), but rather as identifying a series of norms and injunctions that impinge upon all human beings equally, independently of their habits and dispositions. 'The individual' is reduced in this way from a living, thinking being to a juridical abstraction.[20] Most of the paradoxes of liberalism flow from this intellectual shift, for the liberal emphasis upon individualism becomes a doctrine of faceless and anonymous agents constructed by a feat of theoretical abstraction from the very inequalities and characteristics by which individuals are recognisably distinct from one another. Law then exists, not to facilitate private intercourse between persons with widely differing attributes and agendas, but rather to eliminate the inequalities that may otherwise undermine 'agency'. Such 'inequalities' are the natural abilities and aspects of personality that constitute personal identity.

To treat natural abilities and dispositions as matters of relevance to the polity's distributive concerns is to reverse an ethical tradition with roots in classical notions of excellence, in which moral judgment concerns the developmental realisation of a person's qualities in line with an idea of personal wellbeing, for we are instead encouraged to think of personal attributes as if separable from personal identity, becoming rather the randomly distributed products of 'moral luck'.[21] Having achieved this separation, a society may then operate to effect a redistribution of natural advantages in pursuit of overarching values of fairness and equality. Such operations will seem permissible (or indeed possible) only if performed against a tacit background of assumptions that regard personal attributes as the raw material of social assets rather than as properties *of* the person in whom they inhere. The notion of political society then ceases to be thought of as a set of institutions for nurturing and sustaining a way of life, but becomes instead an artificial construct orientated towards the pursuit of deliberately chosen social goals. A view of this kind

---

20 For an argument that the moral persona is itself ultimately an abstract juridical form, see Simmonds, 'Judgment and Mercy', 13 *Oxford J of Legal Studies* (1993), 52–68. My own feeling is that the moral persona is defined within a metaphysical framework which is not essentially juridical in character: see Chapter 2, above, and some further remarks, below.

21 The most famous advocate of this view is John Rawls: see *A Theory of Justice* (Harvard University Press, 1971). For critical discussion, see S.L. Hurley, 'Luck, Responsibility and the Natural Lottery', 10 *J of Political Philosophy* (2002) 79–94; and Simmonds (above, note 20), passim.

may incline us to treat justice and equality as unconditioned ideals, fashioned by Platonic administrators working to create society from behind a 'veil of ignorance';[22] or it may result in a Marxian perspective in which equality and justice become the historically conditioned yet malleable epiphenomena through which political ends are structured.

These intellectual forces govern our perception of the modern political landscape. The same theoretical tendencies that force us to treat the individual as the bearer of rights and duties also incline us to accept the picture of the individual agent as a locus of 'interests'. Where these two ideas combine, the resulting political vision is one that is at once seductive and undermining of the central liberal virtues in which it is enrobed. Private law represents a body of thought which, to some extent, retains the idea of the person as a separate locus of potentialities, dispositions and possible lines of development. It is thus no surprise that an idealistic philosophy in which notions of justice and interest occupy centre stage should fail to discern the value and importance of conventional doctrinal practices. Rather than seeking to illuminate the sensitive exploration of moral value within doctrinal rules and principles, the philosopher will emphasise instead the need for constant reinterpretation of the rules and principles in light of shifting conceptions of justice and equality. Political understandings will have then become detached from the fabric of ordinary existence, and must instead be regarded as fully integrated aspects of a collective juridical vision. Practices of entitlement, then, no longer serve to sustain the presence of personal trajectories from *within* a framework of social interaction, but constitute the juridified persona as an abstract bearer of meaning upon which the public manifestations of value impinge.

In this chapter, I have sought to connect questions relating to the nature of entitlement to a general understanding of the theoretical boundary between public and private law. That boundary is both elusive and problematic; yet the obvious truth that the categories of 'public' and 'private' do not stand readily demarcated before the theoretical intellect should not blind us to the importance of private law as a body of thought differently constituted to that of public law. Only through an awareness of that distinctiveness can we begin to understand the moral nature of law.

---

22 See Geuss, *Outside Ethics*, 32.

Chapter 9

The Moral Nature of Law

The legal order of the English polity might be thought of as an articulate embodiment of a tradition of civility. Embodying such a tradition, it is not immediately clear that legal order should represent an intellectual artefact transparent to theoretical understanding. For given the complex and non-linear nature of English social history and politics, we might instead have expected the law to comprise successive layers of meaning that have become superimposed to form an elusive cultural and historical object. In such a case, we could give univocal expression to our traditions of legality only if we are willing to embrace a certain level of distortion and intellectual blinkeredness in our theoretical explanations. At the same time, we might think, law does not simply *embody* the traditions of thought and practice upon which our civility depends; it also alters and creates forms of social interaction in pursuit of objectives that go beyond the desire merely to sustain present conceptions of social order. If we think of a tradition of civility as embodying certain moral ideals, then it is the case that law not only embodies certain ideals, but in many cases shapes its own ideals in the course of its daily existence. Any attempt to relate the mundane, everyday manifestations of legal practice to those ideals must, of necessity, exhibit a considerable degree of complexity.

It is my purpose in this final chapter to offer some thoughts on the relationship between law (considered as a familiar set of institutions and practices) and the ideals of legality and governance. Given the nature of the concepts involved, my discussion will inevitably remain somewhat suggestive and capable of further refinement. Yet its basic direction should be evident from the concerns of preceding chapters. Modern jurisprudence is deeply wedded to the view that moral ideals are in some sense products of the will, and most jurisprudential writing has therefore tended to focus upon the law's ability to structure social interaction in such a way as to bring about certain goals or conditions, correspondingly less emphasis being placed upon the law's embodiment of informal practices and varieties of social formation. Just because there is no obvious dividing line between the role of sustaining the intellectual foundations of civility and that of manipulating forms of social interaction, there is a perennial temptation to subsume the nurturing function of the law within the latter processes of alteration and change. It is this temptation which, I argue, ought to be firmly resisted.

One way in which to overcome temptation is to understand the source of that temptation. The relevant place to start, in this instance, is with the nature of morality. Where law is regarded as being connected to, or as embodying, morality, the principles to which the law is viewed as giving expression are naturally conceived to be juridical in structure. Thus, the ideals with which law is ultimately connected (if they are viewed as moral ideals at all) are thought to relate the mundane rules and doctrines of legal practice to specifically *juridical* forms of moral consciousness. Such forms typically exhibit the characteristics of the very legal mentality that the moral ideals explain and justify: they therefore frequently embody morally significant distinctions between the 'individual' and the 'state'; between 'agents' and those devoid of agency; and they contain notions of justice structured around conceptions of moral right, power and obligation.[1] The effect of such thinking is to suppress a sense of the degree to which law draws upon planes of shared understanding and experience which lie beneath (and make possible) the conscious levels of political thought. In embodying aspects of the social, such planes of understanding may of course be viewed as objects of 'political' concern, in the wide sense that *any* dimension to social interaction is potentially subject to variability in pursuit of broader goals; but this is to miss the importance of the fact that such social forms constitute in an important sense the pre-political foundations upon which the deliberate processes of political and legal manipulation depend.[2] It is through the neglect of levels of shared understanding that the dominant forms of juridical consciousness have tended to view the moral significance of law as a question of the exercise of public powers of amendment and decision.

My argument will thus begin by addressing the nature of moral understandings which are in an important sense 'private' rather than 'public' in orientation. (In saying this, I do not mean to suggest that such understandings are 'subjective'; rather, I mean to emphasise the connection of such values with the wellbeing of the particular person rather than the general characteristics of the 'agent'.) Having sought to clarify such understandings, I will then offer some general remarks about law's relationship to, and instantiation of, the general guiding ideals of legality and governance.

Morality and Identity

The intellectual shift involved in the movement from classical forms of ethical reflection to moral philosophy is one in which a concern with metaphysical ethical contemplation regarding the human *telos* is replaced with a secular and Protestant

---

1 Indeed, these conceptions may be regarded as second-order properties insofar as both statehood and agency are defined in terms of power, the relations between agents being understood as governed by dyads of right and duty. The exact relationship between these notions is something in which I lack any interest, since I am about to challenge the foundations of this general approach to moral questions. Yet I hope the reader may see in this description something resembling a very widespread and prevalent form of moral thought exhibited in the political and popular thought of the present day.

2 We might initially hope to capture the elusive distinction I am after by appeal to the divide between 'politics' and 'culture'. Yet the permeability or even reality of that divide would of course simply invite the scepticism of those who champion the dominant approach. It is for this, amongst other reasons, that I prefer to think of the areas of shared understanding I have in mind not in terms of any firm conceptual distinctions, but instead simply as a dimension of importance that is overlooked by the dominant consciousness. For an illuminating discussion which highlights the recent origin of the state's power potentially to vary *all* aspects of social understanding, see Geuss, *History and Illusion in Politics*, Chapter 2.

concern for 'the works of man'. Meditation upon the ethical dimensions of the person will then give way to a focus upon 'activity, creation, change and process, goals and purposes.'[3] For once the relevant moral unit becomes not the person but the *agent*, there is little to be gained from sustained reflection upon its particular instantiations: each such instantiation will reflect merely the series of choices, or interaction between choices, exercised by otherwise morally equal agents. It will be, instead, the general social conditions, connections and lines of interaction within which agency is exercised that merit philosophical attention. Where morality centres on the actions of the agent, therefore, it is natural to elevate practices to the centre of moral concern. It is then possible to contrast our philosophical grasp of the natural world, in which insights are brought to the judgment of a perceiving intellect, with our understanding of the social world; for the latter (it will seem) is not something merely *inhabited*, but also *created* by the human will. Being themselves products of human agency, social practices will come to be regarded as somehow transparent to the understanding in a way that natural processes are not; at least, they will seem as transparently open to us as are our own decisions and states of consciousness.[4]

We might hope in this way to escape attachment to the particular social forms and institutions that make up our familiar social existence and ground moral thought in a bedrock of objectivity, as (it will be thought) if morality constitutes a set of requirements that are binding upon all human beings equally, then moral demands cannot derive from the contemplation of an experience that is essentially unequal and uneven, but must emerge from elsewhere. Moral thought that takes its inspiration from current attachments will (it is felt) merely reflect our immersion within the social forms that create those attachments. Thus, the truth of moral judgments must be grounded in an objective bedrock which is itself devoid of particular empirical attachments of form or substance, and which thus reproduces the most abstract and fundamental conditions of human agency. So the dominant conception of morality holds.

It is worth taking time to consider the characteristics of this moral bedrock; for in seeking to cast off present associations and concerns, it reflects its own philosophical associations and preconceptions. The notion of a featureless 'bedrock' invites a distinction between an endlessly diversified experience, on the one hand, and a form of reason, on the other, which imposes upon that experience forms and structures that it has generated from within itself. As with so much of modern moral philosophy, this view finds its genesis in the Kantian notion of the mind's propensity to shape and structure its own experience.[5] Thus, we are led to think of the natural world as lacking form in the absence of animating thoughts and interpretations. The classical ethical idea that the human mind perceives and understands the realities in which it is immersed is thus replaced by the Kantian and essentially Protestant idea that

---

3 E. Craig, *The Mind of God and the Works of Man* (Oxford, Oxford University Press, 1987), 198.

4 *Ibid.*, 121, 228. The issues surrounding the philosopher's classic distinction between acts and omissions should perhaps have put paid to this sense of transparency; yet its presence continues to exert a pull of fascination over much modern moral philosophy.

5 Craig (above, note 3), see especially 149 and 198.

the mind *creates* its realities. It is, then, in the general lineaments of the will and its conceptual creations that moral understanding is thought to consist.

What are we to make of the idea that the mind structures its own experience? In one obvious sense, knowledge of experience does not come before the mind unmediated by conceptual thought, for even the most mundane, everyday observations require the classification of particulars under certain concepts. (My seeing of a tree before me depends not just upon sense-perception, but the ability to recognise the visible form in front of me as one instance of a class of entities, 'trees', distinguishable in my mind from other classes or concepts, such as 'shrubs' or 'rational animals'.) Such concepts and the attendant processes of classification are learned, or rather inculcated, at an early age through the learning of a language. Since language is itself a social construct and thus a product of human will, these simple observations might incline us to reject experience as a ground of knowledge. The line of thought extending from Plato to Kant (and beyond) is thus apt to distinguish two sources or stages of knowledge: first there are intuitions (formed from sense-perception), and secondly there are concepts (based on the internal resources of the mind) through which those intuitions are processed and rendered open to the understanding. Moral or aesthetic notions, such as beauty or equality, then, are too complex to be the straightforward products of sense-perception,[6] and so must be treated as in some sense productions of the will. Since an individual has infinitely many true descriptions or properties, it will thus seem that moral judgments attach not to particular persons, so much as to certain theorised aspects of personhood, such as agency, or the capacity to act as the bearer of rights and duties. When measuring equality as between persons, we can address only certain *dimensions* of equality (and so on).

Despite the Kantian philosopher's tendency to view such theorised strata as *deep* aspects of the human personality, it is clear that the Kantian form of moral thought can address only a superficial concept of the person, understood in abstraction from the very capacities and inequalities that constitute separate personal identities.[7] As Hegel was later to observe:

---

6   For they apply in too diverse a range of circumstances: my possession of a twig and your possession of a twig make us equal in respect of twig possession; yet my twig may also be equal in length to your arm. A concept that applies not only as between objects (in terms of existence or number) but also to properties (such as length) is of too sophisticated an order to be derivable purely through unmediated 'intuitions' (so the Platonic theory states). Similarly, the judgment of diverse objects or states-of-affairs (such as human faces and musical compositions) as 'beautiful' cannot take the form of disjointly formed intuitions, without reference to a concept (beauty) that exists in some degree of detachment from the instances to which it applies. For a general discussion see D. Scott, *Recollection and Experience* (Cambridge, Cambridge University Press, 1995).

7   Simmonds ('Judgment and Mercy') makes the point by referring to the existence within Kantian philosophy and Christianity of a depersonalised substrate. Whilst I agree with this insight, my aim in the present discussion is to trace the philosophical roots of the objective moral bedrock more broadly. I do not therefore wish to imply that my agreement with Simmonds's earlier discussion would lead *him* to agree with *me* so far as the present argument is concerned.

The thing-in-itself is the object, when we abstract from everything that it is for consciousness, all its emotional connotations and all determinate thoughts of it. It is easy to see what is left – total abstraction, complete emptiness, just what is *Beyond*; the negative of every image, feeling, determinate thought. But it is just as easy to reflect that this *caput mortuum* is itself only a product of thought, thought carried to utter abstraction, a product of the empty Ego which makes its own empty identity into an object.[8]

It is this process of abstraction which leads to the Hegelian concept of 'dislocation', for having reduced the complex notion of personality to a single point in 'agency', we will be increasingly drawn to an idea of reason which has as its central concerns the essentially Protestant fascination with the agent's capacity to formulate and address his own concerns, and the possibility of integrating those private concerns within a public framework of political interaction. Concentrating on such features of moral experience, we will begin to see the world (according to Hegel) as a series of opposing forces of fragmentation and division, and our intellectual energy will thus be spent upon efforts to comprehend the dichotomies we see around us: the individual *v.* society; law *v.* morals; life *v.* thought, etc. Thus, as Schiller warned, 'instead of expressing humanity in his nature, [man] becomes a mere imprint of his occupation, or of his branch of knowledge.'[9]

Schiller's warning serves as a timely reminder of the dangers of applying a Kantian philosophy to the central questions of liberal social order, for in seeking to identify such opposing tendencies with the 'interests' of rational agents, we not infrequently yield to the project of levelling the inequalities they entail in a quest to bring about conditions more conducive to the exercise of perfect agency. It is increasingly philosophy, rather than (say) the market, or culture, which bears the responsibility for effecting a reordering of such interests. Much moral philosophy therefore centres on the thought that human welfare is to be attained by the adjustment of social institutions in order to promote the conditions in which agency is jointly exercisable. The effect of Kantian liberalism is thus to bring about a moulding of individual 'interests' to the institutional and political circumstances to which the individual is exposed, decreasing the opportunity for expressions of opposition and plural visions. Yet, as Schiller argued, '[t]he opposed tendencies are in themselves perfectly legitimate, even inescapable; they are therefore not to be erased, but combined, and our problem is to find some way of bringing that combination about.'[10]

As I have argued, this process is to be effected not through the exploration of social practices in terms of an abstract theory of justice applying to faceless agents, but rather by exploring the significance of areas of shared understanding and experience that lie beneath the ordinary political process, and of the existence of instances of fragmentation within those understandings. Common ground in social intercourse is frequently the product of perceiving aspects of oneself and one's

---

8   G.W.F. Hegel, *Phenomenology of Spirit*, trans. A.V. Miller (Oxford, Oxford University Press, 1977), para. 44.

9   F. Schiller, *Werke in 3 Banden*, Vol 2 (6th letter), quoted in Craig (above, note 3), 146. See also Craig's discussion, Chapter 3.

10   *Ibid.*, 149. (The quoted words are those of Edward Craig.)

concerns in others (or in the external conditions in which social interactions take place). Moral knowledge is thus not introspective (in the sense of being concerned with abstract equalities or agency) but concerns the place of human beings within the external structures of society and natural order in which they move. The form of self-knowledge required for moral understanding is thus incapable of realisation in separation from the institutions, concerns and attachments through which our present identities emerge, for, as Hegel argued, self-consciousness is possible only to the extent that one can see oneself reflected in *external* sources.[11]

Here, however, we may seem to hit a snag. If, as seems likely, our understanding of externalities rests upon present *conceptual* dichotomies and associations, then how is moral knowledge to find a grounding in experience rather than in the introspective properties of will? Must we, then, in the end rely not upon sensitive experiential reflection but upon *interpretation*? It would seem so, if we adopt the following line of argument to be found in Nietzsche, but also prevalent in different ways within the moral thinking of the present day: there is no world, Nietzsche argued, that is distinct from the way in which those who interact with it experience its form and substance. Accordingly, we have no *knowledge* of the world as *truth*. Rather, truth is 'a *process in infinitum*, an active determining – not a becoming conscious of something that is in itself firm and determined.'[12] Similarly, it is thought within modern moral philosophy that social institutions and present arrangements can reveal nothing by way of moral insight unless understood from the perspective of some animating interpretation.

Nietzsche here seeks to reveal a disjunct between the processes of consciousness and awareness, on the one hand, and those of participation and determination, on the other. The former processes are presumably to be understood as essentially passive, receptive lines of connection, whereas the latter are active and the product of the conscious adoption of certain interpretative attitudes.[13] Yet the two sets of processes may only be presented as fully distinct elements of thought if the interpretative attitudes which characterise the latter set are regarded as fully detached from the external order in which human beings think and move. The opposition of a static view of human nature to a process of raw constructivism thus depends itself upon a contestable metaphysical position, for human potentialities are not detachable from the social world and from institutions within which they emerge and develop. The will to power is then itself the embodiment of a certain metaphysical understanding of human potentialities (of agency, action, power, etc.) in relation to the social arrangements and attachments that render its existence possible or meaningful.

The moral thought of modernity, in all of its diverse aspects, is united in its assumption of two distinct sources or levels of knowledge. There is the ordinary level of knowledge and reflection grounded in intuitions; and then there is the deeper, more reflective achievements of conceptual thought. This has, so I have argued,

---

11 Hegel, *Introduction to the Lectures on Philosophy of History*, trans. T.M. Knox and A.V. Miller (Oxford, Clarendon Press, 1987).

12 F. Nietzsche, *The Will to Power*, W. Kaufmann (ed.) (New York, Random House, 1968), para. 552.

13 For my argument that such ideas motivate much of Dworkin's legal philosophy (and indeed probably that of many positivists by a more convoluted route), see Chapter 7 above.

led to a general posture of scepticism towards the value of ordinary experience as a source of moral insights. Scepticism of this kind may present itself before the philosophical imagination in two divergent respects:[14] the dependence of thought upon the conceptual structures of language may be suggestive of the character of ordinary knowledge (that is, our 'intuitions') as the combined product of sense-perception *and* conceptual associations, even if the early stages of conceptual reflection are automatic and easy. Being already theorised, our comprehension of our social surroundings would differ from that of the moral philosopher not in kind, but only by degree: both, that is, would consist of 'interpretations', although at differing levels of sophistication and reflective depth. Alternatively, we might think of ordinary intuitions as furnishing an apparently coherent view of the social world that is transparent to understanding *without* the need for deeper reflection. Reflective (that is, conceptual) thought would then be thought of as embodying difficult intellectual processes at even basic levels, and thus as constituting an autonomous form of reflection ('philosophy') that is achievable only by a few. Experience, on this view, would then play a greater role as a source of knowledge for most people, even if it turns out to be ultimately deficient or unreliable.

Both of these alternative explanations of the relation between ordinary and conceptual knowledge leave room for considerable divergence between ordinary moral understandings and those of the philosopher. On the second view, philosophical reflection embodies a deeper level of truth that may diverge sharply from ordinary perceptions, and it is thus suggestive of a view of ordinary understandings as in some sense misleading or deficient. On the first view, ordinary understandings are not actively deceptive insofar as they form a common starting-point for reflection (being in a sense already reflective); yet the level of reflection of which the layman is capable may offer only the slightest glimmerings of moral truth, and thus forms an insufficient basis for a rich moral understanding. The deeper reflections of the philosopher would then contain the potential for significant revisions of ordinary perceptions and understandings.[15] We may regard the existence of moral *philosophy* as itself exhibiting scepticism of either sort, as the presence of complex theoretical systems of morality, which are obviously difficult to grasp and seemingly resistant to mastery, may be taken as an indication of the *difficulty* of morality. The impression frequently given is that of the insights of the philosopher as dimly indicative of the presence of a far-off horizon, and of present experiences, values and social institutions as stumbling in semi-darkness towards the light of day.[16]

The idea that our everyday moral choices are made against a background of confused or imperfect understandings stands in some tension to Judeo-Christian

---

14 I derive the general form of the following observations from Dominic Scott: see Scott (above, note 6), although much of the specific application of these observations to moral thought, and my resultant conclusions, probably differ from those of Scott. It is not my intention to pursue these differences here.

15 *Ibid.*, especially 17–21.

16 The inherent optimism of much philosophy is nevertheless suggestive of the general features of the utopian horizon as resembling to a surprising degree those of the present society in question: for my earlier discussion of this point, see Chapter 7.

conceptions of moral responsibility, and of sin. Much of the emphasis within theological morality lies not in the process of *discerning* rightful action, but in the cultivation of appropriate attitudes towards the *performance* of rightful actions. Inherent in orthodox understandings of sin, therefore, is the belief that most ordinary contexts of moral decision are both perspicuous and readily intelligible, the relevant concerns centring not upon what is known but upon self-discipline and the control of one's appetites and desires. Similarly, the processes of child-rearing (outside the theological context) depend to a considerable extent upon courses of moral instruction that are widely known and unproblematic: for they are premised on the belief that, having received initial guidance, the child will grow up not to challenge the *truth* of moral injunctions, but will rather come through experience to perceive their truth (whilst perhaps refining his understanding). In seeking to distinguish such ordinary contexts of moral judgment from the deeper, philosophical level of learning, we are forced to posit two concepts of moral knowledge: on the one hand, we have the knowledge of rightful action gained from early training and subsequent experience; on the other, we have the more refined knowledge that comes from philosophical insight and 'interpretation'. Unless we regard ordinary understandings as deeply mistaken (or at most coincidentally true), then there is an obvious problem in *distinguishing* the two senses of knowledge – for how can both sources of knowledge embody knowledge *of* 'morality'?

Having grasped this problem, we may begin to perceive more clearly the deficiencies in philosophical insight that give rise to the moral standpoint of modernity. These may be seen to stem from a tendency to be overly impressed with the connection between thought and language. Because language is a human artefact, we may feel, the terms in which we perceive the world are intrinsically human rather than 'real' or unmediated. *Therefore*, (we may be tempted to conclude) moral thought must find its source not in reality, but in the human will as it *interprets* its surroundings. However, the existence of conceptual thought as an autonomous outlook on the world depends upon the thought that the mind does not form concepts *from* experience, but independently of experience. For, whilst experience is not unmediated by concepts present in language, conceptual thought should not (so I argue) be thought of as a *separate* stage of reflection to that of experience. The contemplation of the social world would then not be a question of simply fitting free-floating notions to mundane observations, but rather of recognising the groundedness of our notions in shared experiences and present attachments. A specifically human outlook upon the world may in this way be revealed as connected with processes, not of will, but of cognition, perception and of intellect.

Plato's philosophy itself depends upon a view of conceptual thought as something other than a product of will. To comprehend reality, he argued, 'man must understand the language of forms, passing from a plurality of perceptions to a unity comprehended by reasoning.'[17] Yet we can only do this, in Plato's view, because the soul is separate from the body and, knowing the eternal truth (being itself eternal), enters into the human body. Humans thus participate in the eternal via the soul, which *transcends* experience: the process of understanding is one, not of perception

---

17 Plato, *Phaedo*, 249b5–c4 (various translations and editions).

but of recollection. Now, suppose that we regard Plato's metaphysical explanation as endeavouring to ground human knowledge and experience in a universal order of being, and explaining the processes of concept-formation by reference to a knowledge of the eternal. Might we not reverse the direction of thought, and instead think of human understanding as depending upon some idea of the point or significance of human life within a universal order, itself derived from perception? The processes of concept-formation would then be seen as emerging from experience in a symbiotic relationship with the processes of cognition and perception, and as both arising from and giving content to habitual immersion in a form of life. We would have approached, in this way, something akin to Aristotle's position:

> Since it seems that there is nothing outside and separate in existence from sensible spatial magnitudes, the objects of thought are in the sensible forms, namely, both the abstract objects and all the states and affections of sensible things. Hence, no one can learn or understand anything in the absence of sense...[18]

For Aristotle, the universal does not exist in separation from particulars; rather the particular is the perceptible or intelligible form of the universal. He is thus able to say that although we perceive particulars, *perception* is of universals, or rather of the universal-in-the-particular.[19] In the same way, morality transcends particular or momentary concerns, but moral understanding proceeds from the contemplation of particular situations that are either actually confronted or envisaged. Such understanding is manifested by the ability to give sensitive and careful expression to the dimensions of a situation that mark it out from others before the moral imagination, or which (in a legal context) require intervention of some sort. Moral knowledge does not exist in a manner that allows for understanding in advance of its application or specification in individual cases, for moral ideas are not independent of the contexts in which moral judgments are given specific formulation. The relevant image is thus not one in which a body of acontextually determinate propositions *applies* to actual or hypothetical cases, but one of a deepening sense of the moral flowing from immersion within, and treatment of, particular situations.

Hart famously characterised shared juridical reasons as resting upon an agreement in judgments. These reflections, I believe, help us to understand how the presence of diversity within cultural backgrounds and interests does not prevent broad agreement upon the judgment of particular cases, even where there is sharp divergence between individual reasons for accepting those judgments.[20] For they indicate that moral knowledge might be fundamentally particular, in manner of intelligibility. Furthermore, the above reflections explain the nature of that particularity without the need for problematic distinctions between two sources or levels of moral understanding, or of the existence of 'objective' versus 'subjective' understandings: the understanding of the subject proceeds from reflection upon the meaning of present attachments and concerns as they relate to a universal order in which they participate.

---

18 Aristotle, *De Anima*, III 8, 432a3–8.

19 Aristotle, *Posterior Analytics*, I 31, 87b28–30.

20 See A.R. Jonsen and S. Toulmin, *The Abuse of Casuistry* (Los Angeles, University of California Press, 1989).

The particularity of moral understandings should not therefore be taken to imply that the relevant knowledge is to be found in an endless series of discontinuities that may only be related or combined by will. Discontinuity can only be comprehended within the context of broader continuities between the human person and the external order she inhabits.[21] Such continuities are composed of aspects of human existence that combine to form coherent projects and ordered capacities, for human beings relate to the social forms and institutions which surround them not simply as a disconnected series of moments or occasions of choice, but as integrated personalities defined by interconnecting plans and projects of medium- to long-term range. Only insofar as the social environment exhibits purposiveness and continuity can human life and experience be said to manifest intelligibility.

The moral reflections of the *phronimos* are thus, to an extent, reflections upon how individuals simultaneously construct and are constructed by the social environment.[22] Such moral deliberations might be directed with profit to the consideration of private law, for it is here that the frontier between the individual and a shared environment is most clearly defined and articulated. Propositions of private law cannot without distortion be taken to represent a set of general rules established by authority and imposed upon the civil polity. Many of the forms and concepts of private law exist not to restrict or govern conduct, but to facilitate ordinary transactions by creating determinate meanings for informal understandings. The traditional emphasis within private law has thus not centred on the identification and eventual elimination of instances of fragmentation or inequality within social life, but rather the enunciation of a set of rules that allow for the possibility of a peaceful and meaningful coexistence in the presence of fragmentation. Law's embodiment of a moral ideal does not betoken the attempt to give direct expression to a general theory of justice, in the idealist's sense. The ideals of governance and legality, as I hope to demonstrate, take a wholly different form.

Constructing the Ideal

One way in which a set of rules or principles may be brought together under an ideal would be to identify the general purpose or set of values that the collection of rules or principles serve. Such general purposes or values may then act as ideals that inform and structure our interpretation of the more specific rules and principles. Bodies of law might be said to instantiate an ideal insofar as they exhibit an overall coherence of purpose, at some high level of abstraction. One frequently encounters the suggestion that the purposive ideal, which is given expression in this way, amounts to a general theory or conception of justice. This is, in one sense, not unreasonable; but I have sought to demonstrate in my earlier discussions the extent

---

21 See Porter, *Nature as Reason*, 116. The notion of 'universal order' need not be conceived in theological terms (although it must depend upon metaphysical assumptions as profound as a theological world-view): it may be taken to ground a tradition of civility, or a form of life, in Wittgenstein's sense.

22 See M. Gibson, 'The Historical Nature of Human Nature', 72 *J of Philosophy* (1975), 604–611.

to which such an ideal, insofar as it is operative within the legal order, is an ideal of *public* law. The existence of a separate underpinning rationale in the context of private law should therefore alert us to the fact that a theory of justice can be but an incomplete account of the governing ideals of law, for one cannot state in any clear way, *within* a theory of justice, the reasons why it is felt that human relations ought to be subjected to norms of justice in an organised way in the first place. (The law of the jungle may create unpleasant conditions for those on the lower links of the food chain, but it might for all we know provide optimal conditions for the evolution of the human species in terms of the long-term development of capacities.)

As my argument in Chapter 1 was intended to show, the general purposive conditions for law can be understood not against a theory of justice (or of 'legality' as a state of affairs neutral with respect to ideas of justice), but only against a complex background of assumptions concerning human nature. Only having reached some understanding of the nature and significance of human capacities can norms of justice appear on the intellectual landscape as something other than mere life-denying ordinances. A central assumption lying behind the idea of legality, therefore, is that the subjection of human conduct to governance through rules is a precondition for the meaningful realisation of human capacities and potentialities.[23] Insofar as human capacity is central to legality, it is the underpinning notions of private law that inform our most basic understandings of law, the goals and purposes of public law hinging upon rather than preceding those understandings. I have suggested that the relevant understandings concern the introduction of narrowly formed moral categories for thought concerning the informal contexts of social interaction upon which civility is founded. In the absence of such stable forms of thought we do not have lawless anarchy,[24] but we do have irrationality. Thus, as Fuller said, in one respect our whole legal system represents the attempt 'to rescue man from the blind play of chance and to put him safely on the road to purposeful and creative activity', and thus to 'create the conditions essential for a rational human existence.'[25] Legal concepts of dealing and contract provide, in this way, a moral framework in the context of which judgments are set within certain appreciable limits:

> To say that a man has entered a contract is not just to tip the scales of justice indeterminately toward the conclusion that he may possibly have incurred an obligation. It is to say that he *is* obligated *unless* some specific ground of excuse, such as incapacity or duress, can be established. One may suggest that what is manifested here is an impulse of the morality

---

23 For an excellent discussion see Simmonds, 'Law as a Moral Idea', 55 *Univ Toronto LJ* (2005), 61–92.

24 We would not have anarchy in the sense that we could still rely upon widely shared informal understandings, or shared practices which fall short of articulate understanding. (It is a complex question to what extent such informal understandings may be compatible with the nature of anarchy, as one familiar with the writings of Hobbes may be aware. For even the instinctive, unvocalised actions of men in the state of nature manifest rationality of some sort, and may thus act as a means of penetrating the opacity with which Hobbes surrounds human motivation.) For some important reflections upon the nature of anarchy, see M. Arnold, *Culture and Anarchy* [1869] (Cambridge, Cambridge University Press, 1993).

25 L. Fuller, *The Morality of Law*, revised edn (New Haven, Yale University Press, 1969), 9

of duty, expressing itself within the law, to maintain the integrity of its domain and to protect that domain from the erosions threatened by a view that attempts to solve too many simultaneous equations at once.[26]

Viewing the question in this way allows us to make some sense of the belief that our notions of legality and governance do not simply relate to the substantive purposes served by rules, but are also taken to manifest ideals regarding the means by which the ends defined by the rules are pursued or established – for it is indeed only through the collective experience of pursuing the goals of legality and governance that we can achieve a well-defined understanding of the nature of the ends for which we rely upon law in a given form. In seeking to draw a distinction between the procedural or 'internal' and the 'external' (or substantive) morality of law, and by identifying the ideal of legality with the former, Fuller in fact obscures an important truth: that an understanding of the substantive ideals through which the law is rendered open to philosophical comprehension are not detachable from our understanding of the *form* of law, as the means by which those ideals are manifested. Thus, in a society in which social relationships are worked out against a background of strong theocratic bonds, we might expect the law of contract to take the form of strict rules on usury, etc. without any general investigation taking place into the fairness of bargains outside the scope of the specific rules. It will be taken for granted, for example, that individuals deal with one another according to certain understandings, so that no attention is paid to the *sources* of a bargain in offer and acceptance. There may, indeed, be no fixed rules relating to offer and acceptance at all, but merely a fluid set of notions concerning conscience or honour in dealing. The ideals served by law would not concern, as above, the reduction of irrationality by the elimination of ambiguity in social relations, but the straightforward subjection of human conduct to divinely stipulated moral demands.

Accepting this picture of the interrelation of form and substance, we may be led to a different understanding of the way in which the specific rules and attributes of legal order may be brought under an ideal. For it will then appear that our grasp of the ideal can be manifested only highly incompletely, insofar as our processes of reflection in specific contexts of legal judgment demonstrate levels of purposiveness and intelligibility. There could be no question of imposing a specific form upon the law by 'fitting' a body of acontextual principles to variable and contingent conventions. Rather, we manifest a deepening sense of the ideal through the expression given to the various factors affecting decision in the judgment of particular cases. Ideals are therefore viewed from *within* the practices that instantiate them. That being so, we will not at any point possess the ability to perceive all dimensions of the ideal at once. This aspect of moral thinking has tended to be obscured in modern thought due to the lingering influence of Enlightenment conceptions of knowledge, in which mathematics and, in particular, geometry appear in the position of the archetypal rational science. A line of thought beginning in Grotius and finding its apogee in Kant's doctrine of Right took geometry to represent the most fully rational and secure form of human knowledge, and thus sought to model moral thought upon the process

---

26 *Ibid.*, 30.

of geometric demonstration.[27] Moral concepts then resemble the geometer's figures in taking perfect and fully rational form only in the abstract; any actual instantiations representing very imperfect or corrupted versions of the ideal.

The characteristic feature of mathematical or geometric objects is that they typically possess an independently apprehended form or definition, even if our ability to reproduce actual physical or mental images of the form is always flawed and imperfect. Thus, the mathematical definition of a sphere fully determines the idea of that abstract object, despite the lack of real-world instantiations of the perfect sphere: any such instantiations are imperfect approximations only.[28] In this respect, the imperfections to be found in actual spheres are measurable by reference to a fixed form that is known in definition even if not (as is the case with most actual spheroids) by direct acquaintance. Moral ideals do not relate to moral concepts in this way, for, as Aristotle observed, moral knowledge is to be *contrasted* with technical knowledge precisely because moral (and therefore legal) understandings do not possess a final form. Such concepts have a *telos* not in having a final stage, but in having an indefinite number of *further* stages beyond the present form of instantiation. The ideal-form involved in moral thinking thus resembles that involved in painting: each successive brush-stroke is guided by an 'ideal' in the artist's mind; but in having an ideal the artist has no final form in mind that is independent of the way in which the paint appears on the canvas. Improvements made by the artist might be said to be 'guided' by the ideal even though the human mind lacks a concept of artistic perfection. Similarly, the process of moral judgment moves us towards an ideal, but our comprehension of the ideal does not appear before the mind in complete detachment from the actual judgments that we regard as imperfectly instantiating it.

This leaves open the possibility that our understanding of the guiding ideals of legality and governance may turn out, in the end, to be incoherent, or to be composed of distinct elements that exist in degrees of mutual tension which fall short of exhibiting full incoherence. In the case of governance, I have suggested that the very process of subjecting human conduct to governance through rules carries an internal tension or contradiction: a key reason behind such governance is the creation of meaningful pockets of liberty within which each person may follow their own goals and conceptions of the good; yet the establishment of those liberties requires a concept of 'right' which transforms the full-blooded, unique person into a juridically identical 'agent' whose interests are, to a great extent, determined by the state or wider community. The maintenance of social peace that is a pre-condition for human flourishing thus denies the fulfilment of the Romantic notion of the self-standing person as one who is free to pursue her own determining; for as Humboldt pointed out, the existence of social institutions inevitably shackles the spirit to substantively defined human goals.[29]

---

27 See my brief discussion in Chapter 2.

28 See Simmonds (above, note 23) for a discussion of the archetype of a 'triangle'.

29 The social institutions Humboldt had in mind embraced not only those connected with justice, but also, for example the education system insofar as it produces uniformity, stultification of the spirit, etc. For a discussion see Geuss, *History and Illusion in Politics,*

In a similar way, Fuller noted that certain antinomies arise within the ideal of legality itself, as construed according to his eight desiderata. These, as is well known, include the requirement that law establishes rules capable of some degree of generalisation beyond a concern with the minute particular; that such rules are disseminated in a form that those ordinarily subject to them might easily discover; that the administration of the law coincides with the published form of the rules; and that the rules conform to certain basic dimensions of rationality such as intelligibility, internal consistency and immunity from continual or retrospective revision. Whilst allowing that actual instances of legal order will conform to such dimensions of legality only to a greater or lesser degree, Fuller noted that in fact the various desiderata may at times come into opposition with one another.[30] Thus, the aim of clarity in the expression of legal rules may directly conflict with the possibility of shaping the rules into a coherent and consistently applicable whole; for in clarifying the import of individual rules to specifically imagined cases, one loses sight of the general considerations lying behind the functioning of the rule, which are the direct concern of doctrinal legal scholarship. In the same way, therefore, the form of reasoning within the common law system of precedent advances goals of adaptability and sensitivity in application at the expense of the requirement for the rules to bear a definite public form. In noting these potential contradictions, Fuller did not proceed to attempt some higher reconciliation of the various notions in a way that dissolves the opposition. He instead noted that his specific formulation of the ideal (as manifested by the eight principles of legality) 'is not actually a useful target for guiding the impulse toward legality; the goal of perfection is much more complex.'[31]

Fuller's analysis of the ideal of legality is incomplete in obvious respects. For example, it neglects a crucial dimension of legality that lies in the substantial connection between the goals and values pursued by the rules and the content of informal social and cultural practices which constitute the civil nature of the polity. Recognising such additional dimensions to legality does not however 'complete' Fuller's account of the ideal by creating a more inclusive notion within which the various desiderata achieve a final reconciliation. Rather, it is apt to increase awareness of tension and contradiction within the ideal as presently constituted. We can think of the various desiderata (following Fuller's own suggestion) as dimensions of rationality in human affairs which may themselves conflict in various ways: for just as a painting lacks a final form in which artistic perfection is realised, so human societies may embody conditions that preclude a fully rational expression of human nature. In seeking to reduce irrationality in human affairs, therefore, one must strive after the elucidation or creation of rational attachments rather than eliminating

---

80–83. We might, in this connection, regard private law as embodying a pale echo of the 'liberty of the ancients' in a society fundamentally structured according to the 'liberty of the moderns.' (I do not have space to develop this suggestion here.)

30 Fuller (above, note 25), 45. On the eight principles generally see *The Morality of Law*, Chapter 2.

31 *Ibid.*, 41.

rational attachments that may conflict. The ideals of legality and of governance may, in this sense, be seen as an elaborate articulation of an essentially Hegelian idea.

Legality, Theory and Geist

Law is both a phenomenon brought about through the existence of fragmentation and division in human societies, and a body of ideas which, in some sense, stands apart from, and aims to repair or suppress, instances of fragmentation and division. The intellectual structure of private law, I therefore argue, exhibits the characteristics of the moral wisdom of the *phronimos* in seeking to ground its doctrines and judgments in principles that are capable of fixed or acontextual formulation only at the price of distortion or loss. The underpinning notions of governance and legality are thus related to concrete legal ideas with the same level of complexity as prized aspects of social life (such as promising or reliance) are related to an encompassing tradition of civility. Aspirational forms of public law reasoning, structured around the pursuit of aggregative or distributive goals, are parasitic on the body of civic values rather than constitutive or determinative of them. Hence (so I have tried to argue) the modern tendency to see in a system of constitutionally entrenched human rights an inviting doorway to a new and more just and rational society, is an intellectual delusion, for it is to mistake one aspect of legality for the whole; and it is (as Blackstone once observed) to replace that which is fundamental, immemorial and beyond alteration with that which is deliberately authorised, variable and dependent upon official recognition.

The motivation behind such intellectual developments, I have suggested, lies in a secular form of moral Protestantism for which each person possesses the capacity to formulate and pursue genuinely distinct conceptions of the good. A society aware of its own complexity will then perceive the need for a political process to mediate between plural visions of the good. Law may then embody civility only in the diminished sense of a hypothetically consensual body of rules that establish certain boundaries and conditions in which the joint pursuit of divergent conceptions of the good is possible. It will then seem that a philosophical account of law's nature cannot be illuminated by the notion of a *tradition* of civility, but must instead be directed towards the abstract possibilities presented by systems of moral principles in relation to the conditions of agency. Whilst this view is implicit in most legal and moral philosophy at the current day, I believe it is wholly wrong.

Legality (understood as a series of ideas relating to the form and substance of law) and governance (as the process of ruling through law) represent neither an elevated set of general principles of justice, nor intellectual categories that are neutral as between forms of the good. Instead they ground a tradition of civility. An understanding of the law's moral nature thus does not derive from an abstract structure of ratiocination (in the form of 'interpretations' of legal concepts) but constitutes an immanent form of reflective speculation upon the values for which present forms of human ordering exist. Modern philosophy has, by and large, directed attention to the definition of a complex object (comprised by norms of justice) and has sought to understand personal interests and the relations between them in the light of that objective perspective. Such a strategy, I have argued, is deeply mistaken about the relationship between civility and plural forms of the good, for human preferences and interests are not self-standing objects of the will that operate within normative interstices, but rather take their form from factors within the social environment which are thus external to the 'agent'. Insofar as human action manifests rationality, human actors do not develop preferences or formulate coherent medium- or long-term projects that are incapable of fulfilment within the immediately available conditions. This relates as much to the social as to the natural conditions of life: our bases for action are premised not upon the assumption of a greatly increased lifespan, nor the absence of social norms that structure human interaction, but upon the matrix of social, legal and moral understandings within which each person operates. Forms of jurisprudential thinking that perceive society as being governed by a descending conception of justice thus tend to foster imperialistic rather than liberal understandings of pluralism.

The central question for jurisprudence is how plural visions of the good combine within a tradition of civility. Civility is not a theoretical structure that exists in detachment from plural visions of the good, for (in being civilised) such visions partly constitute the structure within which they move. It follows that the notion of 'the good' is not an ethical category that stands fully apart and in abstraction from ordinary experience. Social ordering, in constituting part of that experience, is thus not a mere *framework* within which pursuit of the good is possible, but forms part of the good that is being pursued. It is for this reason that secular Protestantism is not the most suitable intellectual standpoint from which to pursue a rich jurisprudential understanding. The standpoint required is that of Hegel: one in which plural or fragmented understandings are comprehended within a complex and unified object that embraces their combination. Such a standpoint on the nature of the good, as a finally unified object of understanding, might be worked out within the intellectual structures of either Catholicism or Protestantism, but must finally stand as the embodiment of a theological or a humanistic (though not secular) world-view.[32] Insofar as one's ethical commitments depend upon attachment to such fundamental metaphysical world-views, philosophical understandings of the moral nature of law and society are products ultimately not of will, but of faith.

Law (particularly private law) forms part of the dense fabric of social institutions and understandings that give shape to human endeavour in a context of close and permanent relations. The dominance of public-law understandings of governance increasingly obscures the significance of this dimension of legality by focusing attention upon the descending structures of legal authority. Legality becomes, in such contexts, a concept that is in some ways subordinate to that of governance, rather than a complex series of ideas that are independent of modes of governance: the idea of 'the rule of law' achieves synonymy with the notion of governance *by* law rather than governance *according to* law. In this book I have suggested that the idea of legality ought instead to be elucidated as the embodiment of a tradition of civility.

---

32 A reminder is in order here that in seeking to illuminate the general form of the British polity, one confronts a tradition of civility formed (in at least its 'modern' manifestation) by predominantly Judeo-Christian ethical ideas.

The value of legality within the British polity is thus not separable from national spirit, conceived (as in early-modern philosophy and 19th century literature) as an essentially benign force in the world. The main characteristics of this national spirit are a reverence for liberty[33] and the avoidance of extremes, and a deep attachment to the ordinary moral experience of the 'middling sort.'[34] Moral thinking of this kind is seldom capable of abstract or fully general formulation as a set of principles. Thus, the conception of legality through which an understanding of the law proceeds is one rooted in the value, not of fixed rules or of abstract principles, but of informal understandings and of sensitive and careful reflection upon specific features of each case. The English spirit is captured most eloquently by George Eliot:

> All people of broad, strong sense have an instinctive repugnance to the men of maxims; because such people early discern that the mysterious complexity of our life is not to be embraced by maxims, and that to lace ourselves up in formulas of that sort is to repress all the divine promptings and inspirations that spring from growing insight and sympathy. And the man of maxims is the popular representative of the minds that are guided in their moral judgment solely by general rules, thinking that these will lead them to justice by a ready-made patent method, without the trouble of exerting patience, discrimination, impartiality – without any care to assure themselves whether they have the insight that comes from a hardly-earned estimate of temptation, or from a life vivid and intense enough to have created a wide fellow-feeling with all that is human.[35]

The tenor of such remarks reveals the deep affinity between the English moral sense and that of the wisdom of the *phronimos*, manifested in experience but incapable of full articulation. Legal consciousness within the tradition of English common law involves the direction of legal attention to aspects of this fabric of shared characteristics and understandings as part of a constant process of social self-consciousness and reflection. It is upon such understandings and thought-processes that jurisprudence must seek to cast illumination, if it is to make any contribution to legal thought.

---

33 The idea of liberty was not in this traditional sense a political notion but a social condition of Englishness (being the birthright of every free Englishman): see for example Jerome K. Jerome, *Three Men in a Boat* [1889] (various eds), chapter 11.

34 See for example the profusion of texts in the 'common sense' tradition of moral philosophy in the 18th century, such as Thomas Paine's *Common Sense* [1776] and Francis Hutcheson's *On the Nature and Conduct of the Passions* [1742]. The common law provides an obvious example of thinking in this tradition.

35 Eliot, *The Mill on the Floss*, book 7 chapter 2. See also for example Trollope's remark that the man of principles 'quiets the suggestion [of doubt] within his breast with the high-sounding name of justice – *fiat iustitia ruat coelum*' ('let justice be done though the heavens should fall'): *The Warden*, Chapter 4.

Index